BIC

Management Self-development

Management Self-development

Concepts and practices

Edited by

TOM BOYDELL and MIKE PEDLER

Gower

Published by
Gower Publishing Company Limited,
Westmead, Farnborough, Hants, England

British Library Cataloguing in Publication Data

Management self-development
  1. Management – Study and teaching
  I. Boydell, Thomas Hamer
  II. Pedler, Mike
  658.4'07'124   HD20

  ISBN 0-566-02194-3

Typeset in Great Britain by
Supreme Litho Typesetting, Ilford, Essex
Printed and bound in Great Britain by
Biddles Ltd, Guildford and King's Lynn

Contents

Page

Preface

It might perhaps be appropriate to introduce this book with a quick reference to one small part of our own self-development.

Approximately ten years ago we were both heavily involved in a 'systematic' approach to management education. This involved us in taking great pains to identify the needs of our 'target population', specify behavioural objectives for them, plan teaching activities, devise objective tests, and so on.

Gradually, however, for reasons we didn't fully understand, we became dissatisfied with all this trainer-centred activity, which treated the learners as cohorts of homogeneous passivity. Together with one or two close colleagues, we moved into what we dubbed a 'learning community' approach (see Chapters 5 and 10), which involved the participants in taking active responsibility for their own learning, and in some mysterious way seemed to synthesise the apparent opposites of each person's unique individuality with the commonality necessary for the formation of a true community ('diversity with unity').

This new approach was not only good fun and tremendously exciting, but it also seemed to work rather well for the participants. Part of the excitement was trying to find out *why* it was working, and for the next few years we explored this question, through a combination of reading, reflecting on our own activities, writing about these, and sharing them with others.

We gradually became aware that our new approach was, perhaps, part of something much wider — that some of the underlying ideas could find other forms of practical expression. It seemed that a useful generic title for this wider field was 'self-development', and hence we started to use the term and to play with (i.e. think about) the concept. In so doing we were involved in the preparation of a programme of structured activities for self-development (Pedler et al, 1978), a brief overview of a number of approaches (Burgoyne et al, 1978), and an

annotated bibliography (Boydell and Pedler, 1979). Thus we encountered a number of attractive people and their work, and we felt it
would be helpful to bring them together.

Our intention in this book, then, was to invite a number of people,
who are actively helping managers with self-development, to describe
their work and the ideas on which it is based. We also set out with the
aim of trying to find out what it is they have in common – what is
'self-development'?

As will be seen from our opening chapter, our current view is that
self-development is primarily a process of unifying, or of integrating
the knower and the known, the teacher and the learner, you and I,
the individual and the group, the unique and the common, body,
mind and spirit, theory and practice, participant and experience, work
and leisure, etc. and etc. This is our view of what all the contributions
have in common – of the nature of self-development.

There are, of course, many routes to a particular destination, and
there are therefore many perspectives from which this common view
may be obtained. For example, it may be seen simply as a more
efficient means to certain educational ends. Others may base their
activities on certain values about the rights of individuals to have a say
in their own development. Another way of arriving at similar principles is through a study of certain schools of psychology – either
Western (e.g. cognitive development; humanistic), Eastern (e.g. Zen)
or both (e.g. Transpersonal; Jungian). To some, perhaps, it just makes
more sense, or is more fun, or more rewarding. Others still may see this
approach as part of the task for the age, for the current epoch, of
seeking new forms for the development of mankind as a whole.

Most of these viewpoints are represented somewhere in the contributions to this book, although they are sometimes stated more
explicitly than others. We believe, therefore, that as well as providing
a useful overview of a number of practical approaches, they can also be
seen in a wider context. Each reader can, we hope, thus get from the
book the aspect he or she is most excited by – theory, practice, or the
integration of both.

The preparation of the book has certainly contributed to our own
self-development and, from the enthusiastic way in which the contributors responded, it seems to have helped theirs as well. We hope it
does the same for the readers.

Tom Boydell
Mike Pedler
Sheffield, December 1980

References

Boydell, T. H. and Pedler, M. J. *Management Self-Development: An Annotated Bibliography.* Bradford: MCB Publications, 1979

Burgoyne, J. G., Boydell, T. H. and Pedler, M. J. *Self-Development.* London: Association of Teachers of Management, 1978

Pedler, M. J., Burgoyne, J. G. and Boydell, T. H. *A Manager's Guide to Self-Development.* Maidenhead: McGraw-Hill, 1978

Notes on contributors

Philip Boxer (*Learning as a subversive activity*) is an Associated Member of Faculty at the London Graduate School of Business Studies. His work is focused on the problems of enabling structural change in organisations, and his case work at present involves him in working through problems of personal strategy with senior managers and intervening in group and inter-group processes within organisations.

Ian Cunningham (*Self-managed learning in independent study*) is Head of the Personal Development Division at the Anglian Regional Management Centre. He has a BSc in Chemistry and an MA in Manpower Studies (both from London University). He has been, among other things, a research chemist, a lecturer in science, the National Secretary of the National Union of Students and a training officer in local government. Currently he is trying to divide his work life between research, writing, working with undergraduates and with managers and doing consultancy. His main interests are in how people learn and change and how one can help this process in others.

Sheila Harri-Augstein (*Learning conversations*) graduated from the University of Wales with a first class honours degree in Physiology. She then went to complete a masters degree on the topic of Ageing Factors. Having obtained a Teaching Diploma in the early Sixties, she took up teaching posts in various grammar schools and was, for several years, Head of the Science Department at Dover Grammar School.

In the late Sixties she joined the research staff of the Centre for the Study of Human Learning and completed her PhD, on the Psychological Processes of Learning by Reading, in 1971. She went on to a Senior Lectureship in Education at Loughborough University and later rejoined the Centre as Senior Research Fellow. She has worked on several research projects at the Centre, including conversational uses of the repertory grid in 'Learing-to-Learn' and in 'Cognitive Modelling'. Sheila has contributed to the development of a theory of 'Learning Conversations' and is responsible for running 'Learning-to-Learn' courses in Education and Industrial Institutions, here and abroad.

John Heron (*Self and peer assessment*) is Honorary Project Director of the Human Potential Research Project of the University of Surrey – the longest established growth centre in Europe. He is also Assistant Director of the British Postgraduate Medical Federation of the University of London. He established co-counselling in the UK and Europe from 1971 onwards. Currently, as well as introducing personal growth and experiential methods to medical education, he conducts workshops on varied aspects of human development from radical education to transpersonal psychology.

Anthony M. Hodgson (*Stimulating self-development*) is the founder and chairman of the Oxford based Hodgson Myers Group Ltd, which includes Hodgson Myers Associates Ltd, Self-Development Systems Ltd and Communi-Kit Aids (UK) Ltd. He has been a consultant and sub-contractor to industry in the UK and abroad since 1968. His assignments have been in the fields of computer aided learning, leadership and management training and organisation development consulting.

He graduated in chemistry from the Imperial College of Science and Technology in 1958, and has qualifications in education. His early researches as a Research Fellow of the Institute for Comparative Study were in the fields of creativity and learning, group dynamics, systems theory and computer aids to creative learning. He is the innovator of the structural communication learning method and his publications range over the fields of programmed learning, management training and self-development for managers. He is a major contributor to the 'SYSDEV' library of management development materials. Currently he divides his time between responsibilities in research and personal consulting with senior personnel managers and chief executives.

Andrzej Huczynski (*Self-development through formal qualification courses*) is a Lecturer in Management Studies (Organizational Behaviour) in the Department of Management Studies at the University of Glasgow. Previously he carried out evaluation research into management development programmes and management information systems at the Polytechnic of Central London and at Edinburgh University. He is currently conducting a study into the problems of transferring management training ideas into the trainees' work situation. The findings of this action research project are being applied to the solution of organisational training problems.

Philip Keslake (*Outward bound?*) is with the General Products Division of the RHM Group. His work covers a range of activities concerned with specific training events in project work within the company. Much of his work has focused on developing individual capacities and team working skills in a period of marked business changes.

Malcolm Leary (*Working with biography*) is a senior consultant with Social Biology Associates, a limited liability company wholly owned by the Foundation for the Advancement of Social Education, a charitable trust. It is a non-profit organisation devoted to development, consulting and research in organisational and social life. Its activities include work with individuals, groups and organisations, both public and private, in such fields as organisation development, industrial relations, conflict resolution, communications and counselling. In its aims, methods and approach SEA is closely linked with sister institutions through the NPI Association for Social Development.

Professor John F. Morris (*Developing managers for new enterprises*) has had wide experience in industry, commerce and the public sector as a consultant in management selection and development. He joined Manchester Business School in 1966 as Director of Studies of the Management Course and since 1970 has been closely associated with the School's Joint Development Activities. His current research is devoted to the theory and practice of management development activities. He was Chairman of the North West Region Job Creation Programme from 1976–78 and is a member of specialist panels of the University Grants Committee and the Council for National Academic Awards.

Alan Mumford (*Counselling senior managers' development*). Alan Mumford's wide experience in management development began in the construction industry with John Laing & Son, and continued with IPC Magazines. His role changed subsequently when, as Deputy Chief Training Adviser at the Department of Employment, he conducted surveys on management training, the advisory role of Industrial Training Boards, and was involved in the creation of a planning and budgeting system for the Training Services Agency and Industrial Training Boards. In his next job, at ICL, he had the opportunity of studying managerial work in detail as a consultant on management effectiveness. He is currently Executive Resources Adviser to the Chloride Group, where one of his major tasks has been to work with senior executives on their personal development.

Philip Radcliff (*Outward bound?*) is currently employed by the General Products Division of the RHM Group. Much of his work has focused on developing individual capacities and team working skills in a period of marked business changes. One medium he has found rewarding in this connection has been the use of the outdoor environment for personal and team development. He believes that much of the current work and theory being generated on self-development requires robust application and validation in the business context.

Professor Reginald W. Revans (*Action learning and the development of the self*) is a distinguished author in the field of management. He was Managing Director, Inter-University Programme for Advanced Management, Fondation Industrie-Université, Brussels, from 1967 to 1975 and is a former Visiting Professor at the University of Leeds and at Ulster Polytechnic.

Paul Temporal (*Creating the climate for self-development*) has a degree in Economics from Leeds University, a Certificate in Education and a Post-Graduate Research Degree in Management Studies from Oxford University. He has lectured extensively in management subjects and was a Research Associate and Lecturer in Management Education at the Yorkshire and Humberside Regional Management Centre, Sheffield City Polytechnic. He has gained industrial experience as the training manager with a multi-national group of companies, and has overall responsibility for management development within a large division of that group (within which he has successfully instituted self-development groups as an integral part of the management development process). He has also been a consultant in management and organisational development to a number of small and medium sized companies, and is the author of several articles in leading management journals.

Laurie Thomas (*Learning conversations*) has first degrees in Engineering and Psychology and was awarded a PhD in 1962 for a study of the psychology of judgement and decision making applied to Subjective Standards in Industrial Inspection. Since 1969, he has been Director of the Centre for the Study of Human Learning at Brunel University. He and his associates have developed a person-centred technology of learning: 'Learning to Learn', 'Learning Conversations', 'The Learner as Personal Scientist', 'The Repertory Grid as a Tool for Learning', and 'Learning in Therapy, Education and Industry' are topics which indicate the direction of these activities. Dr Thomas and Sheila Harri-Augstein have recently run courses in France, Ireland, Switzerland and Mexico.

Tony Winkless (*Self-development groups*) gained his early industrial and commercial experience in the fields of publicity and systems work. In 1969 he began his career in training and development as Training Manager for one of Kodak's major divisions. This position gave him the opportunity of building and running a new department covering a wide range of training activities in a setting of large-scale organisational and technical change. In 1974, he joined the Geest Organisation as Training and Development Manager. In this work he was again initially involved in developing a new training function, although this time in a more diverse organisation spanning foods, distribution, shipping, horticulture, computing and engineering. Nowadays Tony Winkless' major interest lies in helping employees (mostly managers) in developing their potential. In this work his approach is essentially individual-centred, employing a wide range of methods, including counselling, small-group activities, and computer-assisted reflection.

PART I

SOME PRINCIPLES OF SELF-DEVELOPMENT

Overview

The contributions in this section tend to dwell not on specific designs but on the defining characteristics of self-development. In our own chapter we present our current views on self-development from two perspectives — social and individual. *Tony Hodgson* with his twenty principles concentrates largely on the individual manager as self developer — what his attributes are and how he can be resourced and helped. *Paul Temporal* relates the individual self-developer to the organisation and finds blocks both within the person and the climate. There is a certain balance and wholeness in these three contributions — the individual self-developer, the organisation in which he lives and works, and the shared, transpersonal reality of which we are all part.

1 What is self-development?

Mike Pedler and Tom Boydell

In this short introductory chapter we examine our current views of the nature of development, which we see as different from change, growth, innovation or even learning. The developmental process appears to follow certain laws – laws which are not associated with most of what passes for management education. Thus, 'most management development isn't'. These laws are in part associated with movement from one developmental stage to another, and we present a summary of a number of stage models; in brief, we see these as having a common characteristic – movement from separation, through relationship, into oneness. Finally, we touch upon the issue of developing oneself without becoming self-ish, without cutting oneself off from the rest of the world, but through working for and with the development of others. 'For self development and quality work we need others with the same impulse . . . who can hold us and be with us at this time.'

This short, introductory chapter is a co-production. We started, as joint editors, to prepare an earlier version of the opening chapter, first by writing separately, in order subsequently to come together. The first step produced two personal statements which differed not only in focus but also in style. A point of dichotomy and dilemma was reached: of self/other; personal/universal. Here were two statements, each saying, 'here I am and I want you to know it'; each resisting being 'lost' in the ideas of the other. In seeking a way out we turned to Malcolm Leary, who happily took on the task of creating a synthesis, a third position. We now had three pieces – one called 'Self and Social Development'; one called 'Self Development' and one called 'Man and Development'. The pieces were certainly related – but had they achieved that oneness required to merit the term synthesis? What we had certainly was over 15,000 words and this particular dilemma was resolved by a fourth party: the publisher. 'Not only is it too long' said he, 'but this first chapter is not the sort of thing which people who buy this book will want to read.' This product, then, in only one limited sense final, is the tip of an iceberg of effort.[1]

By analogy this little tale illustrates some of the aspects of this concept of self development that we currently recognise. We are talking about *development*, not change, growth, innovation, modification or even learning. Development is a much used term as, for example, in child development, developmental psychology, management development and organisation development. The developmental process is governed by certain 'laws' which are an integral aspect of ourselves as human beings in our world. When we begin to examine these laws a little more critically than our modern and unconfined assertion of trademarks allows, then we find that, for example, a lot of management development isn't.

Development implies qualitative as well as quantitative movement. Some of the characteristics of the development process are that it is:

principally discontinuous, involving step-jumps rather than gradual increments;
a process that occurs over time and in successive phases or stages;
associated with crisis, which has a crucial role in the movement from one phase to the next;
marked by a set of characteristic principles and structure at each phase, which are challenged by crisis and are superseded in the restructuring and transformation that appears in the next stage;
a process where each stage is more integrated and more complex than the last and which is therefore irreversible — there is no going back.

Our earlier feelings about the inappropriateness of much that passes for 'management education' have been strengthened by this consideration of what development means. Quite clearly, most of what takes place is not *designed* to foster and facilitate this process (although equally clearly there are examples of development in individuals from the expert-based and institutionalised forms of 'management development' that go on all around us). This leads some people to the view that 'all management development is self development'[2] but this is to confuse some of the products of an ill wind with its general effects. In the occasional paper which we wrote for the Association of Teachers of Management with John Burgoyne,[3] we suggested that self development ideas underlay a wide range of activities which might otherwise be described as the 'new wave' in management education, e.g. action learning, learning communities, independent study, coaching and counselling. Whilst we still hold this to be true, it now seems uncomfortably constraining to limit the concepts of development and self development to the field of management education. These ideas belong to all people everywhere and not just to managers. We would have to be very sure indeed of the current and continuing efficacy of our models for management development to limit our vision thus.

Of-self and by-self?

We have found this distinction to be useful for thinking about the various meanings attached to the term self-development. Earlier it seemed clear that when people were talking about self-improvement à la Dale Carnegie or self-actualisation after Maslow, then they were primarily concerned with the *of* self dimension which construes self-development as a goal or a series of ascending goals. On the other hand there are in common usage several meanings which have to do with development *by* self, e.g. learning without a teacher; independent study; distance learning and the learner taking responsibility for making decisions at all stages of the learning process. In these meanings, the term refers primarily to a process rather than a goal. This distinction gives a 2 x 2 classification which helped considerably to understand the arguments:

GOALS PROCESS	OF self	NOT OF self
Relatively self responsible	A	B
Relatively non- self responsible	C	D

However, as might be predicted, in other ways this neat categorisation did not make sense. To take the last example of a by-self meaning given above: 'the learner taking responsibility for decisions at all stages of the learning process'; we 'knew' from our experience of learning communities that a *by*-self process had *of*-self implications. Once people question the traditional stereotypes of teacher and learner, once they have experimented with new forms, there can be no simple going back.

The 'knew' in the last sentence but one is to denote that characteristic feeling of recognising the glaringly obvious that is a feature of many episodes that we later describe as 'developmental'. A connection is made and a truth revealed — which has perhaps long been clear and available to those not so engrossed, involved and concomitantly self-deceived by accumulated models, theories and ideas. This precious 'aha!' quality is also present in our new understanding of the by-self/of-self dichotomy. Looking back at our work of two and three years ago (*Self Development*, ATM, pages 8–13) it is now clear that we were talking about learning rather than development. To distinguish briefly between the two (something we did not attend to in that publication despite the continual juxtapositioning of the two terms throughout), we may say that learning has more to do with the incremental acquisition of knowledge, skills and abilities than with the qualitative transformational progression of the whole person. It is in this sense of *learning* – i.e. as not normally affecting/transforming the self – that the by-self/of-self dichotomy stands proud and easily seen. With the concept of *development* the dichotomy does not stand: development by-self implies an of-self dimension; development of-self implies the active by-self agency. (Or does it? Can the self be developed in a non-self-responsible way?)

For-self or of-self?

A related dichotomy is concerned with materialism on the one hand and a more spiritual dimension on the other. Within the earlier of-self dimension were grouped both self-improvement and self-actualisation, which in many ways are strange bedfellows. Nevertheless it must be admitted that one aspect of our current concept of self-development has its ancestry in Samuel Smiles' naïve eulogies of Great Victorian 'self helpers' and the more recent and apparently crass exhortations to self-betterment and 'beggar thy neighbour' invitations of Dale Carnegie. At the other pole are the yearnings towards actualisation and transcendence, drawn to our attention particularly by Maslow,[4] but evident in many ancient religious and mystical traditions and described by Aldous Huxley as the 'perennial philosophy'[5] and by Claudio Naranjo as 'the one quest'.[6]

The problem with this dichotomy is that we both feel some revulsion and alienation with the self-ishness implied by the connotations of self-development which have to do with the more materialistic pole, but also some unease and scepticism with the spiritual and mystical flavour at the other. If the former implies an only too realistic and limited view of this world, then the latter smacks of an other-worldly view with which many of us are uncomfortable. This is a very topical dilemma for us; we like to eschew the merely materialistic, knowing that there is more than this, but tend to shrink from the spiritual, handicapped by our modern rational, 'scientific' way of seeing, and feel that it is more to do 'with the next world rather than this'.

Most recently we have been concerned with trying to find a third position on this dichotomy and one which has relevance to management in common with others concerned with the human condition. At the present there are two aspects of this quest, one of which spans the material and spiritual poles through a synthesis of various 'stage' theories of human development, and one which elaborates the concept of learning community from being (merely) a design for management education into a paradigm for being-and-working-in-the-world-together.

Stage theories of human development

There are literally dozens of stage theories of human development, i.e. theories that posit various stages of development, each stage subsuming, 'improving' on and being qualitatively different from previous stages. Most theories are attached to different dimensions of development, for example Maslow's famous hierarchy of human needs or Piaget's stages of intellectual development. However there are obvious links between dimensions and Kohlberg[7] draws specific parallels between his stages of moral development and Piaget's schema. Other authors have made explicit attempts at synthesis of these often uni-dimensional stage theories, including Dale and Payne[8] who make use of Alderfer's three broad stage levels — existence, relatedness and growth.[9]

Alderfer's three levels have the merit of simplicity, but they do not link the materialist and spiritual poles as clearly as they might. In Figure 1.1 we have used the terms duality, relationship and transcendence to emphasise this underlying dimension.

The first stage-level *duality* (Alderfer's *existence*) is the level of separation, where I am separated from the world around me. Everything is seen in terms of duality e.g. separation of:

me	you
knower	known
subject	object
instinct	intellect

At stage 2, *relationship*, I am prepared to live in some sort of relationship with the world. With people for example, social relationships guided by group and societal norms evolve; the world is less simplistic and is seen as a complex of interrelated parts. Ways of thinking and learning are ways of working out relationships between people, things and ideas.

By stage 3, a *transcendence* of the basic duality — still apparent at stage 2 — has happened. Everything is part of everything else, there is a unity of me and you, knower and known, human and non-human. In

TRANSCENDENCE

Collapse of duality – i.e. everything now is part of everything else – good is bad, I am you, he is she, etc. Since I am you, individual differences are cherished, fully accepted and valued. Maslow's self-esteem, self-actualisation and theory Z needs. Moral judgements by individual conscience, involving reconciliation of inner conflicts. In science, recognition that 'reality' does not exist, everything is uncertain and only exists in terms of probabilities (the 'new physics'); predictability gives way to possibility, mental constructs are not images of an 'objective' world, but mirrors of ourselves looking at the world; cosmic wholeness. Education to become, to achieve one's destiny. 'Learning' in terms of thinking without mental models – the silent level, inspiration, enlightenment, satori, intuition, creative genius.

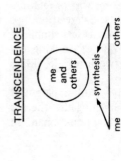

RELATIONSHIP

Everything seen in complex relationship with everything else (systems). Other people respected within certain well-defined social norms, others are entitled to their own views and behaviours (but this is often confined to 'my' social group; other groups' norms are deviant, undesirable; inter-group conflict). Maslow's social and esteem of others' needs. Moral judgements in terms of group/societal norms, rules and laws. Internal commitment to rules and laws as such. In science recognition of complex inter-causalities, no single causes or simple answers, but there is a 'reality out there' with man as detached observer, involved in systematic observation, measurement and verification. 'Learning' in terms of intellectual and empirical knowledge. Education to gain social approval and to carry out jobs and roles for the benefit of one's society (according to its norms).

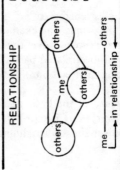

DUALITY

Everything separate, cut off from everything else. World seen as threatening. Other people either enemies or tools to be manipulated/exploited. Maslow's physiological needs. Moral judgements in terms of 'what I want is good' and imperatives; rules are obeyed out of fear of punishment. Clear cut answers to everything – good/bad; right/wrong. In science, emphasis on classification, simple causality. 'Learning' seen in terms of instant, unthinking responses and habits, respect for memory, factual knowledge, 'Brain of Britain'. Education to acquire, to get for oneself.

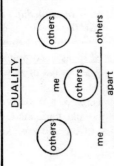

Figure 1.1   A Stage Theory of Development

religious language we have become one with God, attained extinction of self or freedom from desire and karma in union with the supreme spirit (Nirvana).

The value of stage theories is that they link together the poles – in this case – of duality and unity, material and spiritual, showing the unity of both. Over the years such theories have served the purpose of indicating the path to be followed to development, enlightenment, wisdom. Figure 1.1 is an indication of this linking path which can be discerned in the writings of those who have put forward stage theories. For those who would like to pursue this, the following references will make a starting point:

'Dimension'	References
– ways of knowing	Bachelard[10] as interpreted by Bois[11]; Perry[12]; Wilber[13]; Bentov[14]; Bohm[15]; Zukav[16]; Steiner[17]
– individual needs	Maslow[18]; Alderfer[19]
– moral and ethical development	Kohlberg[20]; Loevinger[21]
– learning and education	Bateson[22]; Fromm[23]; Chickering[24]; Naranjo[25]
– duality and synthesis	Assagioli[26]

Being-and-working-in-the-world-together

A criticism often levelled by westerners at eastern models of human development is that they encourage inaction and heedlessness in the face of what are often appalling material circumstances; that 'contemplating one's navel' neglects the very real social, economic and political problems of our time and is more to do with the next world rather than this. Different but related criticisms are made of the varied spectrum of personal development paths which have stemmed from the west coast culture of the USA.

For individuals in affluent, 'developed' societies, the struggle for day-to-day physical survival no longer demands full attention. Although this is something devoutly to be thankful for, the 'out there' problems which we now face, being more remote, have the effect of increasing our feelings of impotence and helplessness. What can the average woman or man do about atmospheric pollution, the threat of nuclear war, a world in which a quarter of us overconsume whilst three quarters of us don't get enough? In the face of such seemingly intractable problems which dwarf our puny will and resources, and perhaps extracting little comfort or peace of mind from consumerism, an increasing number of people are 'inward bound'. Whilst a degree of introspection is doubtless overdue to balance our traditional and unreflective 'busy-ness', this exploration of 'inner space' can lead to a chasing of one's own tail which eventually leaves one with only that same tail for comfort.

Paradoxically an obsessive concern with one's self is a block to self-development. The pre-occupation with self which slides into narcissism is a cause of severe distress in numerous people. In such people, or in such aspects of all of us, the answers seem to lie not in an inward look-ing, but outside, in worthwhile work in the world. This worthwhile work in the world is not just service for others: although it contains this element, it is primarily concerned with the attainment of quality. Like Janus, quality has two aspects, one concerned with excellence (uni-versally recognised) and one concerned with distinctiveness (uniquely formed). Work of distinctive excellence is valuable to others and expressed in a way that is uniquely one's own. Quality work arises from such questions as: what is it that I am here for? What are the skills, gifts, knowledge, characteristics that I can bring to this situ-ation? What is it that I can give to this? Quality work thus consists in a transcending of the duality of self and the world/other; it is the attainment of unity as expressed in the upper band of Figure 1.1.

This model for self-development has three major ingredients. The first of these is the urge to self-development; the second is an oppor-tunity for achieving quality work and the third is the requirement for others. This third element exemplifies another paradox of self-development: that it is in the attempt at self-development and quality work that the need for others becomes most palpable. To develop one's self, to move from duality to unity, to act more skilfully, demands a re-alignment of self with object – a literal losing of one's self. We all have an armoury of defences to guard against this terrify-ing experience which we frequently use to block off development opportunities. We hang on to the old self, investing it with more clarity and rigidity. For self-development and quality work we need others with the same impulse, who are as committed as we are, and who can hold us and be with us at this time. It is also only such people who can challenge our existing clarity and offer us the precious glimpse of alternatives. Such is the nature of 'friends willing to act as enemies' or 'comrades in adversity'. As Torbert has proposed:

> Rightly understood, the search for shared purpose, the search for personal self-direction and the search for quality work require one another.[2]

In the world of management education and rightly understood, Revans' Action Learning embodies these three elements: the development of the manager; action on a currently intractable problem; and with the help of the learning community of 4 to 6 comrades in adversity. The difficulties encountered in establishing Action Learning in our organisations reflect the very real resistances to self-development which exist. We are often not ready to choose our own development (so we continue to allow ourselves to be sent on courses i.e. 'development opportunities'); the intractable problems of organisation are there because some of us, usually those with relatively greater power, 'want' things that way, i.e. they are a consequence of organising in particular ways and of not being willing to change; and most of us lack that sense of community and shared purpose with a few comrades in adversity whom we implicitly trust to both support and challenge us, and without which we feel incapable of either self development or quality work.

What is increasingly clear is that we as human beings, our organisations and our societies, have a number of pressing needs with which this model can help. Perhaps it cannot be brought to the professional management of organisations directly, but only through an outside source and an oblique route. If we were to look for such sources outside our current cultures of management and organisation, then we might light on the ways we manage and organise ourselves at home, in our communities and in our voluntary associations.

References and notes

1 Those who feel that they might want to read the original pieces can write to the editors at the Management Studies Department of Sheffield City Polytechnic, who will oblige with photocopies at cost price.

2 This assertion led us to write an earlier paper 'Is all management development self development?' in Beck, J. and Cox, C. (Eds) *Advances in Management Education*, Wiley, 1980.

3 *Self Development*, ATM, 1978.

4 Especially in *The Farther Reaches of Human Nature*, Penguin, 1976.

5 Chatto & Windus, 1969.

6 Wildwood House, 1974.

7 Kohlberg, L., 'Stage and Sequence: The Cognitive Developmental Approach to Socialisation' in Goslin, D. A. (Ed.), *Handbook of Socialisation Theory and Research*, Rand McNally, Chicago, 1969.

8 Dale, A. and Payne, R., *Consulting Interventions using Structured Instruments: A Critique*, Brunel University, 1976.

9 Alderfer, C., *Existence, Relatedness and Growth*, Collier MacMillan, New York, 1972.

10 Bachelard, G., *La Philosophie du Non*, Presses Universitaire de France, Paris, 1949.

11   Bois, J. S., *Explorations in Awareness*, Harper, New York, 1957; and *The Act of Awareness*, William C. Brown, Dubuque, 1966.
12   Perry, W. G., *Forms of Intellectual and Ethical Development in the College Years*, Holt, Rinehart & Winston, New York, 1970.
13   Wilber, K., *The Spectrum of Consciousness*, Theosophical Publishing House, Wheaton, 1977.
14   Bentov, I., *Stalking the Wild Pendulum*, Fontana, London, 1979.
15   Bohm, D., *Wholeness and the Implicate Order*, Routledge & Kegan Paul, London, 1980.
16   Zukav, G., *The Dancing Wu Li Masters: An Overview of the New Physics*, Rider/Hutchinson, London, 1979.
17   Steiner, R., *The Stages of Higher Knowledge*, Anthroposophical Press, New York, 1976.
18   Maslow, A. H., *Motivation and Personality*, Harper & Row, New York, 1954; and *The Farther Reaches of Human Nature*, Penguin, London, 1977.
19   Op. cit.
20   Op. cit.
21   Loevinger, J., 'The Meaning and Measurement of Ego Development', *American Psychologist*, 21(3), March, 1966, pp. 195–206.
22   Bateson, G., *Steps to an Ecology of Mind*, Paladin, St. Albans, 1971.
23   Fromm, E., *To Have or to Be?*, Harper & Row, New York, 1976.
24   Chickering, A. W., 'Developmental Change as a Major Outcome' in Keating, M. J. et al. (Eds), *Experiential Learning: Rationale, Characteristics and Assessment*, Jossey Bass, San Francisco, 1977.
25   Op. cit.
26   Assagioli, R., 'The Balancing and Synthesis of the Opposites', *PRF Issue No. 9*, Psychosynthesis Research Foundation, New York, 1972; and *The Act of Will*, Wildwood House, London, 1974.
27   Torbert, W. R., 'Educating towards Shared Purpose, Self-Direction and Quality Work', *Journal of Higher Education*, Ohio State University Press, 49(2), 1978.

2   Stimulating self-development

Tony Hodgson

Tony Hodgson sees self-development as important to organisations because existing forms of management and organisation development have failed to meet the economic, political and competitive challenges of the 1970s. Development rather than growth will be the key to survival and success in the 1980s.

The first part of the chapter describes twenty principles of self-development. Development is a breakthrough to a new level of potential when a discontinuity in performance occurs. Challenge from without must be matched by a self-initiated response from within. Taking risks, preferring intrinsic rewards and managing one's dependency/independency are additional attributes. Hodgson thus summarises many of the common themes which can be seen in the applications described throughout this book.

Later the chapter describes design principles for self-development events − reflective learning, action development, transforming perception and input of key concepts and frameworks. Feedback from self-development workshops for managers is used to illustrate the effects which organisations have in underutilising and inhibiting managerial potential. This vision of institutional cultures and the need to unearth individual talent through a self-development approach is echoed by a number of other contributors to this book.

Finally Hodgson describes the possibilities which the new technology of computing, word processing and telecommunications has for stimulating self-development. He paints a picture of terminals which could provide individual managers with self-diagnostic instruments, coaching, guided reading and 'computer conferencing' together with organisational networks and support systems − particularly of peers.

The context of self-development

Development is now important to commercial organisations because the challenges — economic, competitive and political — facing such organisations can no longer be met by 'more of the same'. In the 1980s industry faces a crisis of effectiveness and productivity which is beyond solution by small increments in efficiency and minor changes of management approach. Both survival and competitive advantage will accrue to those firms which concentrate on development rather than simply on growth.

The 1970s have shown that isolated attempts to promote development are very limited in their effectiveness. Management development programmes become increasingly difficult to administer in the face of a turbulent environment and low growth economy. The room to manoeuvre becomes restricted internally or even reduced by management redundancies. Career planning becomes more difficult and the positive open climate essential for good appraisal is eroded under the stress of attrition. Loyalty is no longer present as an adhesive quality to compensate for frustration.

Similarly, despite its early promise, organisation development is rarely able to deliver a breakthrough in organisational effectiveness. These types of intervention are very complex, depend greatly on individual genius and are very vulnerable to changed circumstances. At one level OD requires a basic continuity of relationships however much it may be concentrating on the management of change at another level.

Individual self-sustained development is also rare in that it is regarded as the inherent prerogative of high flyers. Most management, inferred from the samples I have direct experience of, show a 'pattern' of development by accidental crisis. This 'development by crisis' is further sustained by a prevalent attitude of top managers (passing on their own restricted wisdom and experience) of 'drop them in the deep end, and if they don't drown they may be one of us.'

Effective development takes place in an open system in which conditions of organisational necessity, individual aspiration and cultural environment are integrated. This view of total development is symbolised in Figure 2.1.

My hypothesis as to why interventions to stimulate development are so often ineffectual is that all of these relationships need to be orchestrated and any one of them, if missing or distorted, can frustrate any permanent developmental breakthrough.

This framework is an essential guide when we plan a positive intervention to stimulate manager self-development. It illustrates that even with a good programme there are still five major factors that can weigh against our success.

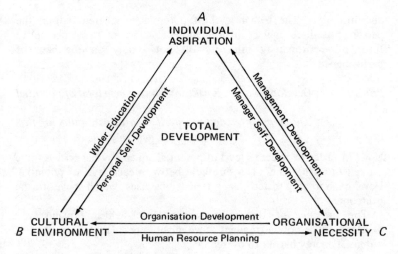

Figure 2.1 Total development

1   The organisation top management does not see the necessity for it.

2   There is an inadequate management development scheme to cope with its success.

3   There is low personal aspiration to develop in the population.

4   The mental and experiental horizons of the managers are too narrow (hence rejective).

5   There is no strategic basis for the proper deployment of self-developing managers.

These are the context factors which influence success or failure in stimulating a manager's self-development. There are also intrinsic factors which are to do with the nature of development itself.

Principles of self-development

Development takes place when an intelligent system breaks through to a new level of potential. Development implies some metamorphosis or change of form. This view of development should prevent us from confusing it with simple change, growth or learning. People certainly undergo change, growth and learning in going through a developmental step, but the converse is not necessarily true.

A developmental step is from a given level of potential to a higher one. It is not a step of 'more of the same'. It is a step of release, a discontinuity. The higher level of potential is inherent within the person, but there may be little obvious evidence of it. A perceptive tutor or mentor may infer it, but not simply on the basis of performance.

Principle 1   Development is a breakthrough to a new level of potential

Principle 2   Development manifests itself as a discontinuity of performance

Now, in order to release a level of potential, an energy barrier has to be broken through. There is a threshold between each level of potential. Development is resisted by internal obstacles which have to be overcome.

The presence of thresholds is one factor which explains why development is not as frequent as we might expect: there is always this potential energy barrier to overcome.

Principle 3   A threshold of difficulty has to be crossed

Particular conditions have to be fulfilled if a person is to be able to cross a threshold and release a new level of potential. Some of these conditions are internal; others are external. Principal in the external conditions is the presence of an appropriate challenge and opportunity for development. The challenge must match in a sufficient number of ways the 'gap' of potential which is to be crossed. A challenge may under-stretch or over-stretch a person, rather than give just the right kind of demand. It is one of the skills of a coach to identify those challenges which best suit the next step to be made in a person's development.

Principle 4   Appropriate external challenge is essential

However, it is also clear that external conditions alone do not really constitute a developmental opportunity. The perception by the subject is the main internal condition which determines whether given circumstances are indeed a developmental opportunity. External conditions can be provided but how they are taken is out of external control: 'you can take a horse to the water, but you can't make him drink'.

Principle 5   Right internal perception of the challenge is essential

Now consider the significance of the term 'self-development'. The prefix 'self' has two distinct meanings. Firstly, it indicates that it is the self, the person, who is being developed as distinct from the organisation or the business. Secondly, it indicates that the impetus to development is self-initiated. You have to do it to yourself. In a great proportion of learning the teacher is seen as the prime responsible agent to invoke learning. In a self-initiated process, however, the prime responsibility must be from the learner to learn.

Principle 6   Self-development is self-initiated

The self-developer, consciously or unconsciously, accepts the view that he has latent potential, that he wishes a breakthrough in performance, that he will have to overcome thresholds and that he needs appropriate challenges. He also knows that he has, like Beethoven, to 'seize fate by the throat' and even turn seemingly negative situations to positive advantage in his maturation. The self-developer always 'makes a profit'. He is involved in the risks of accepting challenges that he cannot compartmentalise into one isolated corner of his life. Accepting this is perhaps the major transition from non-developer to self-developer.

Principle 7   The self-developer accepts challenges to his total self

For example, the lone Atlantic sailor is not simply putting his or her sailing at risk, but the whole of life, even life itself. Similarly, a self-developing manager will put a secure job at risk to take an opportunity to fulfil his potential. People differ in the extent to which they can accept total challenges and this provides one measure of the self-development capacity.

Such a view of life cannot be sustained without self-discipline. Discipline implies a capacity to identify and adhere to priorities, to carry out the apparently mundane tasks which have to be done in order to provide sound groundwork for future action, to recognise and avoid the distractions which thwart development.

Principle 8   Self-development requires self-discipline

One of the hazards of self-development is, therefore, that people must be given the scope to be undisciplined. If discipline is constantly imposed from without it will not lead to self-discipline but to conditioning. Conditioning is at odds with the creative release of potential. Any vigorously imposed pattern of behaviour will inhibit the emergence of insight. Creative insight is perhaps the most crucial qualitative factor in self-development. There seems to be a direct relationship between seeing for oneself and jumping over the threshold. In works of creative art or science this is the spontaneous flash which removes the struggles of seeming to get nowhere. In development it is the inward realisation that what has hitherto been impossibly difficult is now natural.

Principle 9   Development requires creative insight into the self

The person who has cultivated the capacity for creative insight into the self has gone beyond basic creativity in ideas or arts. Insight into the self is not external as is the arrangement of paint on canvas. The canvas is the man himself and the pigments are the various talents and abilities which can be patterned and organised in the self. This requires a power of reflection and impartial self-scrutiny. A person who can face life challenges in this way has learned how to learn about himself.

Principle 10   Self-development requires learning how to learn about oneself

It is not enough to have learned how to learn in the educational sense. Learning about the self is a mature psychological attitude of mind, a kind of pragmatic spirituality and courage to face the truth (and therefore the lies) in oneself.

Beyond the pain of self-learning is the joy when potential is released. A self-developer is oriented towards results but as much because they are a measure of his fulfilment as because of performance. Truly high performers who are secure in that state show a surprising lack of interest in performance relative to those who are expecting it from them. They are more concerned about what they expect from themselves. They have what we can call intrinsic motivation rather than extrinsic motivation. Extrinsic motivation is basically some form of external reward and punishment mechanism.

Principle 11   Primary motivation is through self-achievement and self-fulfilment; external rewards and punishments are secondary

This is one of the crucial conditions for achieving a degree of freedom over the coercive factors in the external environment. If one is seeking to be rewarded by fate or expects to be punished by it, one will be less inclined to seize it by the throat.

Principle 12   A self-developer is willing to undertake personal risks

Principle 13   A self-developer is able to judge whether his intention is strong enough to carry him through

Principle 14   Capacity to self-develop is related to length of time tolerated for receiving intrinsic reward

Principle 15   A self-developer is able to judge how far he is dependent or independent

Principle 16   A self-developer recognises that nothing will be achieved without personal sacrifice

These fundamental judgements facing the person who would undertake a step of self-development make the task a lonely one. For this reason, it is often the case that the influence of other respected people is crucial to the intensity and pace of development. The self-developer, just because he is self-initiating, needs the exemplification and guidance of those who are already pursuing this path or way of life. This shows most clearly in the traditional master—pupil relationship, where the pupil was considered a potential master and had to show considerable self-initiative and self-discipline as well as talent. However, the master was a source of encouragement, a mentor through difficult times and a mirror for evaluating authenticity and honesty. The master was also there to moderate the judgement of the less experienced aspirant. As the saying goes, 'the guide exists because the path is rough'.

We now have a paradox of self-development to consider. It is crucial to the practical problem of stimulating self-development.

Principle 17   Self-development requires the guidance of a more mature self-developer

The provocation of insight is highly fragile and vulnerable unless aided by the objectivity of a person who has experienced the successful over-coming of a number of developmental thresholds in his or her own life. This is where the role of counsellor or adviser is crucial, but to be authentic a further principle must be clear.

Principle 18   Self-development can best be induced by a person who is a mature self-developer

This principle has crucial repercussions on any organised attempt to foster self-development in managers or any other group of people in institutional roles. It poses severe limitations on the role of trainers as facilitators for self-development unless they are actively engaged in the process themselves.

However, it is not sufficient even to be alongside another self-developer for an *acceleration* of one's own self-development. There is the matter of self-understanding which requires certain kinds of psycho-logical and cultural know-how. There is an *art* of self-development and the presence or absence of this art in a culture will partly determine the degree to which self-development takes place.

Principle 19   Acceleration of self-development requires the assimila-tion of specific knowledge and techniques

One of the most potent blocks to self-development is conditioning to wrong assumptions about oneself and one's own possibilities. Part of the know-how is to do with correcting these false self-perceptions which can both overestimate and underestimate a person's real potential.

We need to apply to ourselves knowledge and techniques which help us to break through thresholds. This requires both action and study. It also requires a warm trusting relationship with a mentor or facilitator. Application of this knowledge and technique can be described as 'work on oneself'.

Principle 20   Acceleration of self-development requires conscious work on one's own self

This accelerated form of working already calls for a degree of reflective maturity in the individual manager. He needs to be willing to face weaknesses in a positive manner and to make special investment of time and energy in cultivating strengths.

This set of twenty principles is summarised in Table 2.1.

Table 2.1
Principles of self-development

1	Development is a breakthrough to a new level of potential.
2	Development manifests as a discontinuity in performance.
3	A threshold of difficulty has to be crossed.
4	An appropriate external challenge is essential.
5	Right internal perception of the challenge is essential.
6	Self-development is self-initiated.
7	The self-developer accepts challenges to his total self.
8	Self-development requires self-discipline.
9	Self-development requires creative insight into the self.
10	Self-development requires learning how to learn about oneself.
11	Primary motivation is through self-achievement and self-fulfilment; external rewards and punishments are secondary.
12	A self-developer is willing to undertake personal risks.
13	A self-developer is able to judge whether his intention is strong enough to carry him through.
14	Capacity to self-develop is related to the length of time tolerated for reviewing intrinsic reward.
15	A self-developer is able to judge how far he is dependent on or independent of conditions beyond his control.
16	A self-developer recognises that nothing will be achieved without personal sacrifice.
17	Self-development requires the guidance of a more mature self-developer.
18	Self-development can best be induced by a mature self-developer.
19	Acceleration of self-development requires the assimilation of specific knowledge and techniques.
20	Acceleration of self-development requires conscious work on one's own self.

Designing development events

Developmental events have certain design difficulties not present in the design of a management training course. The main reasons for this difference are:

(a) development events are open-ended; they do not have terminal behavioural objectives;

(b) the risk is much higher in a developmental event since the trainer/facilitator cannot control the outcome of specific sessions;

(c) the facilitation of a developmental event requires the development of trust and hence continuity of relationship throughout the event;

(d) the resource materials/methods brought into the event have to be flexibly administered without necessarily relying on a fixed programme.

The self-development programmes I have experimented with involve two industrial clients and over one hundred senior middle managers. The self-development philosophy was desirable in both cases because of the respective strategic challenges both businesses are under. Managers at the selected level are having to face frequent reorganisation due to top management's responses to the challenges and hence management development cannot follow its traditional pattern. It is easier, in my view, to introduce self-development philosophy in a firm facing a *strategic imperative*. Corporately, the need for a developmental step is recognised and, individually, managers are aware that changes require them to operate at a higher level of potential, even to survive.

A number of key threads were woven together in the course design. They could be considered the rationale for the design process, although it would be misleading to suggest that they were as articulate as reported here at the commencement of the design process. Their formulation is also coloured by the criteria for success and failure which emerged in the seven courses we have run.

Theme 1   Reflective learning

Learning for development is not the same as learning for training. For development there has to be a deeper confrontation which is unusual for most managers not previously exposed to some philosophy and practice of self-development.

To set up the conditions for developmental learning some model of levels of mental function is required. We can distinguish three major levels.

At the lowest, *inertial level*, the mind is functioning by momentum in the well worn grooves of habit. It is very difficult to change direction and also to change pace. If it is a slow pace then the task will inevitably grind along regardless of external urgency. If it is a fast pace, then everything will be insensitively steam-rollered before it.

At the middle, *assertive level*, the mind is energised and actively thrusting in the direction of work. It is more sensitive to obstacles and changes and will knock them down or find a way around them. However, this mind state is strongly ego-centred and is blocked off from external views at variance with it or from deeper insights from the self.

The upper, *reflective level* of mind is very alert and perceptive but not assertive. It is, so to say, standing back from itself and observing quietly the nature of what is being presented, both externally and internally by association. At this level we can speak of an 'open mind' which can appreciate views other than its own, insights from the deeper self, and which can enlarge and extend its ways of under-standing.

The mental life of a line manager is predominantly at level 2 – the assertive level. He is using this to give impetus to the inertia of the organisation and 'get things done'. This fact necessarily puts the manager in a frame of mind in which activity and assertiveness predominate. Yet for the individual manager to *develop*, he or she has to enter the third level of mind where new understandings can come and locked up potential can be released.

This state of affairs leads to a 'culture shock' when a line manager is put into a level 3 reflective climate. It is only when the perceptions and insights begin to emerge that this transition crisis is overcome. The role of the facilitator in this is crucial. The facilitator should:

(a)   sustain a level 3 reflectivity in himself or herself;
(b)   maintain confidence in level 3 whatever reactions occur in individuals or groups;
(c)   transmit, by example and coaching, that confidence to individuals and groups.

To loosen up a manager's mind set and release wider mental poten-tial, a change of perspective has to occur. This is stimulated in several ways by self-development exercises:

(a)   a new basis for assimilating experience is given;
(b)   differing points of view are confronted;
(c)   new information is shared;
(d)   the benefit of reflective thinking is experienced;
(e)   the facilitator demonstrates the way of relating to the materials.

Each exercise is a way into understanding a theme of importance in modern management. The themes have been chosen as a result of intensive consultation with firms facing the many and varied issues of change and development.

Through working at the level of reflective insight with an exercise, a manager can achieve a fusion between his experience and the concept such that his experience is viewed in an entirely new light. He will find this 'learning through experience' has immediate practical consequence for his attitude of mind and his practical decision taking.

Theme 2   Action development

The term action development is used here as complementary to action learning. Generally, the emphasis in action learning has been on task problem-solving in a freshly stimulating environment and on a temporary assignment basis. Project set meetings help plan group learning and consolidate learning experiences. Faced at the right time by the ready person, this task work can lead to developmental breakthrough. The experience and insights gained release a new level of potential which is stable and operable in the job situation. Hence its power compared to conventional management training.

However, action learning can proceed without reference to principles of self-development 19 and 20 above. That is to say that the specific knowledge, technique and motivation of self-development is not actively transmitted. Action development is a process of task problem-solving into which developmental know-how is also fed.

The tasks are personal projects, job related, which are prepared on a course and carried out after it. The project provided a focus for testing the development. Choice of the project is crucial and is guided by the tutors.

Action development can be viewed as a recurring cycle which approximates to the following six steps:

1   Stimulus to self-diagnosis: self-development requires intrinsic motivation. The facilitator can provide a framework against which the manager can assess his own position. Externally administered tests have very limited use for self-development. The problems and opportunities must be seen for oneself.

2   Perception of developmental gap: some kind of experience-based learning is important to establish in depth and detail the nature of the developmental gap. The clearer the perception of the nature of the problem the more chance there is of the manager seeing where he is starting from and what he has to do.

3   Remodelling of experience: associated with the energy threshold of any developmental gap is a mental set which has to be given up (either destroyed or temporarily abandoned to be included in a wider perspective). Development is often blocked by the identification of consciousness with one particular view of the world, one 'concept

window'. This prevents the expansion of consciousness associated with continuous self-development. To break through a threshold we have to experiment with new models of experience and increase our range of viewpoints on the world.

4   Application to need: unless the new models of experience are applied to real action they fade out as empty talk. However, the right situation has to be chosen to make practical experiments in alternative behaviour. Until some mastery at the next level is achieved there are risks which can cause the timid to delay application until the remodelling benefit is lost. This is why focus on some essential task provides a useful vehicle for getting over this gap.

5   Monitoring achievement: at a new level of potential new criteria are needed to judge performance. Too much fixity in the old criteria will prove defeating to the newly emerging potential. Very often the context (e.g. the job environment and culture) will project heavy expectations for the old behaviour. The individual needs to be clear as to how he is to appreciate his own progress. To the extent his mentor, line boss or peers can also appreciate this, he is strengthened at the new level.

6   Growth of confidence: to be a thorough-going self-developer one needs to have confidence in the process. With each successful journey through the action development cycle, the sense of satisfaction and fulfilment builds up and the self-initiative is kindled. The subject of self-exploration with a practical orientation becomes an interesting one.

Theme 3   Transformation of perception

Reflecting for many years on the question 'What will really make a difference to a manager's performance?' I have come to the conclusion that the key is perception.

'As a man sees so does he behave.' It is not quite as simple as belief determines behaviour, although there is a connection. It is his actual mode of perception. Take the issue of freedom to act. If a manager perceives that the only way things can be done is through the rule book or custom and practice, then he will behave within those constraints. If he sees custom and practice as merely one possible way, then he will, if necessary, influence and change custom and practice to achieve results. Equally, if a manager does not perceive certain factors (say assumptions) in his situation then he will act out his work oblivious of them. He will usually feel threatened if they are pointed out to him. Hence learning at the level of questioning assumptions is very hard to achieve.

Theme 4   Key frameworks

The initial concept in Figure 2.1 shows that both the environment — social, cultural, political — and the organisation impinge on the individual. Self-development has to take these two arenas for its working material. To understand the forces at work in them and on them, managers need to understand something of the strategic predicament of the firm, of the changing role of the manager, and of those changes in society which will challenge their assumptions and way of life. To assist in the design of self-development programmes we have already generated over one hundred frameworks for discussion and enquiry, and anticipate a resource bank of some three hundred to have the desired extent and flexibility.

Part of this library of stimulus material is also concerned with individual aspects of development. Such areas as learning how to learn, self-management, self-image and learning through experience are included. These areas are part of the crucial knowledge about self-development which each aspiring manager should have. It includes some basic and practical psychology about strategies of learning, about the nature of insight, about the two sides of the brain and about the nature of creativity in management.

How these four themes are woven together emerges from a combination of:

(a)   consultative investigation of client needs by means of semi-structured interviews;

(b)   the views of the principal client commissioning the programme; and

(c)   the constraints and opportunities of the given programme.

The programme is fairly well prescribed, but in such a modular form that it is easy for the tutor to be flexible with the needs and trends of any given group. Also the precise design varies from course to course if it is a series, due to the joint learning which always takes place.

Achievements and difficulties

In a typical course/workshop we can distinguish the following levels of response to the stimulus to self-development:

(a)   those to whom the idea that they can intentionally develop themselves further is new and the realisation of this is a mind opener;

(b)   those who feel they have not learnt anything new about themselves but who have been helped to reassess their priorities, confirm their self-image and confirm strengths not necessarily recognised by the organisation they work for;

(c)   those who report at least one shock in self-perspective, sometimes upsetting, sometimes exhilarating, which opens up a whole new field of exploration;

(d)   those who are ripe to encounter a threshold and during the course make the breakthrough which really does alter their way of working as a manager.

The projects provide a useful measure of short term benefit. We have cases of managers making a breakthrough in perspective which saves the company substantial amounts (at least an order of magnitude greater than the investment in the programme costs!). On the other hand there have been a couple of occasions where individuals found the developmental crisis precipitated led them to seek more fulfilling employment elsewhere.

Another beneficial result we have noticed is the switch from extrinsic to intrinsic motivation. A group concerned about the increasing difficulties of achievement becomes infected with a new energy to tackle the difficulties, not on the basis of corporate reward, but on the basis of turning it into a developmental challenge.

In Table 2.2 are shown some of the self-reported insights arising from the programmes. They show the range of impact such a programme has.

The main difficulties we encountered in carrying out a self-development stimulus can be related pretty clearly to the model in section one of this chapter (Figure 2.1). A key inhibiting factor was lack of appreciation of self-development as valid and relevant by the boss. Few bosses proved to be the calibre of mentors. The resources to tackle this problem directly were not available. However, some headway was made by introducing a special 'appraisal' document which was used at the discretion of the participant with his boss. Also the theme of 'managing your boss' was explicitly on the agenda.

Another difficulty was the fact that, on the whole, lip service only was paid to the concept of management potential. The explicit policies are often a thin veneer of very static attitudes and assumptions about people. This tended to become clear to participants as their insight developed and could be pretty disillusioning for them.

Some parts of the client culture could be called 'one-concept cultures'. The official view here was that 'for heaven's sake, don't give them another concept. It will confuse the one we gave them last year'. In fact, we attribute to most human beings of modest intelligence the capacity to entertain simultaneously several distinct and useful concepts. Typically, we introduced a dozen or more on our five-day programme.

Table 2.2
Learning points from the workshops

The insights were expressed by managers on the final afternoon of the course in answer to the question, 'What have you *seen* of importance for your own development as a manager?' The points are grouped under general headings to aid summarisation and reading.

Self-discipline
1   Value of methodical approach
2   Engage brain before opening mouth
3   Making time to create strategic vision
4   Managing one's own strengths and weaknesses
5   Truth is difficult
6   Seeing the similarity in the way we all spend our time

Learning how to learn
7   Self development is *active*
8   Learning from experience
9   Shock of recognising one's own preconceptions
10   Evaluation of personal style
11   Challenging assumptions behind objectives
12   Relativity of success and failure
13   Personal diagnosis
14   Getting a framework which enables diagnosis and understanding of the management culture

Influence
15   Power is not such a bad thing
16   Understanding how my power base is composed
17   I am the 'MD' of my area
18   Examining the impact on others of one's own style
19   Seeing how managers have influence

Blockages
20   'It's up there' syndrome
21   Amount of running while standing still
22   Realising how we are playing games

Creative management
23   Idea of the *enterprising* manager
24   Helicopter vision
25   'Radar' anticipation
26   Acting before *events* take place
27   Aim of wealth creation
28   Connection of vision, change and leaning
29   Seeing opportunities in change

Job performance improvement
30   Understanding the effect of different styles of managing change
31   Seeing a choice of management methods
32   Diagnosing the various categories of management actions
33   Seeing room to manoeuvre in terms of one's style

Team work
34   Dynamics of small groups
35   Value of studying how people are different
36   Reasserting authority by example
37   Consciously deciding a management culture

Confidence
38   Hope
39   Stop panic
40   The organisation style need not be crippling.

Yet another difficulty was that our work was positioned under the training function. This encouraged confusion between training and development. It also tended to cut us off from the small population of top and senior management mentors who should be the dynamic driving force to sustain the self-development ethos.

One overall impression from all of these difficulties was their marked contrast with the impression of under-utilised and unfulfilled potential in the managers we shared these events with. It confirmed for us the disabling role that institutional cultures have on personal realisation. Many people cling to the apparent security of institutional life, but inwardly are at odds with the restriction that need for security puts on their creative potential. In its extreme form this creates a kind of organisational paranoia — the idea of developing human potential appeals as long as it is not put into practice.

If practised it becomes too threatening to the pretty low level psychological glue which holds the institution together. This makes the role of stimulating self-development a very delicate task.

Continuing stimulus to self-development

For the established self-developer, all life presents an opportunity for learning. He is not dependent on the presence of formal opportunities. However, self-developers do need resources and do construct or participate in special developmental events. The conventional training function of an industrial corporation is an almost completely inadequate vehicle for stimulating in a varied and continuous way the needs of a self-developer culture.

The philosophy of the self-organised learner has stimulated such concepts as autonomous learning in which managers are left to get on with it with a bank of resources. The difficulty is that that type of learning is most likely to succeed when the need spontaneously arises on or off the job. The particular 'blow' has to be delivered whilst the 'iron' is hot. The delivery systems currently in use are too restricted.

We are now actively investigating with a small number of clients the potential of the forthcoming revolution in combined computing, text processing and telecommunications technology. Picture a world in which every office has access to a multipurpose terminal which can serve as a communication station, an information retrieval station, as a text processing facility and as a computer. Each terminal is in a network communication system. A given company could then operate a central design and facilitation resource providing both materials (frameworks) and personal guidance on manager self-development. Managers in all locations, without having to travel, could:

(a)   conduct self-diagnosis on the terminal
(b)   receive coaching by telephone on the basis of results
(c)   be guided to materials to help remodel their experience
(d)   share that experience with similarly concerned managers whatever their location by computer conferencing
(e)   report on the successes and failures of their application attempts
(f)   receive normative guidelines, special coaching, newly designed materials on the basis of centrally monitored usage and performance
(g)   contribute their own innovations to the system.

The sensitive and experienced touch of mentors and facilitators would still be needed but their effective stimulus would be maximised. Such a system would provide facilitators (e.g. management development advisors) with a very accessible flexible resource which cuts down diagnostic and design time in providing counselling, coaching or workshops. Such a system also facilitates establishment of a network of co-counselling managers − a kind of company-wide 'project set'.
The types of interaction such a system will support are:

(a)   individual self-diagnosis and study
(b)   peer co-counselling
(c)   individual − adviser consulting
(d)   individual − mentor coaching
(e)   team building − line or project
(f)   OD type workshops
(g)   course design and conduct.

Out of these interactions the limitations of conventional performance appraisal systems will be transcended. Relatively continuous self-review will be possible and bosses will be encouraged to learn how to become mentors in the system.
Taking a longer term view, the problems for the realisation of such a system are not technological. The technology is already in the pipeline, some of it spilling out already into the market place. The problems are in terms of the learning software, the diagnostic instruments and the cultural adjustment. The introduction of such a system is itself a major organisation development exercise. It is encouraging that a few corporations of widely differing sizes are willing to take exploratory steps in this direction as a joint development activity.

3 Creating the climate for self-development

Paul Temporal

Paul Temporal's approach to self-development is to see it very much as a process of overcoming blocks within the person — perceptual, cultural, emotional, intellectual and expressive — in order to learn and develop in a non-contrived way. Given this approach it is not surprising that he sees the creation of the right sort of climate for self-development as the top priority. Repressive climates in organisations block the individual every bit as much as any factors within himself. In fact as Temporal illustrates with two short cases, it may not be worth attempting self-development unless the organisation has the sort of climate which will support managers who want to grow and develop.

Introduction — self-development and non-contrived learning in management

Contrived and non-contrived learning and development

The development of any manager — supervisor or director — is directly dependent on the amount of learning that he or she accomplishes. Traditional management development schemes have tried to maximise that learning through the provision of well thought out and clearly executed learning experiences, such as training courses. Furthermore, if we try to pinpoint what management development is and how it takes place by looking at management literature, we immediately learn that management development is the outcome of a whole range of planned learning experiences, such as job rotation, performance appraisal systems and formal training courses. We are given the impression that a manager's learning and development is highly structured and is not a continuous process. Nothing could be further from the truth. In fact, the larger part of managerial learning and developing takes place under conditions that are not planned or deliberate. It is these non-contrived aspects of learning, I believe, that provide the greatest resource for the self-developing manager, who is looking to learn from every possible situation.

It is surprising that so few writers and researchers have given up their time to consider how managerial learning originates and how it takes place, but one particular study of note which reinforces the fact that much of it is non-contrived, is that by Burgoyne and Stuart (1976). Through research interviews with a substantial number of managers, nine major sources of learning were found, ranked in order of importance, as follows (see also Temporal, 1978):

1 Doing the job — managers pick up skills as they go along.
2 Non-company education — spending time in public educational instruction.
3 Living — learning from their experiences in out-of-work activities.
4 In-company education — deliberate training interventions.
5 Self-learning from meditation, reflection, introspection and self-assessment.
6 Doing other jobs — non-managerial jobs prior to taking up a role.
7 Media — newspapers, books, professional journals, television, etc.
8 Parents — home background, upbringing and guidance.
9 Innate learning — gained from the potential existing in an individual, usually genetically predetermined.

It seems clear from this research that the sources of material learning are only partly to do with planned learning activities. Further work by Burgoyne (1976) tells us how this learning comes about, by identifying seven learning processes associated with managerial competence:

1 Modelling — copying or imitating a 'respected other'.
2 Vicarious discovery — observing the actions and behaviour of others and the consequences of that behaviour and acting accordingly in similar situations, e.g. 'It seemed to work for him, so I'll try it', or 'That action failed so I won't try it'.
3 Unplanned discovery — experiences at work, trial and error learning.
4 Planned discovery — going into situations with the deliberate aim of learning from experience.
5 Being 'taught' — being told or shown an approach, ideas, systems, etc.
6 Discussions — the sharing of information, ideas, feelings and experiences.

7   Storing of information – remembering data, facts, during the course of events.

The above learning processes also reinforce the idea that much learning for managers takes place in a non-contrived way and they also suggest that the amount of learning that does take place is very much dependent on the individual's ability to identify and take advantage of potential learning situations.

The self-developing manager – what can hinder him?

It appears then that the non-contrived aspects of learning present the largest area of reward for the self-developing manager and that being a self-developer he will look for and capitalise on such occurrences. However, we have now built into this argument the assumption that the manager knows how to learn from work experiences and that he can dispose of any barriers to learning and self-development that stand in the way. Unfortunately this assumption is not likely to be correct because the majority of managers have not learned how to learn in a variety of ways and every manager, as part of his psychological make-up, will possess some internal barriers to learning and development.

The other point to note – and one which will be discussed later – is that the range of non-contrived learning opportunities may be limited by factors which will vary between organisations; factors such as the physical work environment, the climate for learning development within the organisations and manager–boss relationships.

Section 1   Individual blocks to learning and self-development

The self-developing manager can be the cause of restricted learning himself if he cannot identify and remove the barriers or blocks to learning that he will inevitably possess. Such barriers are of great significance for non-contrived development because they can prevent individuals from making full use of the many unplanned learning situations that occur every day, both in and out of work. There are five main types of internal barriers to learning which occur within the individual:

1   Perceptual blocks: where the manager is unable to see what the problem is, or to recognise what is happening in a situation or to see opportunities for development.
2   Cultural blocks: where the manager denies himself access to a range of new behaviours (and the learning that ensues from them) because he is conditioned to accept a set of cultural norms regarding what is good or bad, right or wrong, etc.

3   Emotional—motivational blocks: where the manager feels insecure in certain situations, which causes him to be reluctant to take action on his ideas and beliefs. As a result he may not start self-development or make further progress in it.
4   Intellectual blocks: where the manager has not developed the right learning skills, the mental competence, or the experience to resolve problems and approach situations correctly.
5   Expressive blocks: where the manager possesses poor skills of communication, leading him to inadequate relationships with his boss, subordinates, peers and others.

To show the extensive impact the above blocks can have on a manager's ability to develop himself and people under him, let us consider a relationship that can result in both contrived and non-contrived learning — the coaching relationship between a boss and his subordinate at work.

Table 3.1 (developed from Temporal, 1978) shows how these blocks can (a) hinder a manager's own learning in general, (b) hinder his learning when he is a learner in the coaching relationship and (c) hinder his ability as a coach in helping others to learn and develop.

Included in Table 3.1 is an example of how blocks external to the individual can also prove to be considerable obstacles to learning and development. The manager's environment in terms of its richness of resources and the climate for development in the organisation, can effectively frustrate him in his attempts to develop himself and may promote internal barriers to learning as well and this area, because it is so important, is discussed at length in this chapter.

As all individuals have some blocks to learning, it follows that the more of them that are present in the learner's psychological make-up, the less effective his learning and resultant behaviour are likely to be and the less likely he is to be a self-developing person. This proposition has been well summed up elsewhere in the following statement:

> Unless the individual perceives his need for continued learning and growth and accepts personal responsibility for initiating steps toward learning, unless he has reduced internal barriers and blocks to learning and unless he has learned to receive help from others in processes of changing, little continuing learning or change will take place in himself or in the social systems of which he is a part . . .
>
> (Bradford et al., 1964)

Thinking in terms of specific management behaviour, it can be said that blocks to management learning, self-development, improved performance and new behaviour may effectively prevent a manager from gaining and exercising the skills of:

Table 3.1
Blocks to managerial learning and the coaching process

Nature of block to learning	Effect on a manager's learning in general	Effect on a manager–learner in the coaching situation	Effect on a manager–coach in the coaching situation
PERCEPTUAL	Manager has limited vision regarding the total range of learning sources and processes available to him.	Manager does not perceive the need to be coached,' or similarly to assist his colleagues.	The coach cannot identify the individual's real development needs, and so selects the wrong tasks.
CULTURAL	The manager's background is such that he wants his source of learning to be planned inputs from specialist teachers.	Manager rejects the idea of coaching because he has been taught to help himself – the entrepreneurial approach.	The manager new to coaching cannot resist the temptation to give a straight answer when the learner comes to him with a question or problem.
EMOTIONAL–MOTIVATIONAL	Manager avoids entering into learning situations that are potentially painful, and that might threaten his security/credibility.	Manager is reluctant to expose his weaknesses to others in the organisation.	The coach feels he is unable to share his own problems, and so prevents the learner from seeing the bigger picture.
INTELLECTUAL	Manager does not believe learning to be an ongoing activity.	Manager cannot apply to other situations what he has learnt from his coaching experiences.	The coach denies the need to give the learner plenty of feedback on both his good and bad results.
EXPRESSIVE	Because of his poor listening/speaking skills, the manager underrates the value of group discussions, meetings, etc., and so avoids them.	Manager cannot explain ideas, feelings, etc., clearly to his colleagues/coach.	The coach cannot translate ideas into terms and language which are readily understandable by the learner.
ENVIRONMENTAL (Climate)	Risk-taking is not encouraged, and so the manager does not experiment with new ideas and behaviours.	The climate is such that a manager does not feel able to be honest and open about problems, feelings, etc.	The pressures from top management are such that the coach consistently checks up on how the learner is dealing with a problem/situation.

being creative
being flexible and adaptive
communicating with others
experimenting with new ideas and ways of doing things
self-confidence, through the fear of making mistakes and taking risks
perceiving problems and solving them with the correct strategies
autonomy and independence
decision-making, judgement-making, judgement deferral
goal setting and seeking
leadership and the ability to influence people
honesty and openness with self and others, building trustful
    relationships
determination, perseverance and emotional resilience
proactivity (inclination to respond purposefully to events)
rule setting and the use of criticism and praise
the transference of learning and the ability to see remote
    relationships and many other facets which have a bearing
    on his development.

Despite the acknowledgement by many people now that personal factors are important in managerial self-development, teachers and trainers have given more thought to developing the existing range of abilities of managers and less thought to ways of helping individuals to reduce or remove individual blocks to learning which would lead to increases in the persons' range of abilities. The argument for reversing the emphasis lies in the fact that the extent to which managers are able to avoid many of these blocks will depend a great deal on their frequency of self analysis, their self-knowledge and their self-development skills.

With the dearth of guidance for managers on how to explore these areas, further explanation of the block areas, with examples, and some activities to try out are given in the next section. Management teachers and trainers can assist managers in developing themselves by designing similar, but more extensive kinds of questions, instruments and activities for use with managers in their organisations.

One further important consideration that can help or hinder managers in developing themselves through the process of identifying and removing any blocks they might have is the climate for learning and development that exists in the organisational setting, of which mention has already been made. Section 2 discusses this in detail.

Section 2   Environmental blocks to self-development

Clearly, the right kind of organisational climate can be crucial to the improvement of managerial behaviour through self-development.

What is meant by 'organisational climate'? A great deal of research has been carried out in organisations to try to identify what the constituent elements of the climate in organisations are. None of the researchers or writers on organisations is in complete agreement, but there are general areas that are considered highly important in shaping the kind of climate that managers will encounter whilst at work. I would describe organisational climate as a range of norms, practices, policies, procedures and relationships that somehow combine to influence the learning, development and behaviour of people in the organisational system, but this statement needs further explanation.

The concept of climate is probably the most important and least understood set of ideas that has been considered in the field of managerial learning during the last twenty years. Most important — because climate is a ubiquitous reality. All organisations possess their own climate or culture and every manager will be subject to the influence of the climate in his organisation. Least understood — because no one has yet produced an adequate theory and explanation of what constitutes climate and how climates influence people and organisations, in other words, how they work.

Before looking at the fundamental elements of organisational climate that influence managers, it is important to mention one more thing, and this is that the climate in any organisation will exist only as an individual's conscious or subconscious subjective impressions or perceptions of it. Each individual will see the climate quite differently from other individuals. To the manager, the climate seen by him in his office, department, section or sub-unit of the organisation will represent the climate of the organisation itself. This means that where organisational sub-cultures exist, there apparently may be more than one climate in the organisation; there may be several micro-climates. Also, because the individual identifies climate through his particular psychological screening mechanism, his responses to and his behaviour within that climate will be based on his own interpretation of events and how they appear to affect him.

The list below contains those characteristic elements of climate that are generally agreed upon as being important influences on managerial learning and behaviour.

Organisational pressure for performance and results	Attitude to authority
Warmth, support and consideration in relationships	Role clarity and relationships
Degree of openness and open mindedness	Leadership styles
Organisational structure and role relationships	Organisational clarity

Type of reward systems in operation

Peer relationships

Management concern for employee involvement

Attitudes to change

Autonomy: freedom of action in doing a job

Administrative efficiency

Organisational rules, policies and standards

Future orientations

Degree of interpersonal conflict and co-operation

Scientific/technical orientation

Attitudes towards risk taking and the making of mistakes

Emphasis on job challenge

It is very important for every self-developing manager to be able to assess the climate and how it might help and hinder his strategy for self-improvement; to identify his organisational support and constraints to development and further learning. After thinking about the above list, perhaps at this stage you might like to think of other items that you consider to be important aspects of the climate in organisations you have worked in. At the same time, ask yourself whether they helped or hindered your job performance and your learning and development. All the above elements of climate and many others, can potentially and actually influence a manager's learning and development. For instance, consider the characteristic of 'autonomy'. A high degree of autonomy in doing a managerial job, if accepted by both organisation and individual, could encourage self-development, by giving a person his preferred freedom of action and behaviour and the opportunity to learn from being able to take many decisions involving many different responsibilities.

The findings from my own research with managers in organisations suggests that there are two types of climate constituents that are considered conducive to self-development — support constituents and pressure constituents. The following instances show examples from the two categories:

Supportive elements

Goals (individual, departmental, organisational) are clearly defined

Experimentation is encouraged

Mistakes are tolerated (provided learning takes place)

Individual and cultural differences are respected

A trusting and accepting atmosphere is predominant

Collaboration is felt desirable

Pressure elements

Bosses delegate heavily a variety of problems and activities

Managers are encouraged to take leadership roles

Constructive criticism is encouraged upwards and downwards

Competition is accepted as being healthy

Open confrontation is a normal relationship

Targets are set that are difficult but

Supportive elements

Feelings are considered to be as relevant and as legitimate as ideas and skills

Systems and relationships are open to inspection and feedback

Pressure elements

achievable

Managers are placed in positions of ambiguity and uncertainty at times and are told why

As much responsibility is given as early as possible

Managers are asked to change roles, jobs and functions reasonably frequently (e.g. twice yearly) i.e. change is a behavioural norm

These generalisations are useful in providing a framework for looking at elements conducive to overcoming obstacles to self-development but what counts to every manager is his own climate and how it helps and hinders him. The following exercises might be useful in helping you to understand your climate and further define the helping and hindering influences.

Environmental blocks to learning and improved behaviour

Exercise A

Supportive environments. This exercise is designed to get you to analyse your ideal and actual work learning environment, with the aim of identifying any gaps. The term 'supportive' means most encouraging, least hindering in nature.

Step 1. Take a piece of paper and list the characteristics of the most supportive possible environment you can think of for your own type of work and learning style. You might want to think in terms of organisational norms, rules and procedures, attitudes, levels of risk taking, etc. You might also consider helping behaviours of others such as your superiors, your peers, your subordinates, etc.

Step 2. Answer the following questions.
  (i) Does the environment in which you work resemble that shown by your list? Outline the similarities and differences.
  (ii) Do you feel that you personally can alter your work environment in any way towards your stated ideal? List any reasons why or why not.
  (iii) If you feel that you can alter it, in what ways would it affect your job as a trainer/manager? The ways in which others relate to you? The ways in which you relate to others?

Step 3.   Find someone else who can complete Steps 1 and 2 and share your answers.   Are their similarities/differences in your ideal and actual climates?

Step 4.   What questions has this exercise generated for you as a learner?   What are you going to do about them in connection with your own situation at work?

Exercise B

Restrictive environments.   This exercise asks you to identify the factors in your work environment that definitely hinder your learning and development.

Step 1.   Make a list of everything at work that you feel restricts you from doing your job the way you would ideally like to do it.   Write down the 5 things that you resent most from the list.

Step 2.   What do you as an individual need to overcome these restrictions, e.g. what information do you need, what experience do you need, what skills and attitudes do you need?   What power do you need and how can you get it?

Step 3.   Ask a colleague similarly to complete Steps 1 and 2 and share your answers.   Are there any similarities/differences in hindering factors?   Are there any similarities/differences in your identified individual needs?   How can you help each other to satisfy these needs?   How can you apply what you have learnt from this exercise to your future development?

Section 3   The link between climates and self-development

The climate in an organisation will always present gateways or barriers to managerial self-development, but the effect of the climate on self-development will depend largely on three things:

1   The amount and extent of the existence of factors of either kind — gateways or barriers (the influential balance of these).
2   The way in which the self-developer perceives the gateways and barriers, or indeed, if he sees them at all.
3   The qualities inherent in the individual's personal learning character, which determine his reactions and behaviours within the climate.

The influential balance of the gateways and barriers to self-development presented by the climate in any organisation is clearly important in being oppressive, supportive or indifferent to individual learning. Nevertheless, equally important is the form and extent of individual perceptions. The way in which the individual sees the climate, or parts of it, as directly affecting him will tend to determine how much influence he and that climate will have over each other. For instance, some managers in organisations might not perceive that there are encouragements to learn present, or alternatively, they might perceive discouragement factors in the climate as being dominant while other managers in the same organisation may view things quite differently.

However, once these perceptions are there, the individual's mix of learning abilities and blocks to learning will determine how effective he is in maximising his development potential and in minimising climatic discouragements to learning and development. To illustrate this idea and to help you consider whether climates always influence individuals or whether individuals can influence climates, consider the model in Figure 3.1.

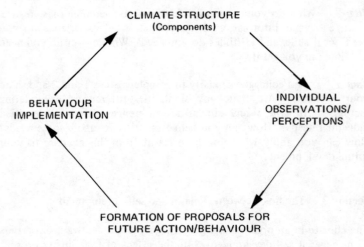

CLIMATE STRUCTURE
(Components)

BEHAVIOUR
IMPLEMENTATION

INDIVIDUAL
OBSERVATIONS/
PERCEPTIONS

FORMATION OF PROPOSALS FOR
FUTURE ACTION/BEHAVIOUR

Figure 3.1   Influence of climate on individuals

This model clearly tells us that climates can influence individuals, but that the reverse might also be true. For instance, if the individual does not perceive any inhibiting factors, or thinks that they do not really affect him, or believes that he cannot change things even though they do not affect him, his proposals for action may be to continue with present behaviour. This will have a minimal effect on the climate and will tend to reinforce the *status quo* of the organisational norms, processes, etc. Alternatively, he might see certain aspects of climate that help him in his development and some that hinder him and believe that he can use this knowledge. If this is the case, he is more likely to attempt direct action in the form of new behaviours designed to maximise helpful aspects and minimise hindering aspects of the climate.

So with regard to self-development, managers are likely to be more effective in learning from the non-contrived work experiences associated with climate if:

1   They are capable of analysing which parts of the organisational climate are helpful and which can hinder their self-development.
2   They believe that they can influence climate and use their interaction with climate elements as learning experiences.
3   They are willing to take direct action aimed at improving the climate for self-development, as they see it affecting them.

This may sound easy but it is not, first, because it is difficult for a manager to analyse the climate in the organisation that surrounds him and secondly, because changing the climate can be a frustrating, painful and sometimes an impossible task for an individual. The following case studies deal with the possibilities for changing climates.

Two case studies in attempts to change the climate for self-development

The consequences of climates that are not conducive to learning and development can be disastrous for the self-developer, as the following case study will show. It deals with the case of a Financial Director who understood the meaning of self-development and consciously tried to develop himself and others working under him for the benefit of his organisation. It shows that in an organisation there are always some aspects of climate and interpersonal relationships that can be changed, but it shows also that there are occasions where the real blocking elements cannot be removed and the individual then has to face a critical decision — to stay and not develop or to leave to further his development.

Case study A: A poor climate for self-development that could not be sufficiently changed

The Financial Director and Company Secretary of a manufacturing firm that employs between 80–100 people has for some time felt that his efforts to increase his personal effectiveness and the effectiveness of the organisation were not productive.

It was suggested that he fill in an organisational climate supports and constraints questionnaire containing 100 items which would help him to clarify his areas of discontent and give him a data base upon which he would start to minimise or remove the perceived constraints to his job performance. He completed the questionnaire and was surprised to find that he appeared to have more constraints than supports to carrying out his work effectively. In fact he found that only one item made it a great deal easier for him to do his job well (that being his own level of appropriate experience, skill and knowledge):

the number of severe constraints was 41 ⎫ the total number of
the number of lesser constraints was 11 ⎬ perceived constraints
⎭ was 52

the number of strong supports was 1 ⎫ the total number of
the number of lesser supports was 8 ⎬ perceived supports was
⎭ only 9

(12 items did not apply to his situation; 27 were relevant but did not influence his work.)

The chief areas of discontent (appearing as constraints) were identified as being:

the poor standards of work of his fellow managers, subordinates and, to some extent, his Managing Director;

the fact that his Managing Director would not allow him the further autonomy and responsibility necessary for him to develop and grow within his job;

the lack of good relationships between managers and directors, e.g. lack of trust, lack of openness and honesty, poor interpersonal skills and the systems of rewards and punishments in existence;

the lack of adequate procedures for setting and maintaining high standards of goals and good systems of information and control.

Outcomes. The outcomes in this case were far-reaching. The Financial Director used the information gained from the instrument to plan his attempts to modify or remove the constraints areas of his job. Over a period of several months he managed to put in additional systems of work to help other staff improve their standards of performance and improve the flows of information. These proved to be highly successful and company profitability improved as a result of their introduction. The Director also managed to improve interpersonal relationships within the management team, partly through his own efforts and partly by utilising an external consultant as a training resource for interventions. Unfortunately, what he could not do was to resolve the problems that surrounded his relationship with his Managing Director and this led to severe conflict. The Financial Director eventually realised that he had done all he could to improve the overall organisational performance and that he could see no further opportunities for self-development or for helping others to develop. He spent several agonising weeks, with a loss of health, before taking the decision to leave the company and look for a position which could give him better opportunities for self-development.

His joining another company has allowed him more autonomy and has led him to work in several areas that he had little experience of before. He has since claimed that he learnt more in the six months after he left his firm than in the three years with his previous firm. He is now a happier person, has overcome illnesses associated with previous work pressures and frustrations and is enjoying considerable personal growth and achievement.

Comment.   Some organisational climates will just not allow for personal growth. It is important for managers to test their climate in various areas to identify the gateways and barriers that are influencing or can influence their development. Self-developers need to be able to overcome the barriers, but if these are insurmountable, decisions like the above become inevitable.

It is easy to feel despondent about the extent of organisational climate influences which are felt to hinder self-development, but managers must be capable of realising that climates can be changed and they must realise that they are capable of bringing about such changes.

Case Study B also deals with climate change. It shows that if people work towards changing the climate, it can be achieved. Although a person external to the company gave assistance in this case, the climate changed because all concerned were committed to changing it.

Case study B: A poor climate for development that was successfully changed

A small distribution company had 'people problems'. The 7 Senior Managers and 3 Directors had all felt at various times that relationships between them left a lot to be desired. Team spirit in the organisation was minimal and references had been made at management meetings to the 'tug-of-war' that existed between Managers and Directors. One Director in particular was very concerned about this for two reasons:

1   He was a very 'people-oriented' person and wanted his managers to have the right conditions within which they could develop. He wanted to develop himself through developing others and through extending organisational effectiveness.

2   He had realised that the right conditions for self-development were not present in his organisation, the main barrier being a lack of trust and helping relationships between the Managers themselves and between Managers and Directors. The atmosphere was, he felt, too humid and stifling for growth to occur.

While talking about this problem, which was clearly a climatic one, he asked for assistance in helping him to analyse the problem in more detail and with greater accuracy and in helping him to put matters right. This led to an in-depth diagnosis of where in the climate the problems lay.

A great deal of time was spent with individuals in getting them to identify clearly their perceived supports and constraints to work performance and subsequently two sets of data were prepared — one for the Manager group and one for the Director group.

Taking each group on its own, members' views were consistently similar but when the data for each group was contrasted, it was clear that each group differed strongly in their views in certain areas with regard to perceived supports and constraints. There were, in fact, clear cut areas of conflict and frustration and a marked lack of confidence in each other's abilities.

Both groups, Directors and Managers, agreed to having all the data presented to them at a residential week-end — they wanted to clear the air. The data was discussed in detail with all 10 people present and the areas of conflict were openly identified and talked through. The week-end continued with activities and exercises designed to remove some of the interpersonal conflict areas and eventually concluded with the members formulating an action plan of objectives, organisational and individual training needs and development activities which would provide a team-building approach to the development of the organisation over the following year.

Outcomes.   The programme was completed and many of the problems identified during the climate analysis were resolved, the result being a great deal more unity, collaboration and trust between Managers and Directors. The programme designed by members was based entirely on attempts to capitalise on perceived organisational supports and attempts to remove perceived organisational constraints. Work performance, job satisfaction and personal development increased for all participants and the year following the programme proved to be the most profitable the company had enjoyed for several years.

Comment.   In this case, there was a clear need to initiate changes in the organisational climate in the area of interpersonal and intergroup relationships. Climate changes can only occur if problems are brought out into the open and this process, while initiated in the above example by a third party, was largely accomplished by the Director himself once he had established his objectivity and commitment to change with others. Managers can change the climate of the organisation by confronting issues and by persuading, influencing and helping people and setting an example for others. I know of several instances where

ordinary managers have achieved climatic change within their organisations and they have been successful because they have been quite clear
about which aspects of climate they wanted to change and equally
clear about the strategies open to them in initiating change.

Summary and conclusions

Self-development requires of managers the following personal characteristics:

the capability of self-analysis in terms of understanding their own
strengths and weaknesses, their blocks to learning and development;
the capability of analysing the environment/climate that surrounds
them in terms of whether it is supporting or constraining their
development;
the capability of identifying the full range of learning sources, processes and possibilities that arise from their work experiences,
whether contrived or non-contrived;
the commitment towards translating all of the above capabilities
into action, i.e. making their development happen.

This chapter has tried to show that the largest potential range of
learning and development activities for managers lies in non-contrived
situations that he can react to immediately or turn into contrived learning experiences. It has also tried to show that the biggest potential
barriers to self-development are those within the individual and those
imposed on him by his organisation's climate. The manager who
develops himself effectively is the one who is constantly seeking for
ways of improving himself and removing organisational constraints.
He can be assisted considerably in this process by trainers and management development practitioners who provide him with the resources
with which he can tackle these problems. He can be assisted by the
organisation if top management openly demonstrates its commitment
to providing a suitable climate within which self-development can take
place, in other words, giving management self-development the credibility it deserves in the form of time, money and personal example;
by acknowledging that the climatic conditions must be right if
managers are to maximise their learning from non-contrived and
contrived work experiences.

Checklist of questions for trainers and developers

1   Do I help develop managers or manage their development?
2   How can managers best be helped to develop their personal

learning skills in the company? How can I be a catalyst to this development?

3   How far can I provide managers with the opportunities to take risks, be creative and set and evaluate their own learning objectives? Do I want to? Will the organisational climate allow for this?

4   Do I encourage self-development in myself and in others? How do I do this? Can I do it better?

5   Can I identify the full range of learning possibilities that exist within the organisation? Are they adequate for all managers? If not, why not? What additional learning activities would be desirable?

6   Are managers openly encouraged to comment on the worth of the learning opportunities and structures that affect them? If not, why not?

7   Is training in this organisation geared to current work performance? Should it be? Why? Why not?

8   Should management development in this company be designed to accord with opportunities for self-development? Are my views consistent with those of top management? Can I talk to them about it?

9   Can I make an assessment of the factors most influential in both helping or obstructing managers in learning within the organisation, i.e. can I obtain some measurement of the climate in the organisation? How?

10   Do my training and development plans and actions take account of these factors? How? If not, why not?

11   Does management training ever conflict with management development in my organisation? If so, in what ways?

12   Have I learnt how to learn? How can I improve my learning style and the range of my learning experiences?

13   Have I any 'blocks' to learning that are stopping me from experimenting with new ideas in training and development?

14   Am I setting an example in the organisation by developing myself?

15   Am I providing managers with the resources they need to help develop themselves?

References

Bradford, L. P. et al., *T-Group Theory and Laboratory Method*, Wiley, 1964.

Burgoyne, J. G. and Stuart, R., 'The Nature, Use and Acquisition of Managerial Skills and other Attributes', *Personnel Review*, Vol. 5,

No. 4, pp. 19–29, Autumn 1976.

Burgoyne, J. G., 'Learning Processes in the Acquisition of Managerial Skills and Qualities: a Research Note', *Management Education and Development*, Vol. 7, December 1976.

Temporal, P. M. E., 'The Nature of Non-Contrived Learning and its Implications for Management Development', *Management Education and Development*, Vol. 9, pp. 93–99, August 1978.

PART II

TWO DESIGNS FOR SELF-DEVELOPMENT

Overview

This section contains six chapters depicting different designs for self-development which share common principles. If there is a patron saint of self-development then it is probably Janus — perpetually looking in and looking out. The balancing of 'inward-boundness', by 'outward-boundness' is the motif of *Phil Radcliff* and *Phil Keslake*'s chapter and it appears in *Malcolm Leary*'s as the inner and outer biographies. The spirit of Janus is abroad in the stress which these chapters place on action followed by reflection — *John Heron*'s 'educated person' who develops competence through a reflective enquiry into practice. It is Janus who demands that our peers be both supportive and challenging: that our friends be willing to act as 'enemies'.

All the six chapters use peer group settings as part of the self-development design. *Mike Pedler*'s piece discusses some of the practical difficulties which such designs do face — shall I pursue my own goals or should I stop and join this other person in the pursuit of his? *Malcolm Leary* points to the common and unique aspects of biography. The significance of the learning community as a cradle for self-development rests on this transpersonal reality, this sharing of the human condition.

It is also clear from these chapters that self-development approaches are 'whole person' approaches. The inter-relationship of personal and organisational goals in *Tom Boydell* and *Tony Winkless*'s self-development groups serves to underline that we are talking about the manager as a person. The role and function of manager may be part of a person's outer biography or part of his professional competence but the problems and opportunities which self-development designs address are those of the person. *John Morris*'s chapter describes one approach to helping people to bring together the development needs of the individual and the organisation.

All the contributors share an optimistic faith that we can be more than we are. Liberation of people as managers to fulfil their rich potential is the concern which runs throughout. The question of whether the individual or the organisation benefits is only superficially valid — the organisation may often seem to constrain the individual, but this in turn is the result of constraining actions of people who are that organisation. Self-developing individuals make for a developing organisation — more flexible, more creative, more responsive to challenge and more easily able to adapt, learn and develop.

4   Self-development groups

Tony Winkless and Tom Boydell

Outlines some useful criteria for selecting people within the organisation who are likely to benefit from a self-development approach – underlining the point made by Mumford *(see Chapter 14) that self-development is suitable for particular people and not for others. This chapter describes the form which self-development groups have taken in the Geest organisation and touches upon the central questions of whether self-development is for the benefit of the individual or the organisation or both. It seems from this example that it is not helpful to draw a clear distinction between personal and work-related goals; at any real depth they are inextricably related. The chapter closes with some self-evaluations from participants. Greater self-awareness and life/career planning were often mentioned as gains. Two out of the eighteen people gained nothing and were perhaps not ready to take the opportunity on board. It is interesting to speculate on* Paul Temporal*'s point about supportive organisational climates here – is the climate at Geest particularly supportive or does this success rest on the skill of Tony Winkless in holding a protective umbrella over this development?*

Introduction

Although perhaps best known for bananas, Geest is in fact a diverse organisation with many interests. These range through food processing, food distribution, engineering, shipping, horticultural products, computer bureaux services, mini- and micro-computer sales and services. The organisation employs about 3,000 people in South Lincolnshire and a further 2,500 in various parts of the UK. Because of the wide-ranging products and technologies there is a corresponding diversity of managerial and technical skills employed.

Interest in self-development activities began in 1977. The reason for this interest stemmed from a number of factors. One was a growing sense of unease over the usefulness of the traditional management training approach of externally imposed objectives, design and content. Strongly linked to this was a belief that for training activities to be of value it was necessary to start from the viewpoint of the individual. In addition, much of the training activity was concerned with assisting people with their current roles, and it was considered desirable to place greater emphasis on helping people to plan and manage their future. At this time the company had established a link with the research work by Sheffield Polytechnic in self-development, and in consequence several pilot studies were implemented. The basis of some of these studies may be found in the exercises given in Pedler, Burgoyne and Boydell (1978).

As a result of these pilot studies, four self-development groups were started: in November 1978, April 1979, September 1979 and November 1979. At the outset we had decided that we would invite people who were considered already to be displaying signs of being a 'self-developer', and this point should be borne in mind when reading this account. Our initial profile of a potential 'self-developer' required that participants should:

(a) display some evidence of having taken initiative for their own development (rather than waiting for something to happen or be done to them);

(b) be conscious of life as a learning experience and display an ability to act on that learning;

(c) be prepared to work with and help others in self-development activities; and

(d) be prepared to confront personal issues.

The majority of participants were invited by members of the Training Department on the basis of personal knowledge of these people. In a few cases, managers who had expressed an interest in the events for their subordinates were given the profile and asked to use this as a guide for selection. All participants were given an explanation of the aims and rationale of the events, and then asked to consider whether they wished to attend on a 'you call us' arrangement. Of the 28 people invited, 25 accepted our invitation.

The aims given to prospective participants were:

(a) To appreciate the nature of self-development and the opportunities available for participants to manage their own development.

(b) To enable participants to examine their personal commitment to their own self-development and to help other participants.

(c)   For those participants who wish to make a commitment, to enable them to take further steps in a conscious programme of self-development; to generate personal strategies; to make concrete short term plans for action; and to consider longer term activities.

The age range of participants was 20–43, with a mean of 29.

Occupational groupings were marketing (2), computing (7), accounting (3), management services (1), personnel (4), production (3), administration (3), sales (2). We restricted the size of the group to 6 or 7 participants, plus 2 facilitators. Because of the diverse nature of the company and its geographical spread, participants in each group knew two other members of that group at the most.

The structure for group meetings involved a start-up event, with a number of follow-up meetings. In the first instance the starter lasted three days, but this was found to be slightly too long, and subsequent events were of two days' duration. Follow-up meetings lasted about half a day each, and were held at approximately 2 to 3 monthly intervals. The contract was that participants were expected to attend the first two follow-up meetings after which it was for them to decide whether or not to continue.

The start-up events

The design of the start-up events may be seen as an extension of earlier work using a 'learning community' approach (see Chapter 5) which had been in use at Sheffield for the training of trainers (short courses) and of postgraduate human resources specialists. A few one-week self-development workshops had been run in this way, but the contact with Geest provided the opportunity to work with people from one organisation over a longer period of time.

A brief resumé of some of the underlying principles might be helpful here:

the learner him/herself is the person to decide what he or she should learn, although
such goal-setting is not always easy, and may be aided by other group members ('learners' or 'facilitators')[1]
significant learning is often a difficult or painful process, and may be helped by a supportive learning climate (see also Chapter 3)
all group members (not just 'facilitators') have resources to offer that can be of help to others, although
as with goal setting, participants often find it very hard to identify what it is they have to offer.

The design of the start-up events themselves has therefore reflected these principles. Although each event is unique when it comes to a detailed description of exactly what took place, they tended to follow a broad pattern that will now be described.

The first phase has been some form of introductions/climate building session. Typically, each group member is asked to take a piece of flip-chart paper, write his/her[2] name on it, draw a picture of himself/herself, state why he/she has come to the group, what he/she expects from the event and write down one other piece of information about himself/herself that he/she wants to share. The papers are then attached to the wall for general viewing. This is followed by some form of discussion, either in whole group or in two smaller ones, followed by a brief input on the processes of disclosure and feedback, the part they can play in development, and conditions that help these processes.

We have then focused on the nature of 'self-development' by each person identifying a number of key developmental events in their lives, together with brief descriptions of their outcomes and characteristics. These are then shared in pairs (further disclosures and risk-taking), and then discussed in whole group, this discussion leading into an exploration of some of the notions, guidelines and principles of self-development as elaborated in Chapter 1.

The stage is now set for individual goal-setting. This may be an overstatement, because very often it is a case of identifying issues or vague areas to work on, rather than setting specific goals as such. Although this has to some extent been done as part of the flip-charting referred to earlier, we nearly always find that this first level of issue-identification is very broad, and has to be narrowed down and/or elaborated more specifically. Even so, as the following examples show, the issues or goals are still, in some cases, pretty broad.

Develop a 3-year plan for my division
Examine my life-pattern dilemma
Get closer to my wife and children
Get promoted
Improve my self-discipline
Determine my aims with regard to work/education
Make allies within the company
Examine my management style
Improve physical fitness
Resolve a conflict between me and someone else in my department
Clarification and confirmation of life/career objectives
Stop working late
Learn to relax
Learn how to channel stress/energy into a productive outcome

rather than a destructive one
I don't want to set goals — I just want to use everything that
happens as an opportunity for development.

The most difficult phase now follows — resourcing and planning.
'Facilitators' and 'learners' offer resources that seem reasonably appropriate to the various issues, but it is very easy to push a favourite activity towards somebody, persuading oneself that it is just what is needed.
This is a trap we find ourselves falling into. Consequently at times,
perhaps, we err in the opposite direction, that of failing to offer something in case it is not, after all, appropriate. The indivisibility of
resources is also a problem; for example, if one facilitator is counselling
person A, then he is not available, for that particular time, to do something else.

Another problem lies in 'tagging along' — the tendency, once someone has decided what to do, for another person to seize this and say,
'I'll do that too'. No doubt this is sometimes useful, but we do feel
that sometimes it is used as a crutch, allowing the person concerned to
avoid the painful task of commitment to something potentially more
valuable.

Nonetheless, after quite a degree of hesitancy, confusion, checking
and double-checking — all of which seems enormously time-consuming
— everybody is at work on some issue or another. Typically we might
have two one-to-one counselling sessions, one pair doing a certain
exercise together, a group of three discussing a common problem, and
two individuals working alone — one perhaps reading, the other using a
computer-terminal for an on-line exercise.

Clearly, it is not possible to list all the resources used during such
an event. However, a broad classification might be as follows:

Counselling skills; one-to-one with a 'facilitator'.
Co-counselling skills; one-to-one with a fellow learner.
Information giving; usually one-to-one, with a 'facilitator' or fellow
'learner'.
Discussion/sharing in small group.
Structured exercises and instruments; usually provided by a 'facilitator'. For example, each participant is given a copy of Pedler,
Burgoyne and Boydell (1978) which consists of such exercises. We
have also used the 16 PF personality inventory, discussing the
profiles with individuals.
Computer-based activities. For example, we have used the Management Learning Project NIPPER program, via a telephone coupler, to
examine the relevance of one participant's present management
style to a new area of responsibility that he was soon to take up.
(See Chapters 11 and 15 for descriptions of computer-assisted
reflective learning.)

On an event as short as two days, participants rarely work on more than one or two issues each. However, this seems long enough to establish ways of thinking and to build a base from which to continue. We therefore close with an immediate evaluation session and, perhaps more important, with planning for individual, paired or group activities between this event and the first follow-up meeting.

From feedback at these follow-up meetings, it seems that a number of participants do get together, semi-formally, to work on something specific. However, this is relatively unusual. A more common link-up occurs when, in the course of everyday work, the individual now knows somebody to contact. This is clearly one of the advantages of an in-house programme of this nature.

Most of the post start-up activity, however, appears to be done individually, either in doing further structured exercises, or straight-forward thinking. For example:

> I've thought a lot. I stop and think about why I feel belligerent and aggressive. A lot of people commented at work that I seemed a lot calmer, less brash and impulsive . . . I now feel I don't need to show I'm better than others. I also feel 'part of' Geest — more involved. But I'm also a bit wary of this — is it good or bad? Have I lost a bit of me? I try to be more tolerant — I still feel I know what's right for me, but recognise that other things might be right for other people.

External and internal facilitators

Having two facilitators even with a group as small as these is useful for a number of reasons. Clearly, it allows us to spend more time with individual participants, and it is also most helpful in giving each of us a co-counsellor to discuss the event in between working sessions. There are also certain characteristics possessed by an external facilitator that an internal one does not have, and vice versa.

The external facilitator

The original reason for engaging an external facilitator was that nobody in the company had the necessary experience to run self-development groups. The aim was that, after an appropriate time, the internal training staff would be weaned-off external help. In practice, however, the company view of the role of the external helper has changed. Without doubt, external specialist help has been very valuable in getting the work under way. However, there is a further role for the outsider in that, because internal training staff are inevitably part of the power and communication structures of an organisation, some participants prefer to confide in someone who is perceived as neutral and outside that organisation. In all our self-development groups, the usefulness of having the choice of internal and external facilitators has been evident.

The internal facilitator

As an outsider, I (Tom Boydell) have a few observations about Tony's role as an internal facilitator. Perhaps this can be summarised thus:

a key agent in the selection process; he usually knows the participant (indeed in most cases he invites him or her) and his or her boss; someone who can be trusted. It seems to me that during his time at Geest he has gradually built up excellent relationships with managers at all levels – partly by running relatively conventional activities – and they are therefore prepared to try out this somewhat unusual approach;
this trust also helps develop an appropriate learning climate, and eases the processes of disclosure and feedback;
a source of knowledge about the company. He is often able to put someone in touch with another person who can be helpful; he is also able to explain various aspects of internal politics. He thus has a key network-building and maintaining role;
a continuing resource/support person. As an outsider I'm not there except at the actual events, whereas the internal facilitator is available at most times.

This last point can, indeed, give rise to difficulties, as it can become simply too demanding to be involved in extensive counselling sessions, as well as doing the other aspects of one's job. This is, of course, an issue faced by all 'professional helpers', although hopefully it shouldn't be *too* severe if the goal of enabling others to develop themselves is achieved.

Follow-up meetings

The follow-up days originally had two purposes. The first was as a means of assessing the outcomes of the 'start-up' days. The second was to allow people to continue, if appropriate, with work on their self-development with others in the group. By November 1979, SD(1) had met four times, SD(2) twice and SD(3) once. The frequency of meetings, decided by the participants, has been about every two to three months for each group. (The first two meetings are part of the original contract with participants. Thereafter, meetings are entirely optional.) Common to all groups has been a progress report from each participant, given at the beginning of each meeting. From these reports stem the pattern for most of the meetings. The nature of the reports fall broadly into either information-giving or help-seeking activities. In the former, participants present their progress to others in the group, without the need for help or depth discussion. It is possible that others may seek more information, perhaps to help in their own problems, but essentially the presenter is happy to go it alone on this occasion. Those who are seeking help usually have identified a problem before the meeting and are looking to the group to help solve it. In this respect, the groups take on the appearance of the action learning set. However, the problem to be worked on is usually, but not always, the self. Here are some examples:

(a) perception of self by others (three occasions);
(b) coping with the disappointment of delay over an expected promotion;
(c) to be or not to be a manager;
(d) analysing the reasons for an inter-group conflict;
(e) acquiring the most appropriate qualification for a desired alternative career (two occasions);
(f) conflict over family and work pressures;
(g) handling a difficult interpersonal problem at work (two occasions).

Now that we have experience of participating in these activities, we feel that two further purposes are emerging. One is that the meetings provide one way of establishing a safety net or life line (as one participant had termed it) for those who may, for example, have found a problem awakened in themselves which was unsatisfactorily resolved during the initial event. For many participants they are at times entering unfamiliar psychological territory and there is, in consequence, a likelihood of people experiencing uncomfortable and possibly highly anxious feelings. (Such feelings frequently accompany key development events, as discussed in a number of other chapters.) Although it is our aim to help people through such feelings during the event, the possibility nevertheless exists that participants may find themselves outside the groups and in need of help when such feelings occur. For these reasons, we now stress the availability of follow-up sessions, the need for sharing, and the availability of ourselves and other members of the group if there is a need. In this way, we seek to avoid some of the risks rightly raised by some workers (see, for example, Mumford, 1979). In this respect, there does seem to be an advantage in in-company events, where such meetings are relatively easily set up. In this respect, it is worth noting that meetings have taken place between pairs of participants outside the set group meeting.

A further purpose of the follow-up days, and we are rather tentative about this, is that some participants seem to value them as a form of retreat or quiet harbour where the opportunity exists for contemplation in a supportive environment. There is some confirmation of this in the evaluation data given below.

Some evaluation data

As one step in assessing the worthwhileness of the events, all participants of SD Groups 1, 2 and 3 were asked to complete, in open answer form, the statement 'What I have gained from being a member of a Self-Development Group is . . . '. Responses were obtained from 15 of the 18 participants. Here are what we feel to be significant extracts.

I can self-analyse my reactions to events both in my working and private life.

More confidence.

Better understanding of people.

Set you thinking, looking at yourself and at others until after a while you both look back and the part of you that needed developing has done just that.

Able to think away from my working environment.

Finding that other people's problems are similar to my own . . . never been able to discuss before.

More confidence in speaking about intimate details.

Meeting other people in the company doing different jobs.

Able to monitor by self-development.

Ability to think more clearly and plan better.

Greater confidence . . . allowed me to readily accept the challenge of my new job.

A more positive attitude and approach.

Has helped me to sort out the priorities I want out of life.

Clarified what I want and think I ought to want.

I have achieved a real awareness of what I really want.

I found the course extremely confusing mainly because of the almost totally unstructured (presentation) . . . I feel I would have gained more from, say, following the textbook more closely.

Some of the sessions were in my opinion a total waste of time, others . . . potentially dangerous to participants . . . particularly the sessions devoted to self-examination and personal performance appraisal.

Although the objectives I set during the session have been achieved it is probable that they would have been anyway, albeit not in the same time scale.

An awareness of myself. I have always been introspective but not constructively so.

I found that . . . I began to consider on a more practical level both the faults and advantages of the various aspects of my character.

The reaction of other members . . . instrumental in enabling me to evaluate . . . aspects of my character.

Clarification of personal goals.

Set of ground rules for (use) when dissatisfaction . . . sets in.

More awareness of personal strengths and weaknesses, ability to detect/read into characteristics and goals of those around me.

Increased awareness of my thought processes and attitudes.

Better understanding of how others see me.

Recognition of a character trait . . . try to moderate it.

Opportunity to stop and think.

Interesting listening to what others think of (a) me (b) themselves.

Chance to sound out others as to where I stand intellectually, status-wise etc.

Concepts of what was going on were similar to my own.

Extremely useful . . . in assessing my career to date, needs for the future, potential, and impact on others.

Continuance allows regular reappraisal in an objective environment.

Useful to understand other members' problems.

Didn't learn anything . . . has not inspired . . . perhaps I have not used others to my advantage.

My career has lifted itself out of a deep dissatisfying rut.

A chance to voice fears, doubts and worries about my working environment.

A degree of self-awareness.

Enabled me to set goals.

Increased level of self-confidence.

Reinforcement . . . no magic formula for success or happiness . . . most things in life require a lot of hard work.

Clarification and confirmation of life/career objectives.

Confirmation . . . that I am on the right tracks.

Check out some of the perceptions of others of myself.

Feel that goal setting is subordinate to goal identification and awareness.

Identified the need for self-control . . . higher intellectual level of conversation . . . change to old philosophies . . . a changed perspective towards social behaviour.

I find it reassuring to find that other . . . people had similar doubts and fears as me.

If your teacher is prepared to accept your help . . . then you must have something to offer.

Although less systematically obtained, participants have also claimed the following benefits:

1   Promotion to a new and more stimulating job in a different part of the organisation.
2   Better time management (several).
3   Confirmed in career choice.
4   Using an activity from Pedler et al. (1978) one participant developed a two-year forward plan for his unit that he had hitherto found impossible to tackle.
5   Improved office systems.
6   Boss 'over the moon' (his words) about the effect on his three subordinates in terms of motivation and job dedication.
7   Encouraging subordinates to form own SD groups — to work better together, help solve common problems.
8   Life planning exercise helpful in getting the right job.

The main theme in the statements appears to us to be related, directly or indirectly, to feelings of greater self-awareness. Of the fifteen respondents, all but three made at least one comment on this theme. In particular, it appears that participants valued being able to discuss how they are perceived or stand in relation to others. This, in part at least, probably contributes to the feelings of self-confidence expressed by some participants. A second theme concerns various forms of life or career planning. It was initially our feeling that participants would wish to spend their time mainly on goal setting and ways of achieving these goals. Although such activities featured strongly in the events, it is our conclusion that participants valued more the opportunity to explore themselves. One reason for this is that it seems reasonable to take stock of oneself before establishing plans for the future. However, a second reason may be that for many people the opportunity to discuss their personal feelings in depth is not readily available in their everyday lives. Several comments refer directly to this opportunity provided by the events. Perhaps goal setting, career plans, etc., are considered more legitimate subjects for discussion with boss or colleagues. As stated earlier, participants did not know most of the others in the group, and there may well be some connection here with the 'strangers on the train' phenomenon.

Two participants expressed dissatisfaction with the events, highlighting the need for flexibility in the way in which they are run – in their cases our events apparently failed to meet their needs. They seem to be telling us that they would prefer a much more structured format, although it is not clear that they would actually have benefited from this. This issue is of course related to the question of selection. We gave earlier our initial attempts at describing a 'self-developer'. A later attempt at clarifying our thinking by the use of a repertory grid analysis suggested that, for us, the following constructs were significant; self-direction, openness, easy to get on with, good at handling ideas, interest in theoretical and abstract matters. Juch (1979) in answer to his own question, 'Who then is this self-developer?' appears to share some common ground. He suggests that a reasonable answer might be found in the studies of the characteristics of the 'so-called healthy personality' (Allport, Jung, Perls, Maslow, Fromm, Rogers, Frankl). In respect to working life, individuals conforming to these characteristics, he suggests find that (a) work is a natural and essential part of life, (b) that working life is enhanced by working with others, and (c) that a proactive or interactive stand is taken. Clearly there are important issues here. For example, are these goals to be achieved or are they necessary conditions for a state of continuous development? How can we validly measure such characteristics in people? Are self-developers born or made? What are the implications for the organisation?

References and notes

1   It will be seen that the words 'facilitators' and 'learners' have been used in inverted commas. This is to highlight the fact that although 'facilitators' undoubtedly do possess certain resources/skills, 'learners' also do, although these may be different in nature. Furthermore, in these groups both of we 'facilitators' have taken part in the various activities, identified our own issues/goals, and worked on these with the help of 'learners'.

2   Five of the 25 learners were women.

Juch, A. H., 'Self-Development within the Organisation', *Management Education and Development*, Vol. 10, No. 1, Spring 1979.

Mumford, A., 'Self-Development — Flavour of the Month?', *European Industrial Training*, Vol. 3, No. 3, 1979.

Pedler, M. J., Burgoyne, J. G. and Boydell, T. H., *A Manager's Guide to Self-Development*, McGraw-Hill, 1978.

5 Developing the learning community

Mike Pedler

This chapter grapples with a number of issues central to learning community and self-development designs. The principles of the learning community approach are given and various questions are explored including the dilemma of whether to help oneself or to help others; the problems of managing the potentially rich array of needs and resources in a learning community; the tricky question of finding structures which are liberating rather than restrictive and the role of the trainer. Echoes of these dilemmas are found in all the other self-development designs in this section.

Introduction

As a design for management development the term 'learning community' has been used to describe a learning event with fixed time limits and existing for a more or less specific purpose. The design involves bringing together a group of people as peers to meet personal learning needs primarily through a sharing of resources and skills offered by those present.

Key points in this definition are:

peers: implying not equality of knowledge or skill but demanding that people meet each other on the same level irrespective of outside rank, status or privilege; that all share the norms of the learning community, e.g. as outlined in the three key points below;

personal learning needs: accepting that each of us has, in part, unique needs for learning which cannot be aggregated or equated with the needs of any other person;

sharing: indicating mutual interdependence in providing and partaking of the available learning resources; seeking to avoid the dominance

/dependency engendered by the fixed roles of giver and taker;

offered: indicating the nature of giving, i.e. that a person has him/herself or part of him/herself on offer in the understanding that this may not be taken up by any other person, and, if it is taken up, that it must be done on the other person's initiative and decision.

Examples of learning events which embody these characteristics are Roger Harrison's Autonomy Laboratory; Reg Revans' Action Learning Set; John Heron's Peer Learning Community and Malcolm Knowles' Learning Community.[1] One of the great ironies of the learning community can be seen by comparing that last sentence with the preceding definition. Although each of the designs named seeks the characteristics of the learning community, namely a relationship of peers, each with unique learning needs, offering and sharing, each of the designs named is associated with a founder. The irony is that learning communities, as e.g. one-week full time, one day a week for six months, or even a one-year full time course, are almost always organised and staffed by an outside agent who is clearly, at least in some ways, not a peer. The problem stems from a central one in all self-development designs, that of 'guiding people towards self direction' and is addressed later in this chapter in a section entitled 'The riddle of liberating structure'.

The learning community then is seen as resting on two major principles:

1 That each individual takes primary responsibility for identifying and meeting his own learning needs.
2 That each person is responsible for helping others identify and meet their needs and for offering themselves as a flexible resource to the community.[2]

The process by which the learning community meets its goals is seen as a community-managed one in which five activities can be discerned:

1 *Building the climate:* establishing openness, interdependence and mutuality.
2 *Sharing needs:* of all the persons present and the legitimacy of these individual needs.
3 *Providing resources:* both without but particularly within the persons present.
4 *Community planning:* to establish a 'programme' to meet needs, share resources, to learn and develop.
5 *Evaluation:* identifying criteria for success; looking at where we've come from, where to go next; resolving conflicts.

The following sections of this chapter are my attempts to reach resolution on a number of problems or dilemmas in the learning community design. As such they may seem more abstract than descriptive. To those who would like a longer account and description of learning community, there is the ATM's *Self Development* which is the first reference in this chapter. Apart from describing various designs in more detail, this publication will take you back to the original sources should you so wish. A further source of more descriptive detail is the case study of a one-week learning community that David Megginson and I wrote some years ago.[3]

The dilemmas considered below are:

the origins of the learning community in both therapy and development, like Janus looking in and looking out, helping self or helping others?

oasis for what?

the tyranny of the majority or requisite variety?

the riddle of liberating structure

the membership and non-membership of the trainer.

The origins of the learning community

The connection between learning and community has been acknowledged for centuries. Mediaeval monasteries served as oases of knowledge in otherwise barbarian environments, and the ancient idea of the university is as 'a community of scholars'.

But to focus on the ancient origins of the learning community distracts from the unique dimensions of our time which make this particular conjunction of sharing, support, self-development and work-in-the-world so apposite.

In our time the learning community stems from the two post-war movements, one concerned with learning, the other with therapy. Experiential learning groups, variously known as sensitivity training, encounter or T-groups, have proliferated since the late 1940s in America. The purposes of people participating in such groups include personal growth and development especially in terms of self image, interpersonal relationships and self direction. A major attraction is the experience of intimacy and intensity with others and the sense of freedom which this close community creates.[4]

The second influence stems from groups as providers of therapy for mentally disturbed people. A British psychiatrist, Maxwell Jones, is often credited with the founding of the first 'therapeutic community' at Belmont hospital shortly after the war. In such communities the usual boundaries between 'staff' and 'patients' are blurred in order to share decision-making and encourage people to act as therapists for one another. A set of norms is generated which emphasise comradeship and open confrontation of problems together with 'helping', i.e. encouraging people to own and be responsible for their actions.[5]

Both the Experiential Group and the Therapeutic Group movements emphasise values of community; close relationships and comradeship; confronting rather than ignoring problems; encouraging individual self-development and direction; and community self-government. There are clear parallels between these and various learning community designs. Self and peers as a prime resource for learning rather than experts; 'comradeship in adversity'; the symbiotic relationship of personal development and problem-solving are, for example, central characteristics of action learning. The culture of the learning community enables participants to find new personal solutions to living in a complex society.

It may at first sight seem strange to link together the learning community as a design for helping managers and other people learn, with therapy groups for the 'mentally ill'. However, the work of Szasz and Laing has blurred the previously defined lines between 'mental health' and 'mental illness' and also underlined the social element in mental disturbance. Indeed Laing's schizophrenic is akin to Maslow's peak experiencer in his transcending of 'ordinary reality'. The current preoccupation with managerial stress in the face of a turbulent environment and pressing internal needs 'to be one's self' is but one sign of this reconsideration. The primarily physical metaphors of 'health' and 'illness' just will not do: mental disturbance is not like a broken leg. Development and change in individuals require a disturbing and forsaking of a given equilibrium. Qualitative development, as opposed to quantitative learning, we think requires crisis or 'perturbation' as a precondition. Even simple psychomotor learning is associated with a higher state of stress or arousal. Therefore is the manager who is learning and developing also nearer to the 'mentally disturbed' pole rather than the 'mentally stable' one?

In learning communities participants often experience the dilemma of whether to pursue their own individual purposes or whether to support someone else. This tension between the personal and the communal, the looking in and looking out, the urge to differentiate self and the urge to integrate, is always apparent in this design. Participants in learning communities have to balance the 'looking in' with the 'looking out' aspects of therapy or education. 'Going back' and 'working through' via introspection and reflection is only valuable if it is used to illuminate the present and change the future. An imbalance between looking in and looking out hinders the learning process either through lapsing into obsessive and morbid introspection or by compulsive extraversion, goal setting and non-stop action.

The advance which the learning community has made on its origins is to add a third item to the duality of education (helping self) and therapy (helping others).

What is missing from both education and therapy is the element of purposeful work or being in the world. The focus of the learning community on purposeful action in the world as a source both of personal learning and of helping others brings in the social as well as the individual aspects of development. So, the objective of the learning community is

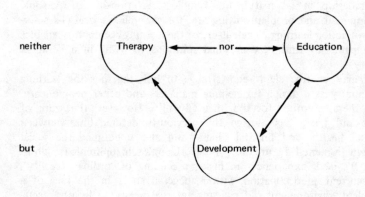

The use of the word 'development' to describe this third position of simultaneous helping self and helping others via purposeful work in the world is perhaps incongruent with some more individualistic construings of development. None the less a feature of most age and stage theories of individual development is a movement away from the individualistic and personal towards the altruistic and transpersonal. In this sense development demands a social contribution — a 'giving back' as well as a personal qualitative leap.

Oasis for what?

The idea of oasis is found in the concept of learning associated with the mediaeval monasteries and universities; in the sheltered environment of therapeutic communities and in the groups of the experiential group movement. Yallom uses the term 'social oasis' to describe the T-group where the individual can retreat from a world in which, measured in terms of outward and material success, he must maintain a façade, repressing any signs of inadequacy or uncertainty.[6]

The learning community as an oasis provides for its members:

a sense of small community, a 'we-feeling' in a situation where the individual can meet his own needs and help others to meet theirs and there will be no comeback — from the hierarchy, from the social system. A real feeling of sharing;

an unusual level of openness and honesty where it is possible to look at oneself and others without feeling the need to defend so much;

a sense of personal depth and worth, not always apparent outside this community, and enhanced by the emotional closeness of other people which develops through this openness, feedback and sharing.

But is this oasis a mere sea of tranquillity? Is it a haven from the intolerable which helps individual members to cope but which in effect maintains the *status quo* outside (and inside)? Oasis marks a point of rest and comfort in an otherwise hazardous journey; without the journey it loses its meaning. The learning community can provide its members with the support and insight which makes a powerful springboard for action, or it can conspire against that purpose in the world.

Personally significant learning or a tyranny of the majority?

The idea of conspiracy is also present in the goals chosen by the learning community and in the resources it generates to meet those goals. The community can legitimate the exploration of the multitudinous variety of personal goals or it can withhold this. As an educational design the learning community gives potential access to a richer field of resources in order to meet a widely varied set of needs. Ashby's Law of Requisite Variety is apposite here — 'Only variety can absorb variety'.[7] The idea of requisite variety is that any system set up to meet a given set of requirements must contain enough variety to match that contained within the requirements. In very simple terms a telephone switchboard with three lines will be very probably swamped by the demands of an office containing fifty insurance salesmen; whilst it might cope very well with a partnership of four solicitors. A modern supermarket copes with many more customers than the traditional grocers by increasing the variety of its response to the demands for speed and ease of shopping, i.e. self service and multiple checkouts.

It has been suggested that the learning community design self-consciously attends to the issues of climate, needs, resources, planning, action and evaluation *as a whole community*. This can be a complex and often time-consuming process which creates conditions of ambiguity and stress for those who are only used to the 'teacher decides' model of educational design. In the 'teacher decides' model, he sets the climate, decides what the goals are; what resources are available; how the teaching/learning shall be done; teaches it and evaluates the outcomes against his criteria. Using a simple systems diagram we may depict the 'teacher decides' model as in Figure 5.1.

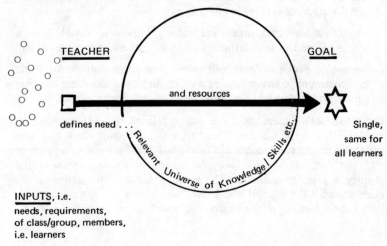

INPUTS, i.e.
needs, requirements,
of class/group, members,
i.e. learners

Figure 5.1   Teacher decides model

Usually then, the teacher decides and provides only one path through the relevant universe of knowledge to one common goal. Naturally enough this goal is one which satisfies his needs as well; the resources will be those which he can most easily provide; the methods for learning those with which he is most familiar and comfortable.

An advance on the 'teacher decides' model is a teacher—consultative, learner—feedback model. Here there is still a single goal, the teacher provides most of the resources and does most of the 'teaching'. However, there is now some greater exploration of the universe of knowledge, some understanding that there is no satisfactory single path to the goal. There may be some sub-groupings amongst the learners from time to time, but basically the group stays together. Splitting up would involve choosing between options, which demands clear personal responsibility for goal achievement. At this stage a widely voiced feeling is that 'I might miss something if we split up, I'd like to do them all'. ('Them' being the options.) The idea of equifinality — that a final state can be reached by a variety of paths — is still beyond this threshold. We might call this the 'lowest common denominator' model, because it pays some attention to the differences in requirements of learners, but tries to satisfy these as a whole group led by the teacher (Figure 5.2).

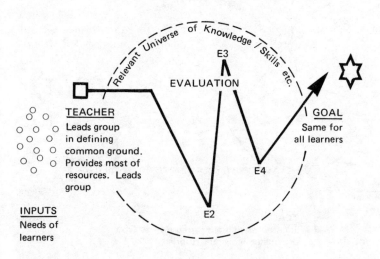

Figure 5.2   Lowest common denominator model

In Figure 5.2 the teacher still has his hand firmly on the tiller, but the crew get a chance to steer the ship from time to time. The 'teacher decides' orthodoxy is still apparent, but modified; the learners fear the extra dimension of shared control and perhaps come occasionally to the brink of the void which is an uncharted universe of knowledge, limitless and allowing of any number of alternative paths of exploration. The boundary of this universe is less well defined and more open to question than in the 'teacher decides' model.

The crew of course are often happy with this state of affairs. They have some feeling of personal influence, but the teacher – the authority figure – continues to carry the can. The conspiracy is often to maintain this pleasant state, occasionally sailing exhilaratingly close to the wind of personal responsibility and personally significant learning.

Model three is the equifinality model where alternate paths to a single goal are allowed (see Figure 5.3). This often consists of several sub-groups pursuing different paths to the common goals, using different resources only some of which are provided by 'the teacher'. Equally it can consist of individual learners pursuing individual paths to the common goal with personal tutorial help from the teacher.

The equifinality model of educational design is a popular one underlying for example programmed learning of the branching variety, various resource based learning designs and also the traditional university tutorial ideal. The tyranny of the majority is lessened in so far as some choice of goal path is allowed but it still remains in the insistence on a single truth, right answer or required performance.

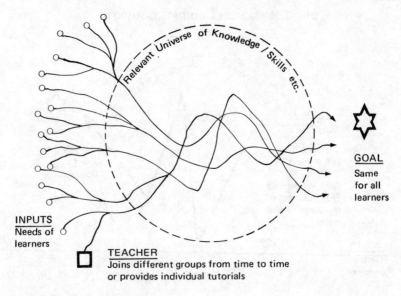

Figure 5.3   Equifinality model

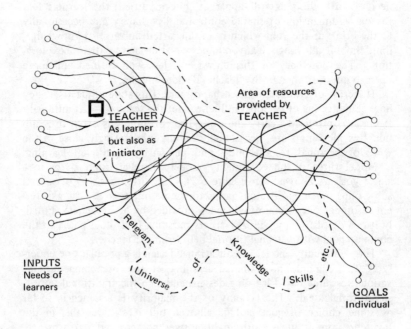

Figure 5.4   Learning community model

By contrast the idealised form of the learning community shows some significant differences (Figure 5.4). The simple system is changing dramatically as more variety is contained within it. Each learner now pursues his or her own individual goals but conforms to a greater or lesser extent to the help/sharing norms of the community. The teacher is also learner in that he has his own goals and purposes. However he fills a multiple role with regard to initiation, exemplifier of learning actions, e.g. helper, sharer, process commentator, etc. He also provides some of the resources. The universe has become ill-defined and problematic, its boundaries permeable; perhaps its existence is called into question. Goals and goal paths have become differentiated and approach 'limitlessness' within the constraints set by the norms and values of the community itself. These are principally the recognition of the shared impulse or direction; the responsibility to help others achieve their goals and the responsibility for the shared management and control of the community.

The learning community is an attempt to introduce more variety into the response of the education system. The purpose of this is literal freedom to learn. In contrast the simple educational design, of 'the teacher decides' model is primitive and constraining:

> Every pupil is a high-variety organiser, and the process of education essentially constrains variety. In other words, the pupil is capable of generating many responses to the question: 'What is six multiplied by seven?'; the educator will seek to attenuate this potential variety to the single answer: 'forty two'.[8]

Designing freedom to learn is a challenging task; it leads us to the riddle of liberating structure.

The riddle of liberating structure

All learning events are structured. If twenty people mill around in a room for a week, and do nothing else, then that is the structure. If the people sit in rows in that room and listen to a succession of speakers who come in for two hours at a time, then that would be a different structure. This latter type of structure is more familiar so we tend to refer to this type of situation as 'structured' and the other as 'unstructured'. Making this black/white and erroneous distinction does not help to answer the critical question, 'What is the right structure for helping these people to learn what they need/want to learn?'.

Structure refers to systems for the exercise of authority, control, communication, planning and decision-making as well as to temporal and spatial constraints and the purpose(s) of the organisation. In traditional learning situations these matters are not usually thought about or discussed much by participants. Tutors and trainers think a little bit about them. In preparing a course or session, we think about the room layout; the visual aids and other materials; the syndicate rooms and, less commonly, whether there is to be any participant choice in the programme or not. But all this is decided by the tutor alone, before the programme. Neither the tutor nor the participants remark much upon this almost entirely tutor-controlled and directed structure; it fits both with their expectations and their expertise in teaching/learning situations.

In directing attention to the question 'What is the right structure for helping these people learn what they need/want to learn?', these conventional expectations and expertise are challenged. As things are, we are usually talking about how to move from a trainer-directed structure to a more liberating one. More liberating in that it helps each participant to achieve his purposes and goals in the company of other, similarly self-directing, people. Once again the joint aims of self-development, shared purpose and quality work.

In responding to the question about the right form of liberating structure, the route must lie through the view of men and women not as fixed but as in a process of becoming, always moving, albeit often slowly, towards a future stage of development. With this model of the person, it is apparent that the commonality at any one time between any two people, however similar in age, circumstances and what we call 'experience', is strictly limited. If each of us is pursuing his or her own personal search for meaning, working out of an already achieved stage of development towards a future one, then learning for any one of us is best conceived as contributing towards this, as yet unrealised, future state. It is a matter of finding out *what* it is that this person is ready to learn — a more existential version of the behaviourists' primarily biological concept: 'maturation'. This data cannot be arrived at by more external observation, i.e. by the outside agent, trainer or teacher. Indeed collective learning events (classes, courses) where the trainer offers common fare, are exercises in throwing mud at walls; knowing it will fall off in some places, hoping that it will stick in others. A crude form of house painting and a crude form of training which, to find a medical analogy, is like gathering twenty back trouble sufferers and prescribing the same treatment irrespective of age, present health, medical history, personality and so on.

Like other people, learners are disconcertingly prone to conform to our expectations about them. Assuming commonality of interests, we see them as an undifferentiated group, class or category. At this level of perception people are very similar and it is only if we choose to see learners, like other people, as unique and disparate, each at the centre of his or her own world 'a wonder, a tragedy and a woe', that we question the efficiency of our standard treatment. How to design a learning event with a vital, rich and confusing individuality to cope, when the development of each and everyone poses a series of complex questions?

A simple solution is community planning, but — like 'free love' and 'workers' self management' — this is easier said than done. There are two issues of importance here; one which concerns the power inherent in the teacher's role, and the other which concerns the actually greater 'knowledge' of the 'teacher' (who is usually the community instigator or convenor).

A whole treatise could be written on the question of teacher or trainer power. The classroom remains one of the bastions of grossly unequal power. As we know, in situations where one party is immensely more powerful than the other, the high power party can be either benevolent or tyrannical, but is always the dictator. The joint control and negotiated decision-making on* structure required for the learning community can only be achieved if the power imbalance is dealt with somehow. To do this the holder of the teaching/training role must drop all the props and accoutrements of the role, seeking, as far as possible, to be as other people. This means dropping the assumptions that 'there is a right way to do things', giving up on the position that the trainer must, as guardian of this right way, always be the instructor; almost certainly forsaking the classroom for more conducive learning environments.

It will never be easy for teachers or trainers to give up their traditional costumes. Some time ago I attended a conference of training people from a particular industry who were bemoaning their lack of organisational power. 'Nobody rates training' they'd say, or, 'We can't get the ear of the top men'. What wasn't apparent was that the lowly level of organisational influence was linked to the high power position in the training centre and classroom. In his bailiwick, the trainer is unchallenged, but the cost of this unquestioned mastery is little learning for himself and little organisational influence. This classroom mastery, this time-served technical expertise, is a barrier to reacting creatively to changing demands and needs. No discovery is possible for either the trainer or his trainees because the trainer's high power position demands that he knows all the answers. In attempting to be participative, perhaps with managers, he hands out case studies to which he has 'right' answers. Because of his position, no one ever really tells him what they think of his training, at least, not in the role of 'a friend willing to act as an enemy', but only as a low power student to a high power teacher.

If the teacher or trainer can renounce his high power position in the classroom, this makes available and legitimate an enormous variety of needs and resources for learning. The teacher can still offer what he (or she) knows, and so can others; he can pose those questions on which he has reached some personal resolution, and also those on which he has not. To operate on learning community lines, the high power teacher role must be diminished or removed. Perhaps only through relinquishing his classroom power can the trainer increase his usefulness and influence in the wider world through enabling this articulation of a wider range of needs and this releasing of a richer array of resources.

In the second block to community planning and design — the actually greater 'knowledge' of the convenor or instigator — lies the very kernel of the riddle of liberating structure. If his 'knowledge', i.e. his awareness, intuition, experience, articulation, is 'superior', i.e. more relevant, lengthier, sharper, more in touch with the collective will, in this situation, then surely he has a duty to make it available. But how can we be freed, made autonomous, through being led by someone with superior knowledge? Knowledge confers power to those that hold it and enslaves those without it. The contradictory stance of many of us seeking to promote 'learner centred designs' through an imposition of what we referred to earlier as 'unstructured', is apparent.

For Torbert[9] this is the irony of liberating structure which we have to accept:

> One quality of liberating structure is deliberate irony. The leadership recognises that participants will initially interpret the organisation structure and particular events based on a different model of reality from the one inspiring the leadership. Moreover participants will not tend to interpret the resulting conflicts as caused by the difference in models of reality, nor will they be inclined to examine or test the different models. The leadership must at one and the same time succeed in 'speaking the members' language', introducing them to a 'new language' through the organisation's structure and leadership style, and motivating exploration of basic assumptions about reality by constructing tasks wherein members feel the limitations and self-contradictions inherent in the dichotomous view of reality. Structures and actions which meet these three demands are deliberately ironic: they both acknowledge and bridge a gap in world views. (p.113)

Later he comments that the leadership must use all the power available to it, to the end of creating a community:

> Instead of attempting to hoard power or to give it away, the leadership uses the power granted to it by institutional status, by its members, or by its own experiential authority to perform a kind of psycho-social jiu-jitsu whereby the members gradually come to question their own assumptions about the nature of

power and begin to experiment with the creative power to constitute a new world. In so doing, the members increasingly join
the leadership in a community of enquiry. The leadership does
not use power manipulatively — i.e. covertly and in order to
maintain unilateral exploitative structures. Instead it uses power
openly to create increasingly collaborative conditions.   (p. 114)

Simply to assert that the leadership does not use power manipulatively, however, is not to achieve it. I may think I'm using power
openly from my ideology, but what do you think from the standpoint
of yours? The ease of Torbert's presumption is not something I can
personally swallow. To assert that, though my purposes may as yet be
opaque to you and that trust and faith are required before all is revealed, is the eternal plea of the con-man and scoundrel as well as the
teacher and saint.

My own doubts give me no easy way out of the riddle of liberating
structure, I can assert no logical or morally simple way of 'leading
others to autonomy'. My own doubts however may often end in my
presenting an ambiguous image of myself — giving the hopelessly mixed
message which Richard Boot described recently as my saying, 'I don't
want to be King, but call me Sire'. This just puts me and everyone else
into a classic double bind and results in disablement all round. Disabled
we hold back from giving in a sort of Rogerian parody of mutual non-
direction; equally we hold back from taking, unable to bear the product
of such agonised effort. Instead of the richly endowed fabric of the
community, all the anxious threads are laid bare and we just scare each
other.

The trainer as stranger: the man with no name

Many of the critical questions about the learning community as an
educational design cohere about the role of the trainer, convenor or
instigator. In a relatively short lived event the trainer will usually be
the focus for issues of leadership and direction. Whilst he may remove
himself from the centre stage of omniscient and single provider and
through individual participant choosing and community planning and
design, he is almost inevitably the instigator in looking at the various
and more opaque processes behind the task.

John Burgoyne[10] has suggested that there are several possible levels
of intervention for a facilitator:

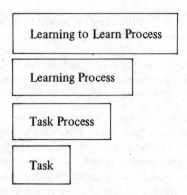

In learning communities and all designs which aim to help participants achieve a greater measure of self direction and control over their development, the trainer is always seeking to move attention to the upper levels of this model. This leadership is what Torbert refers to as the 'deliberate irony' of liberating structure, implying the paradox of leading people to self direction. Traditional learning designs stress task achievement with the upper levels either fixed by the teacher or not paid attention to. Learning community designs give back to participants individual and collective control over the task, i.e. meeting the needs of members, and the task process, i.e. how to go about meeting the needs of members, via some relatively simple and convivial technology. Freed from concentration upon this task the trainer can focus his attention and that of participants upon what lies beyond this task.

Through community control and planning the teacher is enabled to become just another member in that he can state needs and make offers having escaped from the box of sole definer of goals and sole provider of resources. However, because his attention is often directed elsewhere, he is always more than 'just another member'. Because there is this sense in which he is not operating at the same level as other members, he is with them but not of them. It is this marginality, this 'otherness' which allows the particular attention and perception which comprise the most important thing he has to offer.

This role is likely to be seen in a questioning of the activities which spring up in a learning community to fill the vacuum created by the removal of the traditional teacher or trainer. The learning community design removes the old order and reality and demands that each person confronts the existential question 'how shall *I* use these next hours, days, weeks, months, etc., of *my* life?' As Eric Berne has said, structuring our time is the major problem for us, which we can resolve via withdrawal, rituals, pastimes, games, intimacy or activity: 'The external problem of the human being is how to structure his time. In this existential sense, the function of all social living is to lend mutual assistance for this project'.[11]

The learning community, then, is a special slice of social living which sets its sights beyond intimacy and at the level of activity which involves personally significant learning and quality work in the world. This is not easy to achieve and perhaps only the trainer as stranger can ask such questions as, 'Is what is happening now . . .

. . . purposeful activity	or	ways of filling time?
. . . self-directed learning	or	'tagging along' with others?
. . . personal achievement	or	coping with the vacuum/void?
. . . intimacy	or	model swapping – 'I'll show you my TA if you show me your Rep Grid'?

Such questions are difficult to face. Through facing them we may attain a leap in understanding, but not before experiencing the distress or terror of having our routines, rules and rituals cut from beneath us. The immediate cause of this distress is the stranger 'who has put us in this position'. We may plead with him to take on the more familiar guise of teacher. If this fails we are likely to feel aggressive towards him and blame him for the situation 'in which we find ourselves'. If we do find something more of ourselves in this situation, we will feel that 'we did it ourselves'. The stranger moves on after a brief flash of recognition, his purposes once more opaque, but seeking situations and encounters which provide the questions for him.

References and notes

1 For brief descriptions of these designs and for further references see Burgoyne, J. G., et al. (1978), *Self Development*, Association of Teachers of Management, London, pp. 29–40.

2 Burgoyne, J. G., et al. (1978), p. 29.

3 Megginson, D. F. and Pedler, M. J. (1976), 'Developing Structures and Technology for the Learning Community', *Journal of European Training*, 5(5).

4 See for example, Blumberg, A. and Golembiewski, R. T. (1976), *Learning and Change in Groups*, Penguin, Harmondsworth, pp. 9–21.

5 See for example, Almond, R. (1971), 'The Therapeutic Community', *Scientific American*, March 1971, pp. 34–42.

6 Yallom, I. D. (1970), *The Theory and Practice of Group Psychotherapy* quoted by Blumberg, A. and Glembiewski, R. T., *Learning and Change in Groups* (1976), Penguin, Harmondsworth, p. 16.

7 Beer, S. (1974), *Designing Freedom*, Wiley, London, pp. 18–24.

8 Beer, S. (1974), op. cit.

9 Torbert, W. R. (1978), 'Educating towards Shared Purpose, Self-Direction and Quality Work', *Journal of Higher Education*, Ohio State University Press, 49(2).

10 Burgoyne, J. G. (1977), *Some Notes on the Role of the Facilitator in Action Learning* (unpublished).

11 Berne, E. (1967), *Games People Play*, Grove Press, New York, p. 16.

6   Outward bound?

Philip Radcliff and Philip Keslake

The use of a physical environment to stimulate personal risk, exposure and the examination of one's own rules, habits and constraints is the core of Radcliff and Keslake's argument. Self-development is the unearthing and bringing to light of personal capacities and abilities which make the person as manager more autonomous. The physical tasks and activities involved in 'outward bound' are blended with activities designed to help the manager be 'inward bound' as well. The aim is balance – to develop managers not dominated by activity and 'outward boundness' or dominated by passivity or 'inward boundness', but with more awareness and control over both directions.

For many readers the phrase 'outward bound' will no doubt conjure up images of detailed instruction, learning specific skills by rote in an atmosphere characterised by conformity, discipline and external control.   One might well be expecting clearly identifiable roles of teacher/instructor and participant, rich in notions of character-building and personality-shaping. All in all the subject area is one little explored by the theorist and at best dismissed as a fairly traditionally oriented means of training and development for young people. These were certainly fears which were utmost in our mind when we considered our own personal involvement in a *management* training programme based on physical tasks. However, our direct experience of the event and the subsequent opportunities we have taken to develop this programme have cleared us of many of these early preconceptions and enabled us to develop a range of programmes and models of the value of this kind of experience in managerial self-development.

Over the five or six years we have been involved with this kind of training we have moved a long way from the original accent on leadership skills and task analysis.   Fundamentally we feel we have added a dimension to this form of action-centred training based on a variety of elements of group and experiential learning and it is this final prototype which we will describe in more detail later. It has represented a cycle of self-development for us, both as trainers and participants and we will describe at the end some of the notions about self-development which are currently of interest to us. However, before we describe the programme it might be helpful if we present our own views on what self-development is.

What is self-development?

Fortunately we find ourselves without any succinct definition of self-development, because we think to have one would deny the complexity of the subject. We prefer to list a number of criteria which we have found important in releasing our own trainer anxieties and controls of the programmes we run. Increasingly we find ourselves in the position where on a variety of programmes it is essential to share responsibility for the learning design with all members of the course. These then represent our current criteria.

1   Self-development is not about developing learning skills and working on a number of carefully designed exercises — it is about unearthing personal capacities and abilities and using them effectively.

2   The locus of evaluation and judgement becomes the manager himself, combining modes of intellectual and intuitive self-assessment. As trainers we can do little to contest the value or lack of it experienced by the learner in working on any development or training programme.

3   The process of self-development is one of expanding a person's capability to relate and deal more effectively with experience. This by necessity requires the learner to be involved with his environment as a whole person and not to concentrate on using well tried strengths. Fully experiencing reality involves using all senses and capacities — thoughts, feelings and actions, and to have some understanding of their use and interaction.

4   Self-development of necessity demands that everybody takes personal responsibility for their learning, their actions and the results of their behaviour — not just in any controlled learning environment, but fully in their day-to-day working lives.

5   Self-development involves:
    (a) constant process of examining and re-evaluating rules, habits and constraints;
    (b) working beyond artificially imposed limitations and

fantasies;

(c) exposing oneself, taking risks and living with fears in order to learn from points of crisis.

6 Self-development does not have to be a solo activity, it can be carried out effectively in a group context. It is a question of not just coming to terms with internal states, but also of working on the successful expression of our relationship with our environment. In this we can be of help in fostering the self-development of each other, not merely on training programmes, but also in the everyday work situation.

At the end of the day self-development has to be about making people as managers more independent and fully autonomous. It is about becoming personally competent, in the deepest sense, i.e. capable of making decisions about our own development and our own lives and their expression. The effectiveness of self-development will be measured not only in terms of how well managers use their resources to develop themselves, but how effectively they use their time and resources to achieve their organisational and personal objectives. As a radical solution to the problem of achieving managerial performance improvements it requires greater efforts, by all parties involved in the learning situation, poses structural difficulties to many current organisational systems, but also enables individuals to take charge of their own self concept and assume responsibility for managing their own reality. We stress this point at this stage, because as a strategy of personal and organisational change it has often been presented in an all too simplistic form with scant regard for the implications such an approach to development has for the business context within which it has to be carried out.

A programme for fostering management self-development

We have now outlined some of the theoretical criteria we use to guide our own practical efforts to facilitate team and self-development in our company training programmes. In this section we will outline how in one particular instance we have tried to apply some of these criteria in the testing arena of business training.

Origins

The programme is based on a variety of elements which when brought together provide a rich experience in self-development. We have tried to isolate each strand of the experience below, but in so doing it is possible that we move even further away from the synergistic potential of the elements which we still find difficult to explain. In many ways the development of the event to its current status was coincidental. For a number of years we had both been looking, in separate organisations, at ways in which individuals learn and we had personal experience of a wide variety of progiammes in management training, ranging from the work of the Leadership Trust to that of encounter and 'T' groups. In particular we were both interested in the complexities of interpersonal relationships and had explored, quite separately, ways and means of training managers to a higher level of sensitivity and competence than was common in our own experience of organisations.

One major concern, which played a significant part in the design of this event, had been a recurring theme for both of us; we were concerned about the ease with which participants could be and were manipulated through the misuse of trainer authority and training 'games', to adapt and conform to organisational demands for certain approved behaviours.

It was more than a personal concern. Would this potential misuse of training actually serve the organisation sponsoring it? RHM General Products Ltd was prepared to investigate a variety of ways in helping managers cope with the recurring confusion of how to promote effective workgroups in a changing industrial environment. Old models of behaviour seemed ineffective and inappropriate in meeting the modern interpersonal and business needs of managers and we were confronted with the opportunity to develop new ways to meet new needs. How easy and hypocritical it might have been to fall into the trap of using old models of training behaviour to try and achieve new models of managerial behaviour!

It became our objective to create something new and exciting which would give participants who joined us in the event not just a wider choice of activity to learn from, but a deeper experience at the same time.

Our objectives for the programme were severalfold:

For the participant as manager we would provide a series of opportunities for him to take a complete view of himself as a resource and to extend his capacities to meet a complex variety of managerial situations. We would provide him with opportunities to see himself as others see him and to reflect upon those views, adapting his own behaviour if he so chooses.

For the participant as a person we would provide opportunities for him to consider his own managerial style and its effectiveness. However, when it came to making changes in such styles and habits he would need a deeper understanding of himself, his personal identity, fears and capacities. Only by encouraging participants to work at this level could we expect them to truly develop themselves. At the end of the programme participants would be working at their own pace and depth — fully managing their own learning and its transfer.

Design

Tasks.   For five days managers participate in a number of physical tasks, increasing in complexity, each reflecting a variety of situations in which a manager is likely to find himself at work, in terms of resource constraints, length of tasks, and size of group, etc.   The reality of stress and real consequences is built into the tasks, e.g. real bridges being built over real water.

In each task there is opportunity for participants to define per-formance and learning standards and to experience both the anxiety and very often the consequence of poor individual and group perform-ance.   Such tasks bring about real behaviour rather than something which we now regularly describe as *manipulative coping strategies*: we have found particularly on internal training programmes partici-pants come with expectations and models of how they *should* behave on training courses.   Or having attended a number of programmes they have strategies of withdrawal or factual involvement whereby they distance themselves from the actual experience of the course. Such 'manipulative coping strategies' represent ways in which the participant can protect current habits and avoid taking responsibility for his own learning.   Consequently the option for learning provided by the tasks must be very carefully designed to 'distract' delegates away from their coping strategies.

Each task follows a cycle of activity requiring planning, resource organisation, achievement of targets and personal/team commitment. Technical ability is not involved to any great degree.   Managerial and team problems are represented and as such have to be organised by the team.   The challenge becomes a personal and group one rather than primarily technical and the learning is about organisational and sentient aspects of a task system in the group.   Once delegates have familiarity with the vehicle, i.e. understanding the nature of the tasks as learning opportunities, we find that there is a directness about the experience which encourages real rather than coping behaviours, experimentation rather than getting by with old styles and that the learner can set his own personal and behavioural objectives.   At the end of the week although the tasks are more complex, the delegates are in total control of the manner in which they are used to achieve personal learning goals.

Individual endeavour.   Alongside the group tasks runs activity relating to individual endeavour.   The delegate selects the activity, but is largely putting himself into areas of unknown experience.   The challenge is to confront these uncertainties and learn how to manage yourself and feelings. Climbing, caving and canoeing are the activities provided. They generate often deeper understanding and discussion — insights into the fears and blocks to personal growth and development.

The insights are not solely into the processes of growth and experiencing stress, but they provide the participant with opportunities to take charge of himself and his actions with a deeper understanding and confidence. The effects of these activities come into the group and its development, and contribute significantly to the reflection of experience, and sharing and expression of feelings and values.

Intellectual inputs.   The trainers are free to select and introduce intellectual inputs if determined as suitable to a particular group or the whole community. On occasions trainers use brief inputs and methods to help clarify or interpret what is happening at any given time. The nature of the sessions is largely determined on-the-spot by the trainers, but has covered such topics as theories of individual development, systems behaviour and organisational health. They often take the form of a briefing session — limited discussion, but an attempt to pull the strands together. The groups then use the input in whatever way is most appropriate.

Reviews.   Review sessions actually follow each task and individual endeavour, which encourage examination of both task performance and more open group and personal reviews of feelings and values.

During the week we have noticed how the content of reviews moves from examination of the task during the early days of the group through reviews of team development and process until during the last few days personal, individual insights are explored. A spiral of learning at the group's pace into deeper understanding of self.

Task and process reviews merge into personal and group examination and we use a variety of methods, including the use of a personal diary to focus on significant events. Such time for personal reflection is often shared by the group in terms of a number of non-verbal and Gestalt style techniques.

Throughout the week the participants are encouraged to take responsibility for the reviews and the trainer profile becomes lower and lower as the days pass.

Action planning.   At every occasion the programme design encourages each participant to take personal responsibility for achieving progress, seeking and giving feedback and for establishing a personal plan of action. Opportunities are provided throughout for the examination of personal learning goals. Finally each individual is encouraged to establish his own plans for getting back into the business.

Learning goals. Prior to the event participants complete some work designed to initiate discussion with the boss and to identify the 'organisational' reason for attending the event. The output is a series of specific goals stated in terms of explicit behaviours to be achieved.

The programme provides the opportunity for the boss's viewpoint to be tested and for more data to be generated about personal effectiveness, etc.

Refinement and selection of alternative goals, if appropriate is encouraged so that each individual learns to take responsibility for generating data, refining it and using it as a base for experimentation and adapted behaviour.

Trainer role. The trainer role in fact does not really move far from the traditions of sensitivity training and group facilitation – the emphasis is very much on facilitating the processes of growth in the group and in the individual. The same standards of authenticity, competence with feelings and tolerance of uncertainty are merely applied to a different venue of experience. However, the trainer is helped if he can keep in touch with the feeling of novelty, uncertainty and vulnerability experienced during the week. As such he cannot remain distant, but be prepared to confront his own feelings as well as those of others during the week. As the programme necessitates a significant degree of structure and organisation, the trainer has to be capable of letting go of the control of the reviews to the delegates without feeling threatened at a very early stage. His need to be visible as a 'competent trainer' must be low and he must have the skill to provide facilitation without feeling redundant as the delegates take increasing responsibility for their learning.

The design of the programme has convinced us of a number of important points. First how impossible it is to provide any deep insight into the processes of the programme. The written description is a totally inferior medium to that of direct personal experience. Secondly that self-development can be fostered on a variety of programmes so long as the design provides the opportunity to work at sufficient depth to remove individual blocks to using autonomy and the trainer has the capacity to enable the learners to take responsibility for and control of their own learning. Our summation is that self-development is not an easy process to achieve either throughout a programme or more importantly for all managers in an organisation. In the next section we would like to outline some of the concepts which have arisen, particularly from this kind of training programme and which may shed some light on applying self-development to learning and work programmes.

Concepts in self-development

Wholeness and balance

Throughout the chapter we have stressed the importance of achieving a balance of physical, emotional and intellectual experience and growth in order to facilitate personal development. The emphasis not only on training programmes, but also in the everyday working life of the manager must be on physical, intellectual and emotional expression. We have experienced many instances where the balance of the three elements has enabled individuals to gain insights into major intellectual and emotional blockages which have limited their managerial performance over a long period. The learning process involved is often one of achieving total insight into a personal difficulty and finding the capacity to go beyond the customary behavioural habits. We believe such insights are facilitated by a design which enables individuals to push out their limits in all three directions — physical, intellectual and emotional.

The interaction of the three however does not merely constitute a means of stretching each individual and thereby deepening the awareness of the capacities at their disposal. Obviously confidence gained by achievements in one area readily act to transfer into other areas — certainly very different kinds of blocks to expression or action seem to have their roots in a number of common fears. Once that fear has been confronted, the particular technical or behavioural skills can be easily learned. Further the combination of the three very different types of experience seem to offer a further symbolic dimension to learning. A person's difficulties with some managerial or interpersonal situation can often be crystallised by some physical event in a group task or on a rockface. The individual is able to learn often more directly about personal decisiveness, reluctance to be a team member or to lead etc. Often the event represents a kind of 'learning by analogy' and is used in a short-hand fashion to identify where the same feelings or inhibitions are preventing effective action in a management meeting (rather than on the rockface where the original insight may have taken place).

The concept of balance is we believe crucial to any individual intending to manage his own development and thereby his own life. No trainer can specify in any detail each individual's balance of physical, intellectual and emotional; he can only provide a range of opportunities and choices. Each manager must establish his own balance appropriate to the healthy functioning of himself as an organism. Individually we have both learned to build into our own lives the appropriate balance of physical, intellectual and emotional activity and we have witnessed both how different our 'individual regimes' are and the effects on our own overall performance and effectiveness when we are in a period of imbalance. It is our view that most writers on self-development and managerial job design have put an almost exclusive emphasis on achieving only intellectual and emotional balance in their programmes for self-management. Consequently we fear an important aspect of human expression is being unduly disregarded and total balance of experience being avoided.

Inward bound and outward bound

As with the nature of balance and wholeness we have no full understanding of the interaction between processes of 'inward bound' and 'outward bound', but we do have a strong belief that both are required to achieve effective learning and development. As we indicated at the outset we have made efforts to take the richness of experience offered by outward bound style training and add the skills of reflection and sensitivity to experience in order to help delegates gain a greater depth of understanding of themselves. As a result we think we have harnessed two forms both equally important to the self-development of the manager — development is both inward bound and outward bound. To illustrate our point we will paint two extreme caricatures of what we have termed Bound Management.

The 'inward-bound manager'. Strong ability to reflect on his behaviour, identify his shortcomings and to use past failures, often using them as an imposed restriction on his current range of behaviours. He is comfortable in his introspective and analytical world, with no real capacity to take action and assert himself. Such a manager will often be unrecognised and be appraised as retiring and of a low profile. Such a manager may establish a degree of personal acceptance, but be unable to use it in achieving his business and personal goals, because of his fears and lack of skills in expressing himself. He is *dominated by passivity*.

The 'outward-bound manager'. Is too busy acting, responding and asserting his solutions to review and assess the direction of his efforts. Often he is more acceptable to the system in that he is relatively more effective in goal achievement, but his own career may be limited by his incapacity to take a strategic view on matters. At worst he may never learn from his experience and merely develop habitual action-oriented responses with little control and personal organisation. He is *dominated by activity*.

Our caricatures represent managers who can only operate effectively in one dimension. However, many programmes or attempts to facilitate self-development themselves concentrate on one of the two dimensions. This results either in strengthening the manager's inability to act in new ways or merely confuses him with an amalgam of new values, behaviours and feelings. In organising or considering a programme of self-development any person must combine the opportunities to act, give expression to needs and take responsibility for situations with the chance to reflect on events, understand feelings and analysis and learn from experiences. Thereby self-development can help the individual understand the blocks to his being autonomous (inward bound) with the opportunity to feel what it is like to act with greater autonomy (outward bound).

Any learning or self-development programme must combine the capacities of both inner reflection and understanding with those more outward capacities of assertiveness. The caricatures we drew earlier are gross stereotypes, but the tendency to operate primarily in one dimension we think is relatively common. Sometimes it may be linked to the job be it advisory or line; to initial academic study, or more often than not just plain habit – the fear of developing new flexibility in behaviour styles. To help encourage change in such behavioural tramlines we think we need to provide a range of experiences all of which have different but very real parameters. The aim is to make the learning as realistic as possible. Self-development on the job may involve a continuous battle with the constraints imposed by a task predominant system. Any specially designed learning event must provide at least as wide a range of opportunities to learn, but also a context which demands effectiveness and results. Any manager must consider that his development achieves a range of capacities on both sides, otherwise he will find himself unable to respond fully to a range of situations – something which most managers have to accept as characteristic of their working reality.

Awareness and control

Many notions of increasing a person's self awareness involve a loosening of traditional structures and beliefs in long standing models in order to experience more fully his reality. However merely to react with no degree of control is to allow events to dictate our patterns of behaviour. Consequently in order to be a more fully functioning manager or person requires a determination not only to allow the inward processes of self learning and emotional awareness to occur, but to combine these with the capacity to assert one's own needs and take the appropriate action – to take greater responsibility for managing and changing his reality.

One way of considering this growth in autonomy is to consider those processes by which a person interacts with reality. We see two key aspects of the process by which an individual manages his reality – the personal world around him. These aspects are by developing

(1) *a greater awareness* – a sensitivity and understanding of events and experiences of which he is a part – and (2) *an insight* into the feelings created within himself. This is very much a question of helping a person 'to open himself up' to his inner world. This other aspect is not one of establishing greater depth and understanding, but more a question of using such knowledge in a confident, effective and assertive way. We believe that for self-development to continue a manager must possess capacities to influence and survive. Consequently the person must practise and have the opportunity to learn those skills which help him achieve his goals through the results of his work behaviour. Every encouragement must be given to help a person use the sensitivity and understanding at his disposal rather than its disabling him from effective action either temporarily or permanently. Self-development is fostering the skills of managing one's own reality as fully as possible and having the capacities to make changes.

Figure 6.1 summarises our views about the processes in the programme which help facilitate effective self-development, both on the programme and in preparation for the work situation.

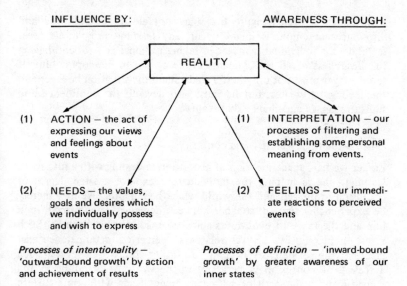

INFLUENCE BY: AWARENESS THROUGH:

REALITY

(1) ACTION – the act of expressing our views and feelings about events

(1) INTERPRETATION – our processes of filtering and establishing some personal meaning from events.

(2) NEEDS – the values, goals and desires which we individually possess and wish to express

(2) FEELINGS – our immediate reactions to perceived events

Processes of intentionality – 'outward-bound growth' by action and achievement of results

Processes of definition – 'inward-bound growth' by greater awareness of our inner states

Figure 6.1

To achieve a fully effective interaction with our reality requires the combination of greater awareness and understanding with control of our behaviours to ensure that our actions lead to the satisfaction of our personal feelings and values. Personal development and growth can be blocked by fears, fantasies or incapacities in any one area. Such growth and effective behaviour can only be achieved when all the elements are understood and utilised in our management of the personal reality we face.

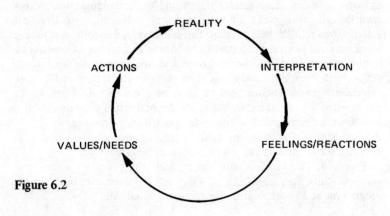

Figure 6.2

Whilst such a cycle (Figure 6.2) may not always be followed and differences in emphasis might occur, any learning programme must facilitate the individual manager in taking personal control and having full awareness of all the elements in the cycle. In developing himself the manager must not only better understand the situation he faces and the feelings it creates, but he must also develop the confidence and skills to manage and change that reality.

Personal identity — clarity and confusion

Earlier we have made mention of how often in dealing with a manager's learning, one is helping the individual to explore a large degree of confusion in himself and the world which he inhabits. We may merely be experiencing some dissonance between demands being placed upon him and the range of behaviours and skills readily at his disposal. Such a fear of incongruity or even relative or perceived incompetence may create a sense of defensiveness and confusion. It is our belief that such a feeling of confusion is pervasive in the world of organisation and management. The path of self-development leads with some pattern and regularity through phases of both clarity and confusion to a deepening sense of personal identity or self-concept.

It is an essential part of the process of self-development for an individual to question and assess his own self-concept. We have certainly witnessed this on the programme. People are not just developing certain skills of learning and acting which can be grafted on to the current amalgam they possess. At times the assessment and feedback which they or others share creates an opportunity to look at their self image afresh. This may be a question of seeing fresh doubts renewing strengths of which they were unaware — either way it can and often is a relatively painful and confusing process. This learning often results from the range of demands, physical, intellectual and emotional, which confronts participants in the programme. The two types of learning are both integral to the development of the self concept.

1   *Incremental development*
    Learning ranges of behaviours, skills and approaches which can be added to those we already possess, without any change in perceived self concept — *learning by elaboration.*

2   *Discontinuous development*
    Is learning arising out of a fundamental change in our view of ourself and the reality we experience. In this instance the individual senses evidence from others, or his own feelings indicate the need for a major change in self concept in order to remove fears and problems. Only when such a change has occurred can he develop further skills and strengths — *learning by crisis.*

It would be erroneous therefore to see the path of self-development as a continuous one, whereby one gradually adds to an array of behaviours. At certain key stages the information we possess about ourselves will be so contradictory to our own perceived self concept, that it will necessitate a fundamental change in that view we have of our own personal identity. Consequently the path of growth will involve periods of extreme confusion when major constructs of our reality come under pressure to change. At other times we can proceed with a greater degree of clarity and confidence as we sense a deeper security in our self concept.

An example of this on the programme is the relatively common dilemma of our sexual identity in the physical tasks and activities. Many participants bring with them stereotypic expectations of the kind of male strengths which they think are encouraged in this type of training. Rapidly these 'macho' stereotypes prove inappropriate to the needs of the intense and complex learning situation. Participants may then share their much more fundamental doubts about using a range of so-called male (assertive and aggressive) and female (sensitive, caring and intuitive) behaviours. Often these mirror the very doubts they have about being seen as either a bullying or a weak manager. Emotionally this is very confusing, throwing participants' self-image into great doubt until they recognise the need to use both without any resulting weakening of their personal identity. The actual practice and learning of the skills be they assertiveness, persuasiveness, sensitivity or caring is much easier. They require no major personal changes and the learning occurs as an incremental process very much under the control of the learner. The managing of the confusion and threat to an individual's personal identity requires greater support from others, but can still be managed by the person themselves. The end result is a much deeper strength of personal identity and ease to learn and deal with experience. However, any trainer must be aware of the full and very possible implications of the process of self-development for the individuals concerned.

Concluding remarks

We have in this chapter tried to examine the benefits of a certain kind of training, particularly in the light of self-development. Many of the delegates have reported significant success in not only achieving their learning but also in being able to apply it to their work situation. We still fear that the impact of this training may outweigh its long term results and this difficulty is complicated by the problems of trying to follow up such an event. Of necessity, we are driven to consider self-development capacities achieved by the programme as one of its major benefits. Most delegates report a battle to apply their personal learning goals, but also report the confidence they achieved during the programme as helping them see the battle through. They have a greater strength of self identity and an ability to continue to learn from their experience by themselves.

'Outward bound' was an unexplored area for us when we started and still requires careful research and evaluation. It has helped provide us with a means of integrating better self-understanding with the skills of action. The programme convinces us of the need both for support in the intensive learning experienced during the process of self-development and of the need to continue to explore new ways of achieving such purposes. Self-development may be easily achieved in educational settings, but has far more severe barriers to its full implementation in the business and training setting. We believe the technology is available (as witnessed by the programme described), but have yet to be convinced that our organisations and managers are fully equipped to cope with, or that we ourselves possess, a deep enough understanding of the processes of self-development and their wider implications. We hope this chapter has shed some further and possibly slightly different light on the matter.

7 Working with biography

Malcolm Leary

We all have our story to tell and the prize for following the developmental path is deeper understanding of the interplay of time in our lives both in terms of general life processes and in ourselves as unique individuals.

Questions form the starting point to development, and the purpose of biography work is to trace the continuities and discontinuities from the past through the present and into the future. Life is seen as a combination of destiny and freedom, in a bending to some of the irresistible forces and events that affect us and in a conscious choosing in what we make of our lives. Malcolm Leary describes the principles underlying biography work in the first part of his chapter and then moves on to the content and format for actual biography work. A spirit of balance and wholeness illuminates this chapter and surfaces in the counterbalancing of past and future, inner and outer, choosing and accepting, individual and social. Development is the product of a conscious bringing together of these juxtaposed forces.

'I keep my life in separate compartments — what happens at work has nothing to do with what I do at home. I don't take my work problems home.' A manager on one of our recent courses summed up what for many has been a guiding philosophy — compartmentalisation and separation. Increasingly, however, this position is being seen as untenable. We are a total person whether we are at work or home. We can block sections of ourselves off for a while but ultimately either our control goes or we find ourselves feeling increasingly denied. There is interest therefore in a total life situation, a fascination with how the bits fit together, how things change as we move through life. For many this means a confrontation with many difficult existential issues, for others more esoteric questions are revealed. These questions can be the beginning of a path to real development. The prize at the end of the road is a deeper understanding of the influence of time and life processes, not just in a general sense but in how they relate to us as unique individuals. We all have our story to tell. How our relationship to this life story, our biography, can be encouraged and enriched is the subject of this chapter.

As well as explaining the purpose of this activity as a development approach, we shall also discuss methods and designs for the work. A beginning will be made, however, with the questions which are raised — the doubts, fears, hopes, expectations perhaps which people have about their lives. The opportunities and the threats, the crises and the possible triumphs which uniquely make up their story.

Issues in working with biography

Initial interest in biography questions

Raising questions about life circumstances.   In looking at life circumstances many puzzles and dilemmas may appear, particularly if we look ahead to an open future. Many of the old traditions have been disturbed, the established patterns of life threatened. In organisations particularly the old ways are under extreme scrutiny. In this kind of atmosphere questions about the future can appear to be full of threat. It is easy to appeal to the negative side and build up real fears. A normal starting point is a feeling of discomfort, uncertainty — things *ain't* what they used to be! For some facing up to this doubt in itself can be difficult, the start, maybe, of a development process. Being used to an environment where certainty, stability and a solid front are encouraged, even demanded, some people allow serious issues to fester. These issues will almost invariably come out later as real evidence of crisis.

Questions as a starting point for development.   It need not be like that. With some guidance and the opportunity to work on the reality being faced, these difficult questions can be a trigger for development. The approach to working with biography outlined here is directed at actualising this possibility. The process of working with biography means first being open to the questions being posed. Perhaps helping others to see the question behind the question, the real issue which is concerning us. There is a counselling orientation to the approach. It makes no attempt to be therapy as such; those with really serious disturbances would be directed elsewhere for help. The biography process is not just for failures, problem children or difficult cases. We believe a more positive relationship to life is possible and open for all.

A starting point has to be however the acceptance that a meaningful life will contain troughs as well as peaks, it will not be a continuous, glorious path to the stars. An understanding of the varied patterns of life which affect us, and are affected by us, opens up the possibility of this new relationship.

Questions managers ask.   The starting questions are, of course, posed in many varied ways. Some come as shouts, others are expressed as whispers:

How can I cope with the many demands which my position and life make on me?
Should I change my job?
How could I face redundancy if it came?
Should I alter my work style?
How can I alter my life style to a more healthy one?
Does my work call forth all my faculties and abilities?
Is my work still meaningful and satisfactory?
Am I needed and accepted in my present work situation?
What should I give up?

These are typical 'work' type questions which a manager might ask. Behind each question might lie a whole world of other connected life issues. Most of us carry with us a complex pattern of life relationships and involvements. To talk about separate compartments under such conditions is nonsense.

Reasons for raising questions.   The people who raise such questions can be led to do so for a variety of internal reasons or external demands. For example we might have:

People engaged in coping with complex and penetrating questions coming from within, denied the chance to explore these with others.
People faced with changes in working, social and personal environments.
A need for a fundamental reorientation towards their present life situation.
Preparing inwardly to meet the challenges of anticipated future events.

Special problems in the managerial area today are posed by redundancies and compulsory changes of job, managers entering the second part of a professional life and issues of professional deformation. Those with heavy demands on their personal ability and involvement find it helpful to spend a quiet, concentrated time looking for answers to counterbalance the outer pressures and strains. It is stressed again, however, that the process described here is not appropriate for those with an extreme or unusual life crisis.

Responding to questions raised.   This does not mean however that all questions will be the same.   Different stages of life make their own peculiar demands and the treatment of these issues needs to be carefully varied to match the circumstances.   It appears that many more of these problematical life phenomena are being raised, particularly in the professional and managerial area.   More questions are being identified than management trainers and developers can cope with.   In order to relate to these questions a more intimate relationship between the trainer and the trainee than is usual in these fields needs to be established.   In the role of a helper, the biography counsellor may begin with assisting the client to clarify the question he is asking.   Later this role moves to encompass other fields.

Respect for the other is essential if the biography process is to work at all.   Interest has to stem from what people are as well as what they have.   An extraordinary change can come about when a person realises that *he* has an interesting story to tell too!

With so many problems inherent in keeping the biography work within reasonable boundaries and under the control of the trainee as well as the trainer, it is important to make the aims as clear as possible before a start is made.

Specific aims of biography work

Biography work builds from the basis of a review of past life events and circumstances through a clear assessment of a life position, moving finally to an anticipation of its future course.   From this point preparation for the next steps can begin.

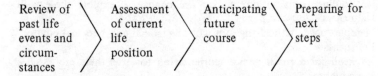

Review of past life events and circumstances   Assessment of current life position   Anticipating future course   Preparing for next steps

The 'biography' element is strictly related only to the past but we are speaking here of a process which uses this past orientated biographical review as a platform for working and current interpretations and future directions.

Looking at our biography and working with it need not be an isolated 'once and for all' event.   It can be done at regular intervals, as a repeated process.   There is, after all, always a new element in events which have just passed to examine.   In addition, invariably we find another scan over old ground reveals something new and significant.

Assessing current life position. An assessment of our current life position does not necessarily mean a sterile listing or mapping process. In fact some of the highlights of a biography work process can occur during this initial stage. The moment when, after telling his story to others, the biographer begins to 'own' his story — 'this is my life, for better or worse, warts and all, this is ME! No-one else has a story just the same as this for sure!' — this can be a magic and significant event for him. Associated with this moment of ownership often comes a realisation that although at the beginning there was a strong feeling of 'poor little me, I've nothing interesting or significant to tell, what a dull life I've led compared to others'; after a while others begin to show an interest, ask questions, explore. After all I have an interesting story to tell — and it's mine. The overwhelming humanity within the context and procedure can be a very powerful force and one of the joys of biography work.

Directions of biography work. Life stories are the grist to work on. Supports and perspectives are then provided to enable participants to enter a conscious planning process for their next stage of life. This can mean different things to people in varying circumstances:

Seeing life crisis as a means of development, not an unavoidable fate

Understanding more deeply life situations, providing images people can work with

Relating to the position I find myself in in a positive way

Understanding the basic issues at each phase of life

Developing a healthy and fruitful attitude towards the problems of a particular period

Preparing for a meaningful future perspective in work and/or the life situation

Helping to discover a more profound relationship with their own biography

Preparing for the next step in development

Looking ahead, planning for the future

Learning to live with a particular character, temperament, set of circumstances.

Destiny and freedom. For many, a real breakthrough is the realisation that life is neither a series of events which are destined to happen to us, over which we have no control, nor a completely random succession of incidents. Life is a combination of both, destiny and freedom. There are some coincidences which obviously have a deeper significance than normal. How we relate to these events, what we do with the raw material which life presents to us is entirely our free choice. We can bemoan our fate, selfishly milk our opportunities, or take ourselves consciously in hand to meet life and do with it what is called for. This kind of thinking often calls for an alteration in the way life is approached. A change in basic attitude to life is being demanded. We make no apologies for doing this. However, some of the beliefs and philosophies on which such an approach is based may need further exploration before we move on to describe in detail the biography work process.

Principles of biography work

As with all work undertaken by Social Ecology Associates, our biography programmes are based on the concept of human development. This development process has certain characteristics which have to be taken account of if we are to encourage people to take their own development in hand. Crisis periods, metamorphosis, qualitative change, seeing things as part of a time sequence, are all familiar characteristics of a life story, a biography. Development is something we understand and appreciate at a very basic level. Biography work with people attempts to bridge the gap between this fundamental acceptance of the reality of human development and the realisation that all this can apply to *me*. Development can be a reality for *me*. I can take my own future path of development consciously in hand. I can plan for and anticipate my next step in development.

Image of man. 'Development for all' is perhaps an adequate statement of our position. This does not mean however that what is being advocated is a way of smoothing out life's wrinkles, avoiding the realities we face or giving up our free choice, giving in to chance or predetermination. Underlying our work with participants on their own biography is a particular image of man. What man as a developing being means is made explicit as an anchor point of the process. Much of the lecture material which is introduced at early stages of the biography process covers this ground. The development of man's soul through his life process is a central theme. Allied to this is the belief that self-consciousness and understanding can go hand in hand with self-responsibility. This does not ignore the fact that strong anti-forces may also be at work. The developed part of ourselves, our higher ego, is constantly in battle with our retarded part, our egoism.

Development psychology. This concept of man as a developing being through life is not new. Development psychology goes as far back as the ancient Chinese at least — A time to learn — A time to fight — A time to grow wise. More recently the influences behind the basic patterns of life have been explored in much more detail. When thinking of life processes and developments, analogies with the biological world are both apt and illustrative. Thus the life of a human being (or a human *bean* as my youngest daughter accurately refers to them) has a time of ascending and unfolding, a time of blossoming and balance, a time of ripening and decline.

The unique path of an individual through life is guided by certain laws of development. Guided but not dictated. Life is a story of potential, of possibility. The realisation of this potential is dependent to a large extent on the relationships growing out of confrontation and encounter with other human beings. Fortunately life for most offers endless possibilities for such meetings. There exists therefore an opportunity for our development in life itself, with all its trials and tribulations, if we care to grasp it. We turn now to look at how this nettle can be grasped.

The inner and outer focus

There has traditionally been a concentration on the outer appearance of man's biography. More interest is shown usually in what a man does than what he is. Studies of man's make-up usually concentrate on outer phenomena first, then the internal states which account for these. Perhaps a start can be made the other way around.

To look at the complete man we must accept both the inner and the outer biography. There is a danger of encouraging participants to itemise their outward appearance too strongly, giving an over-emphasised educational or career bias. This should be avoided by encouraging a statement of inner changes which took place also. Often the inner story can differ fundamentally from an outward face. Outer success is frequently accompanied by inner despair, which makes an appearance later to the surprise of all but the most perceptive.

At a very basic level life processes within us are still largely a mystery. Changes from inside can take some fathoming and sorting out. A great deal of help may be needed to tease out an inner process. At a more conscious level our make-up is more identifiable. We know ourselves just a little. We have this personality, that temperament, a certain characteristic, which is ours alone. These elements are there sure enough. Beyond this we may be in some difficulty. How things hang together and relate is something else. The complexity is almost overwhelming and certainly indefinable in precise terms.

At another level we see ourselves a little from the inside. We recognise our individuality but the real source of recognition, our identity, must lie outside ourselves. In some ways the 'I' does not exist from the outside, only within us. But a real knowledge of the ego can only be obtained from and through others, through a real encounter. You get a real idea of who you are only from other people's reaction to you.

These are some of the dilemmas posed by attempting to understand our inner biography and workings. An impossible task but the attempt is made. For many the only way to counterbalance the outer pressures and strains is to find an inner space. Some feel controlled by circumstances, past ways of working no longer seem effective and block change. When the outside presents a barrier, the inside might release the energy to demolish these blockages.

Finding the task.   This is not to say we totally ignore demands from the outside world but to deal with them in a more effective way, from a position of inner strength. There is work to be done outside, a task for our world, our age, our society, my organisation, this group – ME! The search for this task can be a troublesome and difficult one, particularly at certain stages of life where perhaps new aims to inspire become very important. There is so much in the world to do, so much I could do – how do I identify that task which is for me, which has my name on it. The environment of the biography work cannot entirely bring the outside world in for total examination. Through group work however, the recognition of your own humanity through others can be facilitated. From this recognition the role which that individual has to perform in the future can be more clearly identified.

Approaches to working with biography

The process of working

Two formats have emerged from operating in this field. The first concentrates on a *specific audience*, e.g. managers, and includes a concentration on the particular life/career influences which affect this group. Individuals are helped to work on their own life and career situations.

The second uses as focus a more *general selection* of people, working on all relevant aspects of biography. Group members help each other to work on their overall biography.

There is a strong overlap between the two, the emphasis is varied for particular groups. Within this framework of two basic strands of biography work a variety of different designs are used. Some concentrate just on biography and life planning work, others integrate an element of biography work within a more general programme. A couple of examples of this are:

1   *A two-day biography* element which follows on directly from a one-week social skills programme. This is for managers of a certain level drawn from member companies of a large conglom-

erate. By the end of the one-week programme participants know each other sufficiently to enter a deeper biography process. These two days then provide an excellent course-ending process as well as helping enormously with problems of transferring learning back to the work environment and applying any lessons learned.

2   Biography work being used as part of a *team building exercise.* This helps to cement relationships and establish a new basis for interacting. Team members share their biographies only, although elements of working with biography may spill over into the team building effort.

Such a 'biography' element could easily be envisaged as part of other development/group work.

Time scales.   As far as the more direct 'biography' courses and work-shops are concerned these are designed over a variety of time scales, e.g. a weekend workshop; 3½-day seminar; 5-day seminar; an ongoing self-development group meeting periodically. The design of the bio-graphy work is adjusted for the time available and to some extent to the age range of the participants. Care is taken not to enter a process which cannot be completed within the time allocated. Within these various designs a variety of approaches and techniques can be used. Here we describe a few of them.

Participants' stories.   The basic content of the biography work is provided by the life situations and biographies of the participants themselves. The aim is to help the participants, through the process of the event, to be themselves in time, to become more creative with their own lives.   There needs to be, therefore, some emphasis on counselling (either in pairs or threes) and group discussion. Time is also made available for individual reflection and for answering personal questions. Various relational exercises can then be included to 'work on' some of the issues raised. Lectures are included on major topics. The basic biographical material, the life stories of the partici-pants, is differentiated and broken down to some extent (without compartmentalising) through looking at a variety of possible roles in personal and organisational life, e.g.

Looking at education, talents, abilities, aptitudes
Examining professional career, organisational and managerial sys-
    tems and culture
Personal biography, marriage and family situations
Health, work/play habits, etc.

These are some of the major elements of a biography process. Some attempt is made then to build them into a rhythmic process — not too much group work at the expense of individual reflection, lectures not too long, probably before lunch, exercises after lunch perhaps . . .

Mapping.   In helping to describe our own life stories a number of helpful techniques can be suggested:

   Highlight the main events, work from zero to now or backwards from the present
   Look for major themes in your life — those which began and died away; those which are still with you; those which are just emerging.

Thus the biography is mapped in a variety of ways. Looking behind the events, the person is identified more closely. Participants are encouraged to look at themselves in relation to their education, their talents, inner orientations, temperaments, constitutional types. This is done without in any way fixing people, 'Ah! yes, you are one of those!'. The way in which our basic make-up has been dealt with through life can be looked at, leading on to a questioning of how this relates to the future, e.g.

   Has my education been too one-sided to allow me to develop my talents fully?
   Are my talents out of date?
   How can I live more out of the things I can do well?
   How can I try more of those things maybe I can't do?

Organisational and professional influences often play a vitally important role in the lives of those who choose a career path. The influence of organisational rules and behaviour patterns and the demands these place on individuals can be used as a focus. A useful lead up to this is perhaps some thoughts on the formative forces which affect us in life, particularly the process of professional formation and deformation.

   Descriptions of the biographies of other people (famous personalities) outside the immediate group can help to illustrate some of the steps participants are being asked to take. In this way a new relationship to our own biography is forged. New insights and question openings begin to appear: what have I done with what I have?; what have I done with the meetings I have had in life?; how can I discover my will for the future?

Raising questions about the future.   Emphasising that self-development on your own can be an illusion; the future is explored working in a group. This can begin with an initial scan — what will be my life situation in the next seven years? Areas to work on are then identified more precisely.   These might be: the relationship to a particular development phase of life; organisational/professional formation and deformation; individual creativity and its barriers; organising and structuring workload; developing healthy life styles, rhythms, life hygiene.

Fundamental questions are raised and by working on them development work is made concrete. Preparation for the future can be helped by centring thoughts on specific areas. Lectures on all the above topic/question areas can be included in a programme. Exercises are introduced not only to help with diagnosis but also to help move ahead. These exercises might use colour, sculpturing/modelling, role play to release participants from over-rigid thinking and practices and to aid the process of becoming more creative. Exercises may also be included to help develop particular skills, useful in life situations, but also assisting the workshop group work, e.g. listening to the total person.

Practical suggestions for inner work are given where appropriate, participants help each other and even contract with each other to support their development efforts later on. This help can be very specific and substantial, or can consist of a telephone call just to check on progress.

The development phases of man's life.   Central to all of this process is an identification and association with man and his development path. An essential reference point for all biography work is a description of the phases of life's development. Sometimes this lecture is given on its own. Used as part of a working session such a description can be a liberating and yet stabilising influence for all. The various development phases of man's path through life are illustrated with their specific characteristics, challenges and opportunities. Naturally enough, each person tends to be most concerned with the life phase which he/she is currently living through. Then an interest grows for what has gone before and what is likely to come next. Recognising the major elements of all life phases also helps to see some of the factors influencing other people we have to deal with. If they are much younger or older it may be difficult to put ourselves in their shoes, particularly if we are looking at what they need from us. An appreciation of what each life phase can mean to those living through it is more useful in coming to terms with our fellows. We may have lived through some of the phases ourselves but they always appear different with hindsight! Coming to grips with what it is like to be older is a deep mystery to most of us! Problems of generation gaps may be partly resolved if a more complete understanding and relationship to man's life process as a whole is facilitated. It certainly is a major influence in working effectively with biography.   More specifically the relationship between different life phase issues and periods can be concentrated upon. The way in which previous phases, e.g. adolescence, relate to later phases, e.g. the 40s, is determined. How approaches to the second half of life (i.e. after 40) need to be adjusted from those which were appropriate to the first half are looked at. However, it is the impact of man's life as a whole which has greatest effect. We are all part of this picture and development can be for us in terms of an individual and social reality rather than being merely a self-indulgent flirtation.

Reference

Lievegoed, B. J., *The course of man's life*, Steiner Press, 1980.

8   Self and peer assessment

John Heron

John Heron's concept of the peer review audit has been developed mainly in his work with medical practitioners. However, his idea of the 'educated person' — an aware, self determining person who sets objectives, criteria for excellence against which he/she evaluates his/her work — is universally applicable. Institutions of higher education clearly do not prepare students for such self-determining competence, but the peer review audit utilised by a peer learning community can progress personal and professional development through action research enquiry into practice.

John Heron describes the seven stages of his peer review audit and illustrates these with case material from a peer group of National Health Service Education and Training Officers. A final section of the chapter discusses the role of the facilitator, the size of groups and problems in 'criteriological thinking' or formulating criteria by which to assess the excellence of the groups' own work.

Two interesting aspects of the peer review audit are the 'hot seat' in which each participant presents his work and his own assessment of it and then listens in silence whilst his peers follow the 'devil's advocate procedure' designed to reflect back inconsistencies, delusions, uncertainties, and so on. Heron's design, like all learning community designs, including action learning, demands simultaneous and balanced peer challenge/confrontation with peer support and care.

Background

The background to this chapter is the field of medical audit in particular, and beyond that wider issues in higher and continuing education. I will outline this background since it brings into focus the design issues which are relevant in any use of peer review audit. I will then present a formal model for any peer review audit interspersed with case study notes of its application with a small group of Regional Education and Training Officers within the NHS. I conclude with a brief survey of further general design issues.

First then, the educational background. I have long argued (Heron, 1974) that an educated person is an aware, self-determining person, in the sense of being able to set objectives, to formulate standards of excellence for the work that realises those objectives, to assess work done in the light of those standards, and to be able to modify the objectives, the standards or the work programme in the light of experience and action; and all this in discussion and consultation with other relevant persons. If this is indeed a valid notion of what an educated person is, then it is clear that the educational process in all our main institutions of higher education does not prepare students to acquire such self-determining competence. For staff unilaterally determine student learning objectives, student work programmes, student assessment criteria, and unilaterally do the assessment of the students' work.

This sort of education has generated a classic anomaly in professional development in medicine. On the one hand, medical education is highly authoritarian and unilateral in its processes: staff typically make all the crucial educational decisions and of course unilaterally devise and apply the assessment criteria. On the other hand, the profession in the UK has become increasingly alert to the need for medical audit — that is, the maintenance and advance of standards of medical care through some kind of periodic review of what doctors actually do and know. And in a recent report (1976) the profession recommended to itself audit based on self and peer assessment — peer review audit — as the most appropriate method of audit for mature professional people, rather than any kind of audit imposed from on high by some centralised body of medical authorities. Hence the anomaly: the profession acknowledges the ideological case for self and peer assessment as a method of audit, but the educational system from which the profession emerges has not equipped its members with the sort of self-determining and co-operative skills and competences required. So there has been a sort of developmental stalemate.

Peer review audit: design issues

In medical audit, as in any sort of audit of professional competence, there are two basic design issues: (a) what is audited? and (b) who does the audit? And within each of these there is complementarity or polarity of options. First let us consider what is to be audited: is it process or outcome, that is, is it the processes, the working procedures which the professional adopts, or is it the outcomes, the effects of those procedures? In medical audit, do we look at what the doctor does, or at the effect of this on the patient? It might seem that patient outcomes provide the ultimate touchstone, the final test of medical competence. But only to a degree — since a great deal of the effectiveness of many medical interventions depends significantly on patient compliance, co-operation and self-help. So outcome studies may report ambiguously on both medical intervention and patient self-determination, and indeed on other unsuspected variables. Because of this ambiguity, trial audit procedures, including mine, often focus on professional processes. Probably the most advanced medical audit would be done by a peer group of doctors and patients in which both process and outcomes are conjointly audited. But apart from its administrative difficulties, this plan is far too radical in the present climate.

The other main design issue is: who does the audit? Is it a group of experts in the profession who specify standards of good practice and then organise some sampling of general professional practice to see whether the rank and file are measuring up to these expertly determined standards? The medical profession has rejected this approach, I think wisely, as likely to lead to conformity, playing safe, and as lacking a proper regard for individual professional flair and judgement. The other approach is that the professional people audit themselves; peer groups meet together to generate agreed standards of good practice and then audit their own practice using some form of self and peer assessment. The medical profession, as I mentioned above, have endorsed this method, but so far have had difficulty in getting it going in any very systematic way, for the reason I have already outlined.

Following from my general educational interests and ideology I have used a form of audit on process using self and peer assessment, which I call peer review audit. It combines three strands: it is a form of professional development; it is an advanced continuing education procedure; and it is an action research enquiry into professional practice. As a method it is non-specific to any profession; all professions can use it and the basic design issues remain constant — process or outcomes, experts or peer groups, or any of the various hybrids that blend the poles. I have introduced peer review audit to doctors, dentists, behavioural science researchers, group leaders, co-counselling teachers, managers, management trainers (Heron, 1979a).

Formal model for peer review audit, with case study notes

There are seven stages in the peer review audit procedure. In what follows, I present: first, each stage in general, formal terms, applicable to any profession; second, some of the key design issues that arise in that stage for any application of it; third, case-study notes of that stage applied to four Regional Education and Training Officers within the NHS. The contract with these four RETOs was that they wished me to introduce the method to them, to facilitate their application of it to themselves, so that they could evaluate the method through first-hand experience. General design issues, e.g. the facilitator's role, size of groups, multiple groups, criteriological thinking, and so on, are covered in the final section of this chapter.

1   Central procedures

A peer group of persons doing the same sort of job in the same profession meet at this stage to do two main things. First, they identify and agree on the procedures that together constitute and are central to competent practice of their profession. They list the main sorts of activities that define their job. Second, they decide which of these central procedures to choose for the first audit cycle.

Design issues. It is usuaully unrealistic and unmanageable for a group to audit more than one main activity at a time. Each main sort of activity is itself internally complex and includes several subordinate activities. It takes time to sort these out and to prepare to audit them, in stages 2 and 3. And to have too much self-assessment on the job (stage 4) to do is self-defeating — it starts to detract from the competence it is supposed to be sustaining and enhancing. However, there may be one main activity that itself symbolises all or many of the others (e.g. for doctors, keeping medical records). If there is one such activity, then this deserves special consideration.

Case study stage 1: choosing a RETO activity to audit

(a)   Each RETO spent eight minutes listing his own account of his actual job functions.
(b)   The lists were shared and displayed on the blackboard. Key common functions were then identified as follows: managing staff and resources at the education/training centre; designing courses/preparing programmes; advising on training; doing training; budgetary control.
(c)   Discussion to choose one common function to audit. It was agreed to choose *managing staff* (of all kinds) in the immediate centre or office of the RETO. This was chosen because, among other things, it was most immediately available for audit over the seven working days before the next session of the peer review group.

2   *Criteria for the chosen procedure*

The group continues the first meeting into its second stage, which is to identify, clarify and adopt criteria for doing the chosen procedure well. Again there are two parts to this: first, identifying and clarifying the criteria; second, adopting the criteria.

Design issues.   There are at least three main design issues here:

(i)   Many people in the culture have difficulty with criteriological thinking. I take it that this is because our educational system simply does not train people to think clearly about, to formulate concisely, and to apply, standards of excellence for the work they do. So facilitative help may be needed here. But it's no use the facilitator having too high standards for the group at this stage. People need gentle encouragement to discover and articulate in their own way their own criteria. I deal with the issue of criteriological thinking more fully in the final section of this chapter.

(ii)   The group members can identify minimal criteria, i.e. what it is to do the chosen procedure to the minimal acceptable standard – the bare bones of competence. Or they can identify maximal criteria, i.e. what it is to do the procedure with the greatest thoroughness and excellence. Or they can do both: identify the maximal criteria, and mark out which of these or what modifications of these constitute minimal criteria.

(iii)   Whether minimal or maximal, *whose* criteria are to be adopted? There are two extremes. Either each individual formulates and adopts his own criteria, and runs the subsequent stages of the audit through on that basis, or the group pool individual lists of criteria, discuss and debate these until they all agree on a consensus list of criteria. An intermediate possibility, used in the case study, is for each person to generate his own list of three or four primary criteria, then all the lists are displayed, and each person is free to adopt a total of three or four selected from any list including his own. The rationale of this model is that it seeks to balance the claims of person idiosyncratic values on the one hand, and the claims of the collective wisdom of the group on the other.

Case study stage 2: defining and adopting criteria of competence for auditing the chosen RETO activity

(a)   Each RETO took ten minutes to list three most important and relevant criteria for assessing his competence to manage his staff in his immediate environment. The criteria for each person were as follows:
RETO 1:   Setting objectives with staff

Agreeing standard with staff
Agreeing time scale with staff
RETO 2:   Setting clear objectives with staff
Balancing monitoring of staff with autonomy of staff
Giving staff my time
RETO 3:   Collect and offer ideas with staff to generate policy
Set objectives for staff
Plan implementation with staff
RETO 4:   Giving objectives to staff
Supporting staff
Making sure they 'conform to what I want'.

(b)   Discussion on selection of criteria. The following three models
were offered:
    (i)   Each person uses his/her own criteria
   (ii)   Each person uses any three criteria chosen from the twelve
above
  (iii)   The group evolve one set of three agreed criteria to be used
by everyone.

After discussion the group agreed that each person would use any three
criteria from the total list, including his/her own.

3   *Self-assessment method*

The group now continue the first meeting into its third stage. This
involves: first, devising some way whereby each person can *sample*
his everyday professional behaviour in order to self-assess it in the light
of the criteria adopted in stage 2; second, designing a method of self-
assessment to apply to the sampled behaviour.

Design issues

(i)   If I sample and assess too much of my professional practice
then the sampling and assessing may distract me from my work, so the
whole audit becomes self-defeating. If I sample and assess too little,
then the audit loses validity. The potentially conflicting claims of the
work as such and the audit as such have to be balanced and reconciled.
In the early stages it is better for the claims of the work as such to have
clear precedence over the claims of the audit. Too much rigour in the
audit will be too demanding of time, energy and attention; and people
will rapidly lose motivation to sustain it. It is better to devise a somewhat weaker audit that stands a good chance of being applied in a
continuous way. There are actually two design issues wrapped up in
this point: first, the *frequency* of sampling and self-assessment scoring;
second, the *complexity* of the scoring method used. Both need to be

kept in modestly low profile.

(ii)   The sceptic may argue: if you know which bit of your professional practice you are going to sample for self-assessment then you can skew the performance of that bit to conform to the criteria you are going to apply in assessing it, and then afterwards relapse back into the old slack ways for the unsampled bits. There seem to be two ways of dealing with this issue. One is to make a virtue of the supposed 'contamination' and rather see it positively as quite intentional reprogramming of professional practice: the satisfaction derived from doing the sampled bits really well may lead me to seek equivalent intrinsic rewards from the other unsampled bits. The other way is to have someone else, such as receptionist or assistant, trained to pick out on a random basis bits of my professional work and tell me, *after* I have done the relevant bit, that that's the bit I am to assess myself on. Thus I never know beforehand which bit of my work I am going to assess. And this also will incline me to keep my standards up. So either way, whether I do or do not know beforehand which bit of my work I am going to assess, there will be a tendency for me to keep my standards up. And this, of course, is all to the good. For the whole idea of the audit is for me to do what I do better; not for me to be sure that I keep doing it badly so that I can catch myself out at it.

(iii)   The bit of professional practice to be assessed can be assessed while it is being done, immediately after it has been done, or some time later on the basis of memory, of normal professional records taken at the time, of audio or video tapes taken at the time. Usually the assessment will be done immediately after the relevant bit of work has been done, or some time after, e.g. at the end of the whole day's work.

(iv)   The self-assessment itself can typically be in the form of a rating scale for each of the adopted criteria, with brief notes about each bit of behaviour assessed, notes which mention, among other relevant things, any special or extenuating circumstances.

(v)   At any given occasion of self-assessment, I can assess just one instance of the relevant procedure the group has chosen to audit, or I can assess a batch of instances and give myself an overall score for the batch. The RETO group really chose to do the latter as you will see in the study notes.

(vi)   As well as self-assessment, which is the primary sort of assessment used in the audit, the group may also want to incorporate elements of on-the-job assessment by peers, by clients, by supporting staff. On-the-job assessment by peers means that one of my professional equals, ideally a member of the peer review audit group, is present while I do a relevant bit of work and then assesses the work I have done in his presence. This is an excellent and complementary adjunct to self-assessment. Unfortunately it is often seen to be impracticable: professional people argue that they are too busy to take time off to go and be present at the side of someone else's work. However, subordinate or supporting staff are more accessible. In the case study the use of assessment by such staff was built into the design as an optional extra. Of course, the sort of assessment done by subordinate or supporting staff may well be different from the sort of assessment done by professional peers.

Case study stage 3: designing a self-assessment method.   The purpose of this stage is to design a method whereby each person can assess his on-the-job competence in managing staff according to his chosen criteria.   After brainstorming and discussion, the following self-assessment method was agreed:

(a)   Keep a daily diary outlining your staff management activities for the day with sufficient detail to key your memory in to the events that occurred.   Some variations suggested: only record pertinent activities; record everything then edit the pertinent activities; record both what you did and did not do.

(b)   At the end of each daily entry in the diary, score your self with respect to that day's staff management activities on three self rating scales from one to five (1 = very low competence, 3 = medium competence, 5 = very high competence), on scale for each of the chosen criteria.

(c)   An optional extra, depending on personal preference and local circumstances: ask one or more members of staff to assess you, using a 1 to 5 rating scale for each of your chosen criteria, over any appropriate period of time, i.e. the whole seven days or any appropriate shorter period.

(d)   Note beside each of your self rating scales points that indicate why your rating was pitched where it was.

(e)   If you forget to fill in the diary and then fill it up in a retrospective block of two or three or more days, please note this in the diary.   In this way the group can gather data about how tendencies to forgetfulness affect the procedure.

4   *Professional practice: first cycle*

Stages 1 to 3 can all occur on the first peer group meeting. For stage 4, the peer group members return to work, and for some agreed period they sample and assess their everyday professional practice. So they are taking one sort of main activity that their work involves, sampling instances of it, and doing a self-assessment on those instances, applying the criteria adopted in stage 2 and the sampling and scoring methods devised in stage 3. During this period of on-the-job self-assessment members of the group will not meet each other, unless of course they happen to be professional colleagues in the same place of work, or unless they have arranged some on-the-job peer assessment sessions with each other.

Design issues.   The main issue is how long this period of on-the-job self-assessment is to last. If it is too short, there is no time for the positive cumulative effect on professional standards to work; and no adequate sample of behaviour is taken. If it is too long, then commitment and motivation to sustain the audit task may falter through lack of peer support and stimulus.

Case study stage 4: applying the self-assessment method to professional activity.   Each RETO returned to work with the commitment to apply the self-assessment method designed in stage 3 to all relevant activities on a total of seven consecutive working days.

5   Peer review session: part 1

The peer group now meets for the second time and each takes a turn in the 'hot seat': first, to share his self-assessment scores and findings, plus any other assessments, from stage 4; second, to receive assessment and feedback from his peers in the group on this presentation and its content, being open equally to their confrontation as well as to their appreciation and support. So when I say that peer review audit uses self- and peer assessment, the peer assessment is *on the presentation and content of the self-assessment* — unless, of course, members of the group have been able to make reciprocal on-the-job peer assessment arrangements, in which case the peers' on-the-job assessments can be reported at the peer review session. As I have already said, such on-the-job peer assessment is usually regarded as impracticable, hence the emphasis on the sort of peer assessment I have just defined. The whole procedure for this first part of the peer review session is as follows:

(i)   One person takes the hot seat. He mentions the activity being audited, the criteria he has adopted, the method and frequency of sampling the relevant activity, the self-assessment method he has used, and any other assessments used. He then presents his self-assessment (and any other assessment) findings, using any convenient way of presenting summaries of records and scores, identifying strengths and weaknesses of performance, identifying also typical extenuating, enhancing or distorting circumstances, and emerging with some general estimate of his current level of competence with respect to the activity under audit.

It is also helpful if he briefly assesses his competence in doing the self-assessment. So this is a piece of self-assessment on the primary self-assessment. How often did he remember, how often did he forget to do whatever his self-assessment method required? Did he try to catch up with himself by doing retrospectively all at once a batch of self-assessments from memory which were originally to have been done one at a time? How thorough was his recording and scoring? How honest was it? What conceptual or other difficulties were found in applying the criteria? How did motivation and commitment stay the course? What were the positive, what the negative effects on daily work of the whole procedure? And so on. To do some at any rate of this higher order self-assessment provides the group with relevant data for reviewing and maybe revising the audit method – see the next stage.

(ii) The same person stays in the hot seat and listens without comment or reply while his peers follow the 'devil's advocate procedure' (DAP). This procedure entitles the peers to raise any slight (or of course strong) doubt about what he has said; to reflect back inconsistencies, anomalies, uncertainties, hesitancies, insecurities, defensiveness, evasions, delusions, self-inflations, self-denigrations; to say that the self-assessment ratings appear to be too high or too low; to share concern and anxieties about his competence in this or that respect, on the basis of what he has said or how he has said it; and so on and so on. The point about DAP is that the peers don't have to worry about the justice of their remarks, whether they are based on adequate evidence, whether they are projections or not. They are invited, without inhibition, to amplify and feedback any impressions of anything that *seems* to be unsatisfactory in what the self-assessor has said or how he has said it, provided only that (a) what they say is expressed in a fundamentally respectful manner and therefore (b) that it is free of any trace of malice, of destructive and hurtful attack. This, of course, is a basic interactive skill.

The hot-seater's task, meanwhile, is to listen to the DAP with great discrimination, weeding out and discarding mentally what is obvious misconception or projection, but being open to attend carefully to genuinely perceptive if confronting comments. Above all, he does this silently, without comment, reply, argument, self-justification – mentally using the incoming remarks to refine his self-assessment. There will be a great temptation for the hot-seater to defend himself verbally. This misses the whole point of the DAP. Invariably when it happens the whole procedure rapidly deteriorates. The facilitator has an important task to help keep things on the rails here, until the group has grasped the rationale of the process and built up the simple but basic interactive skills required.

N.B. Before DAP begins, the peers may request a brief period to ask the hot-seater questions simply and exclusively in order to clarify their understanding of his presentation and its content. It is important, in my experience, that the end of this period is clearly marked, so that everyone can make the appropriate change of mental gear into the DAP.

(iii) With the same person still in the hot seat, the peers then give their positive appreciation of the self-assessment, underlining what they valued, what they perceived to be the human qualities and strengths of the person, the work reported on, or the way of reporting on it. Again, the hot-seater listens, without comment or reply.

(iv) The hot-seater, finally, has a brief period which he can use if he wishes to revise, modify or confirm his previous self-assessment, in the light of the peer feedback. Often the hot-seater doesn't want to use this time to say anything because he is still busy digesting all the peer comment and feedback. It is therefore helpful if this comment can be recorded so that the recipient can continue to review it later at his leisure.

(v) The whole of the hot-seat exercise, (i) to (iv) above, is now repeated for each other member of the group in turn. Taking the hot seat is, as a matter of basic principle, entirely voluntary (self-assessment can't be genuine self-assessment unless it is freely chosen) and no-one should be pressed to do it. However, justice does seem to require that you shouldn't be at the giving end of devil's advocacy unless you are willing to be at the receiving end of it. It may be as well to remind people of this.

Design issues

(i) The whole of the procedure just outlined (i) to (v) above is time-consuming. It is also very demanding emotionally, morally and cognitively. If each member of the peer group is to get a fair deal, it all needs to be strictly timed by the watch: say 20 minutes for each person. This means, for example, 10 minutes for self-assessment presentation, 4 minutes for DAP, 4 minutes for appreciations, 2 minutes for final self-assessment statement. For a group of 8 persons, very strict timing, without breaks, would take up 2 hours 40 minutes. It's usually a good idea to do 4 or 5 persons, then have a break — so that no-one gets the thin end of the energy/attention wedge.

(ii) This is the stage where skilled facilitation is most needed, until the peer group members have got the hang of it. The facilitator needs to explain carefully the rationale of the whole hot-seat procedure, especially the DAP; to help the hot-seater find the mid-point between self-inflation and self-denigration in his self-assessment presentation; to help the hot-seater resist the tendency to defend himself verbally during the DAP; to help the peers *use* the DAP thoroughly and courageously, not degenerating either into collusive mollycoddling and evasion, or into malicious, hurtful, destructive attack; to help the group adapt to following the time structure rigorously. This is the stage where the greatest degree of interactive skill is required of all concerned, including the facilitator.

(iii)   Above all, the facilitator's task throughout this stage is to bring out that it is designed to affirm the primacy of self-assessment while still making the fullest use of the discriminating assessment of others. The purpose of the peer feedback is not to browbeat the hot-seater into conformist submission, but to provide a powerful crucible in which he can refine his self-assessment. The hot-seater in presenting his self-assessment is being accountable primarily to himself, and only in a very secondary sense to his peers.

Case study stage 5: peer review session part 1.   This was the second meeting of the group of RETOs. It was on the day following the seven working days which the group had agreed to audit at the first meeting. So this was the stage for the hot-seat exercise, for presenting self-assessment with peer feedback, on staff management activities during those seven days. I shall not give here details of the self-assessment presentations, of the DAP comments on each person and of the appreciative comments on each person. This is primarily for reasons of confidentiality; but secondarily because it would make this chapter far too long. What follows then, is in effect a brief resume of the general hot-seat procedure already fully described above:

(a)   Each person in turn took the hot seat and revealed his self-assessment ratings under the three criteria chosen for each relevant working day. He also revealed the way in which he conducted the self-assessment, i.e. did he do it daily, or forget a few days and then do it in a retrospective block, or forget it altogether?

(b)   He then listened in silence to a devil's advocate round in which each of his peers amplified and verbalised any doubt, negative impression, misgiving about the content of the assessment and its presentation. He discriminated the incoming information, rejecting projections and distortions, but using the remainder to refine his self-assessment. This was done in the mind only.

(c)   He then listened in silence to a round of positive impressions and appreciations about himself, his work and his self-assessment, from each of his peers.

(d)   He then had a short period to express any modification or confirmation of his original self-assessment.

6   Peer review session: part 2

The second meeting of the group continues with an interim evaluation of the whole audit process so far. So the peer group is now briefly auditing the audit. This is necessary, first, to see whether it is sufficiently worthwhile for the group to want to continue into a second cycle, and if so, second, to see whether experience of the method in the first cycle suggests any improvements and modifications for the second cycle.

I usually start this stage off with an open-ended discussion prefaced by the question 'Has the audit process so far been meaningful?' and then let everyone say what they want to say about it. If everyone agrees that the exercise so far has been useless, then we all pack up and go home; but I haven't encountered this phenomenon yet. If the general consensus is that the exercise has been useful and worthwhile, then I ask whether any parts of it could usefully be modified. This is potentially a vast field of enquiry since each design issue under each stage of the process could come up for discussion and review. In practice, however, only one or two do.

Design issues

(i)   The group members have now been asked to shift from assessing their professional work to assessing how they are assessing their professional work. Sometimes they cannot sustain their category shift and drift back from the second-order level to the first-order level. So the facilitator may need to give a little help here.

(ii) Fundamentally the group is being asked at this stage to make the audit model — into which I have initiated them — its own, by modifying it in relevant ways in the light of the experience of using it. Too many modifications introduced too soon will probably mean a degeneration: group members may be avoiding the challenge and discipline of the original model, whose rationale they have not fully grasped. Where I think this applies I can point it out to a group (I haven't encountered it yet). But in the last analysis the important thing is for the group members to make the model their own in their own way — whether this means that it becomes an interesting and useful modification of the same sort of model, whether it turns into exercise of a different sort, or whether it disintegrates entirely.

Case study stage 6: review of all stages of peer review audit so far. The RETOs continued their second meeting and then discussed the whole process so far:

(a)   Was it meaningful?

Yes, *now* after the peer review.

Yes, diary was a useful discipline, peer review session made me look at my use of time.

Yes, peer review session was useful, it made me look at myself.

Yes, the daily self-audit was most powerful, it made me confront some things, the discipline of a diary most useful. The
peer review session conceptually enjoyable, but not sure of its
benefit.

(b)   The hot seat exercise: need for more time to discuss issues after
each person had been in the hot seat. This point suggested the
next step; an action planning stage, so that each one can get out
there and change things.

7   Planning the second cycle

The second meeting now continues into its third part. The purpose of
this is to plan another cycle. The group members have to decide, first,
whether to continue to audit the same sort of professional activity as
they did in the first cycle, or whether to audit another sort of activity.
If they choose the latter, then they go through stages 2 and 3 again, i.e.
adopting criteria for doing that activity well, and designing a self-
assessment method to use on the job. If they choose to continue the
audit of the first cycle, then do they want to modify in any way the
criteria and self-assessment methods used in the first cycle? In the
case study, the RETOs wanted to continue auditing the same activity,
but honing in on aspects of it that the hot seat exercise had put
questions against. This meant that they modified the criteria, but kept
the same basic self-assessment method.

Design issues

(i)   Stages 5, 6 and 7, in this account, are all being done at the same
meeting. This was also done in the case study: but with only four
persons this was quite manageable. If there are six to eight persons,
then all three stages together would be demanding and time-consuming,
needing a whole day session perhaps rather than a half-day session, with
lunch and other breaks to recoup attention. Each stage will need its
time allocation fairly strictly adhered to. There may be a case for
doing the hot seat exercise (stage 5) on one half-day, let everyone
digest the experience, then do stages 6 and 7 together on another half-
day, e.g. next morning.

(ii)   If the group decide, in stage 7, to choose another professional
activity to audit, what happens to the activity audited in the first cycle?
Either a much reduced and skeletal or occasional audit on it can be
continued; or all explicit self-assessment can be dropped on the assumption that a tacit or purely mental self-assessment will tend to continue
on, at any rate for a period. In practice, where a group has changed to
a new activity to audit, it has automatically dropped the audit on the
first activity, and I haven't challenged this on the grounds that having

too much explicit self-assessment to do would be self-defeating, especially at a relatively early stage of mastering the method.

Case study stage 7: planning the second cycle.   This is now the third main part of their second meeting. On the basis of the hot seat exercise and in relation to specific issues picked out from peer feedback by the person in the hot seat each RETO:

(a)   Made an action plan to assess himself with respect to a particular area of practice which the peer review session had shown up as in need of revision or change, or at least careful monitoring to see what goes on.

(b)   He did this by specifying the particular managerial issue, by specifying the criteria to be used in assessing it and by specifying the self-assessment method he will use.

RETO 1:   *Issues:* do I consult or order? Work with or work at? How much of each/how appropriate in each case? *Criteria:* degree, appropriateness, time. *Self-assessment method:* diary, with rating scale for each criterion, with equivalent staff diary rating me on the three criteria.

RETO 2:   *Issues:* use of my time, also confrontation. *Criteria:* for time, awareness of priorities, balancing needs of others with my needs. For confrontation, did I do it? How successful? *Self-assessment method:* diary, with rating scale for each criterion.

RETO 3:   *Issues:* do I work on too low a level, with too much detail? *Criteria:* level of objectives, standards of performance, planning. *Self-assessment method:* diary, with rating scale on each criterion.

RETO 4:   *Issues:* how far do I support staff? *Criteria:* approachability, effectiveness, i.e. resulting satisfaction both to me and to them. Speed. *Self-assessment method:* diary, with rating scale for each criterion.

8   *Professional practice: second cycle*

The group members return to work and commence the second round of self-assessment on the job, doing whatever they planned to do in stage 7. The RETO group members took off on their own at this stage, so I have no more case study notes from my interaction with them.

Design issues

Once a peer group's members take off on their own, leaving their initiator or facilitator behind, they are on their own. They make the thing their own in whatever way they wish, and they are not accountable to their erstwhile facilitator about it. Nor is it the facilitator's business to do 'follow up research' on them. For his job was to initiate them into a way of doing their own follow up research on themselves. He must let them get on with it, and not anxiously tinker about on the edges to see whether they are shaping up. Of course, he may be interested, as a friend, to hear about what they are doing and how they are getting on. But that is a matter of human interest, not of formal research enquiry. If *qua* researcher, he wants to do a sustained research enquiry into peer review audit, then he must become a member of a peer review audit group and audit with his peers *his own* professional activity. This approach, of course, takes us into the whole field of new paradigm research (Heron, 1979b; Reason, 1977–79).

Some more general design issues

In the introduction to this chapter I mentioned two very basic general design issues:

(i)   What is to be audited, is it process or outcome?
(ii)   Who does the audit, 'experts', or peer groups?

Here are some more, presented more or less in the order they occur to me.

(iii)   Several groups of the same profession can run through peer review audit cycles, each group doing so independently of the others for some period. They can then meet in an inter-group exercise to compare and contrast: professional procedures identified and chosen for audit, criteria used, what central issues of professional practice emerge, and so on. In this way a profession can research its own emergent and developing culture; constancies and variations in norms, values and practice. In the inter-group exercise they can also compare and contrast: self-assessment methods used, peer review session structures, cyclic patterning, and indeed anything about the whole audit method. And this then constitutes a higher order enquiry into the peer review audit method as such. At the time of writing I haven't managed to organise anything so extensive as this.

(iv)   The point of peer review audit, is, of course, lost if the professional standards and practices generated and confirmed by one group for itself are then used to *prescribe* professional behaviour to others. The *process* of the peer review audit group is more important than any prescriptive products it formulates to tell itself where it has got to. And it is this process that is to be commended to other groups within the profession so that they can generate *their own* prescriptive products.

(v)   Is a facilitator or initiator needed? My own view is this. If the professional group concerned have had virtually no interactive skills training and are relatively naive about interpersonal and group process issues, then it is necessary to have a skilled facilitator present to help the group acquire the basic interactive skills and discipline without which the whole exercise simply will not work. If the professional group know what's what, then on the basis of a description such as the one given in this paper they can probably get the thing working, appointing one of themselves as facilitator to keep an eye on timing, behavioural lapses and so on. But when an outside facilitator is used, then he needs to make it clear to himself and the group that he is simply helping the group to do without him after a certain initiation period.

(vi)   I come back now to a point I raised in the design issue comments on stage 2: people in our culture have difficulty with criteriological thinking because our educational system does not train students to think about and formulate criteria which they choose to apply to their own work. So when professional people are asked to generate criteria or standards for good practice, they first need to be trained to occupy the quite simple logical territory involved and choose their resting place. The issue is an hierarchical one. Thus doing an activity well is defined in terms of a sub-set of more specific activities. And doing each activity in the sub-set well is defined in a further sub-set of even more specific activities.

For example, in dentistry, doing a filling well is defined in terms of more specific activities such as removing decay, providing retention, eliminating ledges, supporting enamel, lining, contouring, etc. What it is to do each of these well is defined in terms of a still more detailed set of activities, one set for removing decay, another set for providing retention, and so on.

Now for practical purposes of audit, you have to rest at a quite early stage and *assume* the criteria for doing well the set of activities you have chosen as criteria for doing well the activity you are going to audit. Otherwise you are launched in pursuit of ultimate micro-activities, and to audit each of these would, for a busy professional person, become impossibly time-consuming.

It goes without saying, of course, that an external facilitator will never prescribe criteria, but simply help the group master the simple logical issues.

(vii) What size of group? Not less than two and not more than eight, I would say. If there are more than eight people, they can form into two smaller groups, and then you can derive the benefits, at a later stage, of comparable audit groups.

(viii) As well as peer audit groups, there are hierarchical audit groups: for example, managers and subordinates, staff and students, doctors and patients. These are inevitably democratising and dramatically reduce the steepness of the hierarchy profile. If it's a two-person group of manager and subordinate, then each assesses his own work and gives feedback on the self-assessment of the other, and also on the actual work of the other if they are in everyday working relationship.

(ix) Finally a reminder that peer review audit is a professional/ organisational change and development method: it is an education and training method; it is a new paradigm research method. Because of this sweep and scope I imagine it will be greatly used in the future.

References

Competence to Practice, London, Committee of Enquiry into Competence to Practice, 1976.

Heron, J., *The Concept of a Peer Learning Community*, University of Surrey, Human Potential Research Project, 1974.

Heron, J., *Peer Review Audit*, University of London, British Postgraduate Medical Federation, 1979a.

Heron, J., *Experiential Research Methodology*, University of London, British Postgraduate Medical Federation, 1979b.

Reason, P. (ed.)., *The New Paradigm Research Group Newsletter*, University of Bath, Centre for the Study of Organisational Change and Development, 1977–79.

9 Developing managers for new enterprise

John Morris

Another way in which the development needs of the individual and the organisation can be brought together is for the individual to set up his own organisation as a means of developing himself. This chapter describes one approach to helping people to do this. Clearly, as in action learning (Chapter 13) the emphasis appears to be primarily on the task. However, again as with action learning, the success in doing something that really matters to the individual can provide a very developmental experience – 'a crucial turning point in one's career, and a flood of self-confidence and heightened awareness'.

The chapter also illustrates another form of self-development, in that its final section takes the form of reflection, or of a 'learning-conversation' (cf Chapter 15) between the writer and his alter ego. As such it reveals much not only about the theories behind John Morris' programmes, but about himself as well – as though the two could be separated, anyway!

People can develop as owner-managers for new enterprise in many different ways. Before proceeding to describe some current forms of management development in new enterprise, it seems worth asking some key questions about the underlying assumptions that we bring to these activities. *Who* is doing the 'developing'? Is it the owner-managers themselves, in the light of their individual conceptions of their needs? That is the answer I would like to give, since there are few things more interesting and useful than to work with people who stand for the things that you stand for yourself, and to provide practical and theoretical support to people who have some idea of where they are going (Morris and Burgoyne, 1973; Morris, 1975, 1980). But the phrase can be interpreted in at least two other ways, which also find strong supporters. First, there are the sponsors at every level who are convinced that Britain needs more new business, rather than small changes in deeply-entrenched established business. They want to find and develop managers who can bring about this valuable state of affairs. The sponsors stand by with funds, at a price, and can often provide various other forms of necessary support, but usually expect to enjoy the rights and privileges of sponsors throughout history: that they make the final decisions about who is to be developed, and how.

Second, there are the new-look programme staff — tutors, learning-consultants and so on — who are interested in New Enterprise and Small Business as a field in which their resources of knowledge and skill in enabling people to learn seem clearly appropriate. The concern here is rather different from the concern of the 'developing managers' themselves — who may not feel that 'being helped to learn' within an organised programme is their major need. The sponsors may also feel that entrepreneurs are best developed by experience, rather than through 'training'. So a question that might be asked is this: *Can we find ways of bringing the interests in new enterprise of the would-be entrepreneurs, the sponsors and the staff consultants together into workable forms of activity?*

Two attempts to establish such forms of activity are the New Enterprise Programme, described and partly evaluated in a recent paper by my colleague David Watkins (Watkins, 1979) and the New Enterprise Promotion activities in Mid Wales. In this chapter I take six aspects of these activities: (i) a description of the basic design, (ii) the programme participants, (iii) the role of the management committee, (iv) the role of staff consultants, (v) impressions of the effectiveness of the programmes, and (vi) the implications of these activities for self-development.

The basic design

Both programmes are designed as development opportunities for those who are interested in forming an independent business. The New Enterprise Programme is easier to describe, because for over two years it has retained the same basic objective and design. These are set out in the programme notes, sent to prospective participants, in the following terms:

OBJECTIVE
New Enterprise Programme (NEP) provides a framework within which individuals or prospective business partners seeking to start a new business can test out the feasibility of their ideas, modifying these and implementing them accordingly. Each Programme comprises about sixteen individuals — women and men — who

learn not only from experienced MBS Faculty and outside experts but also from one another. The businesses formed should have the potential to employ others besides the initiator and his immediate family.

LOCATION, DURATION AND STRUCTURE
Participation in the Programme lasts a maximum of sixteen weeks of which the first month is spent in residence at MBS.

The first four weeks (Phase I) are spent in developing and revising business skills relevant to the analysis and implementation of new business ventures. This Phase culminates in the development of a work programme for the following twelve weeks. This latter period (Phase II) is spent in whatever location is most appropriate to the conduct of the feasibility study and initiation of the business. This may at different times include the participant's home and residence at MBS. Almost certainly, other periods will be spent 'on the road' in the UK or abroad. Workspace, telephone telex and secretarial backing are provided at MBS during Phase II.

The emphasis is strongly on the work to be done. This is new work for each participant, since it is concerned with the possible establishment of a new business. The emphasis is strongly on 'learning from one another' as well as from staff consultants. The first four weeks reveal some of the familiar features of conventional training courses – lectures, group discussions, case studies, exercises and simulation projects. But even here, the time available for programming by the participants, to meet their individual and group needs, steadily grows from the first to the fourth week. The view is strongly expressed: 'This is your programme: take a hand in organising it!' The fourth week and most of the fifth are taken up with detailed planning of the final stage: the feasibility testing. Plans for this are discussed with fellow participants, before being presented in confidential meetings with the management committee, at which agreement is reached on how the time and the budget is going to be used. In the next three months, each participant works to the agreed plan, with whatever modifications experience shows to be necessary. Every three or four weeks, there are further meetings with members of the management committee in order to review progress.

So much for the basic design. But although this has not changed much, many other things about the programme have, and these will be taken up in later sections. The design of the Mid Wales New Enterprise Promotion activities, sponsored by the Development Board of Rural Wales, is somewhat different, since it is a regional rather than a national programme, and takes place in close conjunction with a wide range of other development activities which this extremely vigorous Board has initiated.

The activities are in three stages, spread over roughly six months. The first phase is a week-end conference tightly packed with interesting people and useful information, including the opportunity of sharing experience and ideas with fellow participants in reasonably small interest-groups, and hearing candid accounts of business development from successful entrepreneurs in the region. A month or so later, the second stage takes up the themes of marketing, sources of funds, management accounting, and basic business planning. The work here is concerned with business fundamentals, with plenty of opportunity for discussion and practical exercises. Finally, in a further month or so, the third stage begins, and combines a short (3–5 day) introductory programme with a feasibility project along similar lines to the New Enterprise programme. But there are several differences: the participants work more as a group during the feasibility stage, combining one-day meetings to consider shared concerns and individual meetings with members of the management committee. The Development Board staff, working on the programme, are able to draw on a much more tightly linked range of support resources that can reasonably be offered in a national programme, such as the New Enterprise Programme.

The three-stage design of the Mid Wales promotion activities enables a substantial number of people to take part. It is not unusual for eighty people to take part in the initial week-end conference, up to thirty in the workshop, and a dozen or so in the intensive final stage. The reduction in numbers through the three stages is the result of several factors: the different demands on the participants' time and degree of commitment, the availability of support staff, and the question of timing of the different stages in relation to the stages of business development of the participants. One of the advantages of the three-stage design is that people can attend the early stages of one programme, and then take part in the third stage of a later programme.

The problem of using a partly metaphorical term like 'design' in referring to complex and changing sets of arrangements such as the two New Enterprise programmes is that one can talk of 'design' on so many levels of abstraction. In the most general sense, the design of both programmes is strikingly similar and has changed little since their inception: they provide a flexible framework of time and resources within which people interested in new enterprise can work with one another, and with support staff, on their business ideas, with limited financial support from sponsors interested in developing new enterprise. If one comes down a step or two towards the individual programmes, the differences outlined above begin to be apparent. If the description and analysis were more specific, the differences between a regional development activity and a national development programme could seem enormous. My sense of the difficulty of finding the right level of approach in discussing these programmes is greatly deepened when we turn from questions of 'design' to an account of the participants.

Those taking part in the programmes

One might expect people who are interested in forming an independent business to be independent and highly individual. And so they are. A glance at the business ideas put forward by participants in a single programme reveals an impressive range, even though it is limited to ideas that might have some chance of being launched with limited resources in a short time. On one programme alone, the following ideas were being worked on: toys and games, audio-visual materials for industry and commerce, micro-computer marketing information systems, PVC shower-curtains, up-market country wines, professional updating services, assembly and sales of safety equipment, buoyancy apparatus, pipe linings for food processing equipment, and small-scale textile finishing suitable for industrial development areas. This does not exhaust the list for one programme of fifteen people: but it may give some impression of the variety.

The participants are from very mixed backgrounds, and have varied in age from the mid-twenties to the mid-sixties (the oldest members of the programmes so far has been perhaps the most successul in his business venture, in partnership with one of the youngest members). The programmes, especially the promotion activities in Mid Wales, have taken people at different stages in business development (Watkins, 1977, 1979), and this has proved a decided advantage, since it greatly increases the opportunities for participants learning with and from each other about the early problems of business formation.

In the New Enterprise Programme notes cited earlier, a special comment is made to the effect that 'women are as welcome as men. It has also concerned us that very few applications have been from immigrants to Britain, a traditional source of vigour and enterprise in business.' Despite these encouraging noises, we have never had more than two women on the national programme, and only a very modest number of immigrants. In the Mid Wales programme the picture has been somewhat different, since many of the business ideas have been in the craft field. On the first programme, 5 out of 12 participants in the final stage were women, and in the second programme, 7 out of 15. If 'immigrant' is reworded as 'incomer', many of those taking part in the Mid Wales programme have come from outside Wales, and we trust that they will prove in the later stages of their business development to be a 'source of vigour and enterprise' in that delectable and supportive environment.

Despite the diversity of the participants, a few general observations can be made about many of them. They have a strong drive to independence, to being free from close supervision, but have a keen sense of business realities. They accept objective constraints much more readily than those embodied in 'authority'. Many of them are quite willing to control others, as employees or associates, but feel oppressed by thought of complex legislation and 'industrial relations'. Their feeling is that if their companies can provide a continuing sense of growth and opportunity, many of the 'labour relations' problems will solve themselves.

They tend to be practical and outward-looking, rather than analytical and inward-looking. If asked what issues they want help on, answers come quickly: marketing and sales, sources of funds, premises, accounting on a realistic 'cash flow' basis, and details of business formation. There is not much sense of 'organisation' or 'relationships' as presenting problems: these, I suspect, are thankfully deferred until success forces them on the owner-manager's attention at a later stage of business development. The nature of one's own motivation, and how it will stand up to the day-to-day stresses and strains of business operation, *is* of interest, but it is rightly felt to constitute a very different kind of problem from the practical 'nuts and bolts' that can be offered in other problem-areas.

Even with a four-month programme at their disposal, those taking part in the various activities feel a constant pressure of time. This means that they often want the fruits of professional expertise, rather than the drudgery of acquiring the expertise for themselves. Not surprisingly, they are greatly impressed by people who have established themselves in a successful business, but are still close enough to recollection of their own early stages of development to be able to pass on their experience, in an unpretentious, down-to-earth fashion.

The emotional problems of reaching a decision with such far-reaching consequences for oneself and one's family as starting a business are considerable. The decision to take part in the programme is an important one: but it permits a deferment for some weeks or months of the actual decision to begin trading. At such crucial points of decision, people are swayed between varying moods: excitement and depression, dependence, and aggressive independence. The programme and its management must be sensitive to these changing states as well as to the more obvious needs of participants for information and basic techniques. The very mention of 'management' of a programme for would-be entrepreneurs raises quite fundamental questions. How does one manage those who — to be successful — must be self-managing? In both programmes, part of the task of management is the responsibility of a management committee.

The role of the management committee

The idea of having a management committee for each of the programmes was drawn from the 'joint development' line of work (Morris, 1977). A management committee composed of sponsors and staff-consultants can start a programme with a group of participants without having to set up a 'selling apparatus' of a glossy brochure, a fixed offering, and lengthy statements about staff qualifications. An effectively working management group can set up its own standards of effectiveness, in close collaboration with the interested parties with whom it is managing. They can use 'audits' and 'evaluation' as flexible devices for improving current and future effectiveness, rather than as formal monuments to research endeavour. If circumstances change, so can the programme. Instead of being a fixed commitment, the programme is seen as part of a network of agreements between people who have a personal stake in it. They are people who want the programme to be effective, because it is an important part of their lives.

This, of course, is a statement of an ideal. Programmes often become rigid control devices, dominating the activities of those who are part of them, rather than fallible human arrangements for getting things done in a difficult world. We have only to look at the programmes in numberless training centres to see how rigidity rules the day. Split off from the hurly-burly of everyday life, they prescribe the course of each day with fantastic precision. This point is often missed by those taking part in them, because they are replete with dramatic and ritual elements that obscure the formal rigidity of the whole arrangement. Because many of us expect education and training to be a combination of heart-stirring rituals and technical instruction, the fundamental irrelevance of much of the activity is obscured. It is left to the outside observer to note that the marvellous orderliness and efficient use of resources that are the pride of the company training centre and the business college are achieved by shutting out the world that we are supposed to be dealing with. Reality only breaks in when the budget is cut or the support staff go out on strike.

The fundamental task of the management committee is to help maintain and develop a flexible programme that helps us to understand and cope with the world and at no point to lose touch with it. The purpose of the programme is to help us as human beings to move purposefully towards an *agreed* objective in a confusing world. The management committee is a way of enabling the nature of the agreement to be open to inspection, and worked with as a key issue rather than being taken for granted.

The realities of managing the programmes can perhaps be seen more clearly when we realise that they are very much 'new enterprises' in their own right. They have had their own problems of securing adequate funds, suitable premises, and initial staff. They are a continuing test of the commitment and of the competence of the small group of people at the centre. There is much the same sense of initiative and ownership of the activity as in the new enterprises that are being fostered. But there are important differences. The New Enterprise programmes are joint ventures, rather than independent businesses. Shrewd observers have not failed to notice the nature of the parent-institutions and to ask: how can a university business school and a government agency do anything useful for entrepreneurs?

Closer inspection of the people working on the programmes, and the nature of the two parent-institutions reveals some reassuring features. The Manpower Services Commission is a relatively new 'executive arm' of a national manpower policy, and displays much of the imagination and energy of an enterprise in its pioneering phase. The Development Board of Rural Wales has been recently formed out of earlier agencies in the field, and has seen the enterprise promotion activities as part of a set of exciting new ventures. Those who have joined the management committees from the sponsoring side have been willing to lend their energies as well as their skills to progressing the programmes. And they have been enterprising people, with wide-ranging experience outside as well as inside public service (one of the Mid Wales committee members, Grenville Jackson, is active in development planning and research, and has recently contributed an interesting paper to a small business research conference: see Jackson, 1979). Manchester Business School, for its part, has a strong commitment to innovative development programmes, and has a form of organisation which favours rapid grouping of staff into programme management and support teams. There are no academic departments, and even the degree programmes are focused on projects and optional studies — including a very popular option in entrepreneurship.

All of these factors serve to delay the process of institutional hardening. But there are many disturbing features of the economic and social scene that threaten every kind of new enterprise, including joint ventures. At the moment, the parent institutions are greatly worried about cut-backs in the public sector, and its effect on their whole range of programmes. Will the recognition, at very high levels of policy-making, that new enterprise is an economic necessity for Britain, help or hinder the new enterprise programmes? At first sight, they would seem to be beneficiaries of the slow move in public-sector finance towards looking for demonstrable results. But new enterprises can be effectively destroyed by trying to do too much, and trying to grow too quickly.

My hope is that the management committees can use their collective skills and experience to advantage here. They can work with the various 'stakeholders' to assure a reasonable rate of growth. They can, perhaps, point out that development programmes are always a delicate balance of personal interests and skills, rather than the application of a routine 'success formula'. Even allowing for the important fact that much of new enterprise is shrewd application of well known ideas and approaches, they need to recognise that each new owner-manager must find a combination of the new and the old, the innovative elements and the routine, in his or her own distinctive way.

Since I have drawn a parallel between new enterprise and the programmes themselves, it is important to note that entrepreneurs often pay insufficient attention to their own management styles, and to the complex relationships between the tiny core group of owner-managers and those on whose skill and goodwill, as key workers and associates, they depend. I am afraid that as far as I am concerned, the parallel holds in this respect too.

Staff consultants on the New Enterprise programmes

A useful way of looking at consultants to New Enterprise programmes is to see them as a combination of programme managers and project consultants. Since each participant in a programme is usually deeply concerned with being the unchallenged manager of his or her own business, as a personal project, there is not much scope for consultants to be *project* managers in an immediate sense: though as they warm to the opportunities that they see in a proposed new business, they often fall into the tone of a partner rather than a consultant ('we could do it this way' or 'If I were you, I would go for the second product at least six months later than you've got it in the plan' . . . and it becomes apparent that in every such consultant, there is an independent businessman halfway into a business of his own).

Both the programme manager and the project consultant have a difficult job: and for much the same reason. New enterprise is a matter of getting a lot of different people and things to come together at a particular place and time, to meet a particular need. There is no end to the specialist expertise that the new enterprise can use, from filling in export documents to knowing the best source of supplies of a rare commodity. But the key task is getting it all together: and through the agency of the owner-manager and the very small group of people with whom he works. Much of the subject matter of academic disciplines and business specialisms is made up of well ordered materials, in the form of theoretical frameworks, analytical techniques, cumulative research, custom and practice and so on. The teacher of an academic discipline and the staff specialist working within a big company are much more alike than they care to recognise. They are working with bodies of knowledge and well established procedures. They know what they know, and exude the air of self-confidence proper to one who treads familiar paths in a well ordered domain.

Parts of the work of the owner-manager may be well established and familiar, though not usually in the early days of business formation. But even when he has become 'established', there is little in his head in the form of explicit knowledge. In its place is a vast array of rules of thumb, detailed understanding of complex and changing situations, a sense of the continuing need to keep a small number of key people satisfied. And, above all, an overriding sense of purpose and personal commitment.

If the consultant tries to respond to this kind of business reality, he is faced with a dilemma. The safest course is to be a recognised expert in a general purpose business specialism, such as marketing or accounting. Not the kind of expert who would be valued highly in a 'centre of excellence' in the educational world, but one who has developed a broad understanding of small-business life, with its flux of opportunities and problems. A valuable but less appreciated expertise is in being able to think clearly about priorities, the oddities of human personality, and the tortuous paths through which we move in everyday life. Such thinking might earn the consultant the label of 'useful sounding board' or 'catalyst', but it will often be seen as 'just common sense'.

Many of these difficulties would be mitigated if one gave up the attempt to model the form of development activities — the New Enterprise programmes — on the form of new enterprise itself. One is reminded of the way in which many well run management training centres deal with the challenges of an increasingly turbulent world by bringing bits of that world into the training centre, but always in a form that does not disturb the tidiness of the programme. Thus, it is commonplace to find exercises in the 'management of uncertainty' which are guaranteed to end one minute before the scheduled coffee-break: and simulations of aggression, deceit, and rivalry which leave the syndicate members in good fettle for getting together in the bar for an agreeable evening's discussion. 'Self-development' can also be neatly encapsulated within a programme that is conceived and managed in a fashion which allows little room for the participation of the members. In the New Enterprise programmes of the kind described here such dilemmas are revealed rather than concealed by the design and management of the activities. The difficult switch from 'support' to 'control', the painful oscillation between trust and mistrust, become glaringly obvious when real time, real funds and real outcomes are the focus of the activities, and not a complex web of real and unreal issues, resources, roles and relationships.

Impressions of the effectiveness of the programmes

Is it possible at this stage in the development of the programmes to establish the nature of their contribution to fostering new enterprise? The most obvious indicator, which the objective of the programmes makes possible, is the actual number of independent enterprises established, and their survival and growth rates. Table 9.1, reproduced from David Watkins' paper on the New Enterprise programme, (Watkins, 1979) gives some impression of the outcome of the first programme (NEP I), which ended in late 1977. The evaluation exercise was conducted in late 1978. The alphabetical letters in the first column of the table refer to the 14 participants who established or re-formed independent businesses.

An initial evaluation of NEP II (which ended in mid-1978) shows that 9 companies have been formed, with a total employment level by the end of 1979 of 111 (full-time or equivalent). The turnover of the NEP II companies was significantly smaller than those of NEP I, but this is very much a function of the type of product. The range of products and services in the companies so far established is very wide: fashion lingerie, micro-processor applications, photo-copier refurbishing, metal finishing, specialist wall-coverings, toys, games, specialist adhesives, site electrical installations, printing, roof insulation, furniture, stainless steel stockholding, pressure gauges, vinyl paste products.

What is it that the programme seems to offer the participants? They are very much aware of the value of constructive criticism of their business ideas, of a clear statement of the success and failure factors in new enterprise, and of helpful, specific pieces of advice, or useful contacts on premises, sources of funds and other vital resources. If one had to pull together the essential contribution of the activities, it seems to be a sustained opportunity to bring together (or find that one has *not* brought together) two tasks: (i) the task of establishing the business idea as a feasible proportion, within the available time, competence and other resources available; (ii) the task of confirming one's own commitment to establishing or joining an independent business, with *this* idea. And not only one's own commitment, but that of the key people with whom one would be associated − as family, partners, key workers etc.

When these two tasks have been related positively, and a decision is made to go ahead, there is a sense of having reached a crucial turning point in one's career, and a flood of self-confidence and heightened awareness. It might be added at this point in the discussion that the

Table 9.1
Selected characteristics of NEP I enterprises as at final 1978

	Turnover in first year £ p.a.	Full time (or equivalent) employees (excluding directors)	No. of employees previously unemployed	Break-even achieved	Pre-tax profits + total directors' drawings
h, i	31,200	4 (all unskilled)	2 or 3	x	
m	4,000	0	–	x	
d, e	260,000	13 (all unskilled)	13		
c	60,000	2 (1 unskilled)	1		
n, o, p	204,000	20 (1 unskilled)	Few, if any		
a, b	12–15,000	2 (all unskilled)	½		
f, g	120,000	4 (1 unskilled, 1 semi-skilled)	2		
j	95,000+	15+casuals (all unskilled started with 5½)	13		
Approx. Total	¾M+	60	30–35	6 out of 8	£115,000 plus 8 company cars

Approximately 20% of first year's production was in exported goods and services. This is likely to double in year two. If current expectations are confirmed, total turnover in year two will be £1.75M and employment about 100.

management committee and staff consultants try hard to keep a balance between astringent reality testing and enthusiastic boosting of the participants.

Implications for self-development

At first sight the New Enterprise programmes present a classical example of the self-development philosophy at work. What could be better example of confidence in one's own capacities than deciding to set up an independent business? The sponsors have been eager to identify and support 'self-starters' who will provide enhanced employment opportunities in the slow-moving British economy. Within the Manchester Business School, the programmes have emerged from the pioneering work of David Watkins in education for entrepreneurship and also from the growing range of joint development activities, of which it has been remarked (Burgoyne, Boydell and Pedler, 1978, p. 39):

> It is this core belief that client responsibility is a necessary ingredient for development that links joint development activities to the self-development philosophy and differentiates them from either standard or tailor-made in-house courses where the educationalists keep fairly tight unilateral responsibility of what goes on.

Even from the brief accounts I have given of the programmes, it will be clear that 'client responsibility' is not a simple concept as applied to the development of independent businesses. In one sense, the sponsor is the client, but shares the responsibility for managing the programme with the senior staff consultants from the School. The participants are in an important sense the clients of the staff consultants working with them, but they are also part of a complex set of 'understandings' within the programme as a whole. The management committee is the crossing point of varied lines of influence: and, not surprisingly, has found difficulty in establishing a role *vis-à-vis* the set of participants and staff consultants that is clearly understood. It is interesting to observe that despite the commitment of staff members of the committee to the self-development of the participants, there is no formal representation of the participant group on the committee. My impression is that committee members would feel that their role as confidential advisers of the individual participants, in their particular projects, would be jeopardised if there were to be formal representation. The critical awareness of the two programmes induced in me by drafting these notes leads me to wonder why so many of the fundamental questions about the management of the programmes have remained latent. But then, the basic nature of management as an 'inter-face' activity, working constantly on the boundaries between tasks, people and resources, obscures some of the fundamental activities of management. On many occasions, one can recall issues being raised, an eager discussion following, to be ended by the need to take rapid and decisive action.   And the very practical, and urgent needs of the participants — which drive them hard even though they are taking time out to explore the feasibility of their business ideas — discourage deep reflection, and replace it with brisk analysis, persuasive conjecture, and a concern for what the participant is going to do, rather than what the management is trying to do.

Perhaps this is a good point at which to return to the question raised at the outset of these notes: can we find ways of bringing together — in workable forms of activity — the interests in new enterprise of the would-be entrepreneurs, the sponsors and the staff consultants? The two related programmes that we have discussed here certainly appear to be 'workable forms of activity', in the sense that they are working associations of people expressing those three sets of interests — entre- preneurs, sponsors and staff consultants.   And they are working associations that have continued over some years and appear to those taking part to justify continuation. Furthermore, they are forms of association that have stayed close to their guiding purposes, though with much room for critical conjecture as to the level of achievement in relation to the purposes. For me, a major virtue of the form taken by these programmes is that they enable those taking part to relate to one another as persons; partly because of the urgency of the task, partly because of the small scale of each programme and — not least, in my view — partly because the individuality of the participants and their business ideas would make nonsense of a standardised approach.

The forms of personal relationship that the programmes encourage are, not surprisingly, strongly linked with the overriding task of testing business viability and business commitment. But my impression is that adherence to the task brings about a very complex sense of 'self' in relation to others. The participant is left in no doubt as to his or her vital significance to the new enterprise, not just as a source of informa- tion, energy, funds or some other necessary and identifiable resource, but as the very *meaning* of the enterprise, both the spirit and the body of the business. However small the enterprise, however narrow its range of activities, that is a great personal responsibility. Being an owner-manager is to be an agent in a very distinctive sense, not only one who responsibly acts on behalf of others, but one who is acting on his or her own behalf, in relation to investors, suppliers, clients and work associates.

John Morris discusses 'Developing Managers for New Enterprise' with John Morris

I must say that I found it a rather odd kind of chapter. You start with a bang on the various meanings of 'developing managers' but you say astonishingly little about *learning.* It's as though you've got so caught up in the managing of these things that you've casually thrown the baby out with the bathwater.

Surely it's pretty obvious that I've used 'developing' throughout the chapter in the sense of 'learning'. With one main difference: in the educational world, learning is firmly seen from the point of view of teaching. In these programmes, developing is seen from the point of view of self-development.

That sounds fair enough, but by leaning over backwards to avoid any notion of teaching you leave some doubt as to what's actually happening on the programme, in the way of specific learning.

You're quite right about the 'leaning over backwards'. In my last paper — which was about moving from Practice to Theory in Joint Development Activities — I commented on my lack of a learning theory, and suggested that it was probably because the obsession with getting into new forms of action had — Oh, Lord!

Yes?

Well, led to the baby being thrown out with the bathwater. That very phrase. And here I am doing it for a second time. I suppose the poor baby learns to be philosophical about that sort of thing. Learning the hard way!

That's a bit heartless! And lets you off the hook rather too easily.

All right. Here's the learning framework that I've found in joint developments. Ability to get quickly into action on the basis of a plan, which can be turned into a workable programme with available resources of time, money and so on. Some quick and effective monitoring of the activity once it's under way: looking especially to threats to its integrity, the kind of things that grow very fast in the wrong direction. And, by the way, the monitoring isn't just looking for cracks in the woodwork. It's also looking for opportunities to get where one wants to get. It's not just slavishly following the programme step-by-step, but always guided by the over-all *pattern* — the guiding purpose of the whole activity.

When the programme is over, or a phase of the programme is over, then it's vital to look back at it while it's still warm, while the feeling is still there. This is *reviewing* — because it's looking back, rather than forward or at currently running activities. Now — the crucial point — if you lump planning, programming, monitoring and reviewing all together — what have you got? You've got a flow of practical awareness that is illuminating the flow of activity, enabling it to be matched to the surrounding circumstances, which are often in continual change. *That's* what the learning is all about. It's learning to do things freshly; guided but not controlled by an overriding, sensible plan that clearly

links with a purpose. And the whole business of exercising practical
awareness is that, as its name suggests, it is an awareness of what is
going on, and how it links up with past and the foreseeable future.
When awareness and activity are as close as this, in the manager as a
person, then you find that the results of the activity are quickly
registered in awareness, and changes in awareness – in understanding, if
you like – are quickly expressed in action.

Phew! That all came tumbling out with suspicious readiness! Did
you have some notes on your shirt cuff?

It's straight from the heart! But it's odd that I didn't feel the
need to put it all down in the chapter.

And that's a pity. Because if you had put it like that, I wouldn't
have felt that there was a missing baby.

As I look back over this chapter, reviewing it if you like – I'm
painfully aware of something else that's missing. I suppose I left it
out because of the danger of it being seen as a bit of rose-coloured
'small is beautiful' commentary. I wanted to say that new enterprise
enables people to relate to one another as people, to get back to the
human scale from all the false 'objectivity' of the big company.

And yet I've heard you say more than once that people who go into
new enterprise as a way of getting out of the rat race often find that
they've dropped into the middle of the mouse race. And the mice run
faster and bite harder than the rats!

That can happen. It's the other side of being your own boss. You
find that there are plenty of people that you have to take very
seriously into account, and can influence – often directly – what you
do. Even if there is a sense that there's no-one standing directly
above you – in charge – capable of breathing down your neck and
telling you to jump to it.

So what's all this about 'relating to one another as people'? Isn't
the distinction a bit academic?

There's quite a lot of middle ground between the roses-round-the-
door view of small business and the mouse race! There's an enormous
amount of work to be done – simply seeing what's needed, and can be
paid for, and then arranging for the need to be met. That's what small
business is particularly good at doing, especially, of course, when the
need is local and particular, and being quick off the mark is important.
I admit that some big businesses are pretty good at that kind of thing
too, especially the ones that work as a kind of federation of profes-
sionally run small businesses.

But despite your comment about the big businesses that run as – if
you like – federations of little ones, you're implying that big business
is out of touch with people as people.

You're right: I am implying that. It always seems to me that it's
extremely hard for big firms to have a feel for anyone as people,

other than the little group of people at the top. And, unfortunately, they become like super-people. Not so much persons, as 'personalities'. Or even personages! And when they try to get people lower down to act like people, they can't trust them enough to give them the freedom to do so. So it's more of a well trained performance — 'service with a smile' — 'Fly me!' — either a bit of a bad joke, or — well — bloodless.

If I had to choose between that kind of bloodless efficiency — like some Chinese restaurants — and being personally ripped off by a bloodthirsty cowboy entrepreneur, I don't think I'd pause for long!

We're back to working down the middle — between the smooth big boys and the hungry cowboys. And although I'm sure that there's a lot of work to be done in the middle ground, it often takes some time to find it.

Could you spell out in a bit more detail what you would have liked to say in this chapter on this 'personal relations' business?

I was thinking about the way in which a very impersonal thing called a 'market segment' becomes a set of people who are 'my clients' or 'my customers'. They may be difficult and demanding, and not inclined to be loyal if you're not doing a good job for them. But they *are* seen as a set of particular people. And the same with the people you are working with. There's not many of them, and many of them are likely to be family. In Britain, I believe that most murders are done within the family, so it's not always smooth running. But whatever you feel like about them, there *are* strong feelings, because they're seen as people.

You seem to be suggesting that it's a good thing to see people as people, even if you are abominable to them!

I'm saying that new enterprise enables us to work on a human scale. And, yes, I suppose I am saying that it's a good thing to see people as people and not as market segments or socio-economic groups or the workforce or the labour market. The moment you stop relating to other people as people, you usually begin to treat them as objects, as sources of revenues, or perhaps some half-human organism with 'needs' which can be identified and measured by a needs-expert, and made into a dependable source of revenue.

All the words you mention, like market segment, socio-economic group, and so on, seem reasonably harmless labels for regularities of one kind or another in human behaviour. And you were going on a minute or so ago about seeing needs and meeting them. You seem to be having it both ways!

I must say that I'm more inclined to take back that wretched word 'need' then agree that all these bloodless concepts and techniques are just harmless labels. They're nothing of the kind. I agree that *any* word can be used warmly or coldly. But some ideas — and especially the techniques that they link up with — seem to me to be straight from the Arctic.

I'd like to know how business, even the small ones, can be carried on without techniques. And isn't what you're calling 'cold' just hard-headedness?

Fine to be hard-headed about hardware, and cash flows, and all those things that don't have any life or feeling. Oddly enough, people who are cold and tough about people are often very warm, even passionate, about the money and the new machinery!

So you're saying that you hope that the new enterprises don't succeed!

Eh?

And become nasty, cold big ones.

I've already said that some of the big successful businesses aren't cold and hard. Anyway, let's wait and see. Maybe a new kind of independent business is beginning to emerge, which can keep the personal touch, and a real concern for people (not a sloppy sentimentality) even when it does very well indeed. One where people don't lose themselves, but find themselves!

I hope you won't misunderstand me if I say: Amen to that.

References and notes

I am grateful to my colleague David Watkins for comments and fruitful discussion on earlier drafts of this chapter.

Burgoyne, J. G., Boydell, T. and Pedler, M. (1978), *Self-Development*, Association of Teachers of Manager, London.

Jackson, G. (1979), Identification and Development of Entrepreneurs: Experience from New Enterprise Promotion in Rural Mid Wales (unpublished conference paper).

Morris, J. F. and Burgoyne, J. G. (1973), *Developing Resourceful Managers*, Institute of Personnel Management, London.

Morris, J. F. (1975), 'Developing Resourceful Managers' in *Management Development and Training Handbook* (eds B. Taylor and G. L. Lippitt), McGraw-Hill, London, pp. 109–25.

Morris, J. F. (1977), *The Use of Social Science Research: The Fenner Example*, (unpublished SSRC conference paper available from author).

Morris, J. F. (1980), 'Joint Development Activities: from Practice to "Theory" ' in *Advances in Management Development* (eds C. L. Cox and J. Beck), Wiley, London.

Watkins, David (1977), 'Technical innovation and entrepreneurship in the UK', Proceedings, Academy of Management Conference 1977, Orlando, Fla., USA.

Watkins, David (1979), 'The New Enterprise Programme', *Manchester Business School Review*, vol. 3, no. 2.

PART III

SELF-DEVELOPMENT AND QUALIFICATION COURSES

Overview

Many management trainers and educators find themselves, for one reason or another, in the position of having to teach on somewhat conventional courses, with required syllabuses, external exams, sceptical or hostile colleagues, and other such characteristics not particularly conducive to self-development. The contributions in this section describe three strategies of tackling the challenge that this situation provides. *Andrzej Huczynski*'s chapter shows how one specific 'official' part of such a course can be designed in a way to encourage self-development. *Philip Boxer*, on the other hand, provides students with an unofficial 'optional extra' — the only time available being last thing on a Friday afternoon. The other end of this spectrum is represented by *Ian Cunningham*'s chapter, which shows how a whole qualification-oriented programme can be designed around self-development principles.

10 Self-development through formal qualification courses

Andrzej Huczynski

Huczynski builds on the concepts of Learning Community (cf Chapter 5) and Peer-learning (Chapter 8), using the term 'learning organization'. He describes how this has been applied to various part-time programmes – an area that many teachers find particularly difficult. It is interesting to note how his efforts to become more student-centred evolved gradually, over a period of years. Huczynski feels that the student-centred approach is necessary if the learners are to become flexible, creative, and if they are to learn to learn – abilities which are becoming increasingly necessary in a world of ambiguity and change – a theme also stressed by Harri-Augstein and Thomas. In this sense he may be seen to be linking the notion of development as integration or unity (cf Chapter 1) with current views on the desired goals of management education.

This contribution describes how a colleague[1] and I have attempted to implement our ideas of self-development within a university Master's degree programme using the Learning Community approach. The chapter is descriptive and focuses on the methods used. Readers interested in the underlying philosophy are referred to the writings of Boydell (1976), Megginson and Pedler (1976) and Pedler (1974). The aim of this description is to suggest ideas to those lecturers who are excited by the possibilities that self-development offers in the classroom, but who believe that institutional constraints such as syllabuses, contact hours and examination procedures prohibit its application to diploma and degree programmes at colleges and universities. The paper offers a personal account of the route we have taken in the past three years. It is not suggested that this is either the right way or the only way. Rather the intention here is to demonstrate that such applications are possible and that they are worthwhile in terms of both student and

153

tutor satisfaction.

The chapter begins with a description of the aims of our course and highlights the sources of dissatisfaction with past approaches and methods. It goes on to define our working concept of self-development which is seen as both a method and an objective. The reasons underlying our choice of the Learning Community approach are discussed as well as the objectives that such an approach seeks to achieve. The course itself is described and the chapter concludes with an account of student reactions as well as an identification of issues which merit future consideration.

Life-long learning

For a significant number of centuries, universities have been in the business of self-development. Burgoyne, Boydell and Pedler (1978) acknowledged academic education as one form of self-development considering universities as ' . . . large resource centres for independent study by members and as learning communities with concern for the whole person as well as learning with specific disciplines'. Since much of this ideal has disappeared in the 'crowded lecture rooms of the modern university' we have tried to recreate the essential character and purpose of university education by recreating it in microcosm within the Learning Organization. Life-long self-development has always been the primary objective of our universities.

In recent years the need for our educational system to help students to deal with change has been stressed. The microchip revolution has taken this imperative a stage further. Not only will students need to be prepared for training and retraining as the economic structure changes, but also a significant proportion will need to be trained for leisure. How then does one educate for change, for what is presently unknown? Pedler (1974) emphasised the need for flexibility in the design of educational experiences, 'to help people cope with new situations and new problems which have not yet arisen, objectives cannot be set in the normal way. What we can do is to try to prepare the individuals themselves for the difficulties involved'. Dunbar conducted a survey of businessmen in the United States to identify what abilities and skills they most desired of students and which they felt most present graduates lacked. The items mentioned included:

> an ability to see for oneself, rather than depending on others, where and how one could make a contribution;
> an ability to organise oneself successfully to achieve assignments;
> an ability to communicate concisely in speech and writing;
> an ability to find workable alternatives in less than ideal conditions;

a willingness when given an assignment to research details before arriving at a conclusion.

These items complement what Juch (1979) considered to be the future needs and problems of organisations. He argued that manpower planning would become less predictable and less specific in the turbulent environments of organisations which would characterise the future. Since life-long job security could not be guaranteed, organisations would prefer individuals to become more flexible and mobile. He also suggested that individuals who were prepared to accept change and who were realistic in their career aspirations would be preferred.

From these sources one begins to build up a picture of the manager of the future. He or she is a person who knows that change is constant and as a result acknowledges that his skills and knowledge are constantly becoming outdated. Such a person has developed the skill of relearning, considers it as an opportunity for growth and does not need to depend on 'experts' to keep updated. The manager of the future is one who is committed to a process of ongoing self-development. In my view, self-development is about de-schooling management education and placing the control of learning in the hands of the learner. Successful self-development involves helping the student to 'learn how to learn' and in the process modifying the teacher's role to that of advisor. Three important beliefs underpin our approach. These are summarised by Abercrombie and Terry (1978) as follows:

(a)   the main aim of education must no longer be thought of as that of transmitting information, but rather that of encouraging autonomous learning; and consequently,

(b)   the relationship between teacher and pupil must not be regarded as that of giver and receiver of information, but as that of co-operating explorers of knowledge; and

(c)   the relationship between pupils, instead of being ignored as of neutral or negligible value in the educational process, must be recognised and fostered as a powerful medium for interaction or collaborative learning.

Course aims

The context of our experiment was initially a class in Behavioural Science in the Master of Engineering in Production Management programme (M.Eng.). It was soon after extended to an option course in Organisational Development on the Master of Business Administration programme (MBA). Both programmes are attended by experienced practising managers employed in public and private industry in the West of Scotland. Both are at postgraduate level and entry is restricted to those with first degrees (or equivalent) in a recognised subject. The programmes are organised by the Department of Management Studies in association with the Faculty of Engineering and the Scottish Business School. Their distinctive feature is the fact that all students attend on a part-time day-release basis. They come to university on Saturdays and Mondays over three consecutive academic years, continuing to perform their normal jobs for the rest of the time. Successful completion of the programme leads to the award of a Master's degree (MBA or M.Eng.) of the University of Glasgow. The Behavioural course described takes place in the second year of study. Running parallel is another full course on Finance and Accounting and a half course in Marketing. These courses are traditionally designed and make extensive use of case study approaches.

Our initial ideas developed out of the realisation that it was impossible to deal in depth with behavioural science in the fifty-four hours allocated on the timetable. What topics should be excluded and which included? Would our choice be relevant to student needs? Instead of focusing on the subject content, we tried to identify longer term objectives which would assist the manager's self-development. Thus instead of arguing about whether to include a session on the Health and Safety at Work Act, we redefined this as the ability to seek out and understand current industrial legislation pertinent to the student's organisational context. We gave the label of 'process goals' to these longer term objectives since they would be acquired in the process of learning content. Instead of regarding these as useful, if erratic, spin-offs of the educational process, we heeded Handy's (1973) dictum to make subject content *the context* of learning, rather than the primary objective, and consciously planned instead to attain agreed process goals by a combination of subject content and learning method. Harrison and Hopkins (1967) used the term 'meta-goals' to refer to the content-process distinction, but we prefer the latter since we have found it more useful in communicating our ideas to students. In essence, therefore,

> We use the term 'process' to refer to the way people do things, as distinct from what it is they do (which is 'content'). In learning terms then, process objectives are taken to be those objectives which focus not on specific matters of content, but on what they do as they learn about content — such as developing their skills of learning, of asking new questions, finding and using available resources and so on. As these skills tend to be of major long term significance as they can help a person to keep up to date independently as currently imparted knowledge becomes obsolete, we place considerable emphasis on process objectives, alongside the traditional content ones.   (Boddy, 1979).

A content syllabus, unilaterally imposed by staff, would not be conducive to developing autonomy. Moreover, we did not know what the students wanted to study. If self-development was an objective of the course then it had to begin in the classroom. From these diverse ideas, hunches and dissatisfactions, we began to develop an outline of the kind of course we wanted to create. It would focus on the long term process goals, would use subject content selected by students and would be taught in a learner-centred way. This last imperative was particularly difficult for us to implement. As Suessmuth (1976) asked, how does one overcome seeing learner situations from a tutor's viewpoint? How does one change aspects of one's instruction to being learner-centred when one has no idea what should be changed? This chapter describes our attempt to find answers to these and related questions.

Over the years we have tried to move away from a vague statement of intention about the course towards a more precise definition of our aims. We became aware that our early articulation of objectives neglected to incorporate the affective dimension of learning. As a result, a cognitive-affective dimension complements our initial content-process distinction and our current list of some twenty primary working goals falls into the matrix described below:

	Cognitive	Affective
Content	Type A	Type B
Process	Type D	Type C

These are described in more detail and exemplified below.

Type A cognitive/content objectives

This category of objectives is most commonly pursued in traditional university education. It concerns imparting, passing on, or otherwise enabling the student to acquire 'knowledge', 'facts', 'theories', etc.

Example: To enable students to develop a thorough and critical knowledge of the basic patterns and determinants of human behaviour in organisations (i.e. to develop a strong theoretical framework relating to behaviour in organisations).

Type B affective/content objectives

Objectives in this category relate to the acquisition of knowledge about affective issues.

Example: To develop an understanding of similarities and differences (e.g. in attitudes, values, beliefs) between self and others, or between one's own group and other groups.

Type C affective/process objectives

Objectives in this group focus on the process by which we learn about our own and other people's values, feelings and beliefs.

Examples: To increase students' awareness of their own capabilities and limitations, particularly those concerned with learning methods and skills/thinking styles, interpersonal skills, team or group skills.

To encourage students to take responsibility for their own learning and for their continuing professional development.

Type D process/cognitive objectives

The final category of objectives is directed towards helping students develop their skills, etc., in relation to certain basically cognitive matters.

Examples: To develop the ability to analyse a problem systematically, evaluate the possibilities and reach an appropriate conclusion, taking account of behavioural as well as financial/quantitative factors.

To develop improved learning skills, in particular (a) the skills of finding and using resources; (b) the skills of learning from everyday experiences at work.

With the exception of Type A objectives which are subject-specific, all the other remaining objectives can be achieved through the use of any subject content – accounting, marketing, English or history.

It is through the conscious selection of teaching and learning methods as well as the tutor–learner relationships which are established, that they are attained. The elements that make up our approach are summarised as follows:

process goals	content goals
learning method	tutor–student relationships

Course structure

In trying to achieve the goals outlined, we rejected traditional teacher-centred approaches, believing that they would increase the student's dependence both on the tutor and on received knowledge. Experiences of Open University students also suggested the need to plan on the basis of the group rather than the individual. Since the course was concerned with the study of organisational behaviour, we tried to build in some of the pressures present within real life organisations. For example, we anticipated that a group approach, where one individual was dependent upon another for the achievement of his learning goals, would itself generate conflicts between the needs of individual students and those of the group and/or among the course as a whole. Such experiences would match real organisational pressures which could provide the basis for learning. Unlike some experiential group approaches, we saw the group learning process as a means to an end rather than as an end in itself.

In the search for a method to meet our needs, we came across the work of Heron (1974) on the training of General Practitioner trainers. Heron's concept of the Peer Learning Community had been applied by Megginson and Pedler (1976) in the field of management education and training. These authors, together with Boydell, had applied it to short courses for training officers as well as to a polytechnic diploma course. The Learning Community approach stresses that the responsibility for the planning and implementation of all learning within the community is shared by tutors and learners. It also encourages the expression of the affective dimension of learning. Finally, it acknowledges the individual needs of learners and emphasises the range of learning resources available to community members. The objectives of the Learning Community approach fitted well with our needs and seemed to have the potential to put our students on to the road to life-long learning. However, we were uncertain whether the method would stand the rigours of a nine-month course attended on a part time basis, especially since that course would be only one of three taken in parallel. We were also unsure of our expertise to apply such a model but at the same time were reluctant to retreat to a tutor-centred approach. Our response to this dilemma was to develop a similar structure which was capable of incorporating the underlying philosophy of the Learning Community, but which contained more of a formal structure.

From Kolb, Rubin and McIntyre (1971) we borrowed the term Learning Organisation. The structure, which will shortly be described, seemed to us more suited to the circumstances of the present course. Being part of a wider degree programme, flexibility in the disposition of the scheduled number of contact hours is limited by student commitments to other classes, while staff have other teaching commitments. The wider Master's programme — which for the most part is highly structured and traditionally taught — must also affect students' expectations about the way a course should be run. Moreover, the time required for study and reflection must, for these students, compete with work and family commitments. The staff of the programme accept a professional responsibility to build in the necessary structure to help students to use their personal and study time effectively. Within the degree programme there is a requirement that the cognitive components be examinable and once again staff take a professional responsibility for students' performance in assessed work.

These considerations led us to favour the notion of the Learning Organisation rather than the Learning Community and the main features of this structure are now described. Broadly it consists of a number of fixed and predictable features in the course which nevertheless leave considerable areas open to student decision-making and participation. The fifty-four contact hours of the course are split into five subject blocks. Each block is approximately ten hours in length and spreads over a fortnight. Past experiences of students' learning needs indicate a high degree of predictability from year to year, which mean that it is possible to label these blocks in very broad terms beforehand. The block format is illustrated in Figure 10.1.

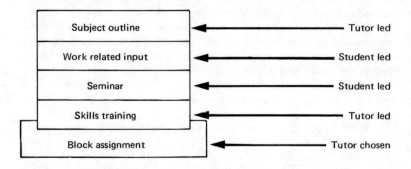

Figure 10.1   Block structure

An outline session is used to help the students map out the subject field they will be tackling. Feedback from students indicated that such formal introductions have been found useful. They nevertheless take up valuable contact time which could be better used. In order to transmit this descriptive content, we are experimenting with the use of audio-cassettes and work books (see McDonald and Knights, 1979). This is not a retreat from our group-orientated philosophy but a way of providing a security base for those students who need it by giving them a common input while not using up scarce classroom time. The work related input is a time slot allocated to students to fill themselves. They take the responsibility for using it in any way they consider suitable while the tutors act as advisors. The only condition imposed upon choice is that the presentation must seek in some way to relate the presenter's work experiences with the subject of the block currently being studied. This is an attempt to overcome the separation of theory and practice that has been observed in the past (Huczynski, 1979). Traditional seminars have been introduced at which articles pertinent to management practice are critically discussed and evaluated. Too often practising managers receive fifth hand simplified and summarised accounts of published empirical research. We have found Hill's (1977) discussion framework a valuable tool with which to organise debate. Once again the students select the articles and take turns to act as seminar leaders. The staff act in an advisory capacity. The fourth element of each block is the skills training session. The aim here is to translate the theoretical and empirical knowledge presented into more effective practice. Thus a session on staff selection interviewing would be underpinned by a consideration of personality theory, while role theory might provide the basis for a consideration of role-set analysis as a managerial problem-solving tool. Finally, the assignment essay, the title of which the student chooses himself (though subject to agreement with staff), offers him the opportunity to explore in greater depth any aspect of the block topic he chooses. This block structure seems to go a long way towards meeting the learning needs identified by participants. It is a framework which our students can understand and which forms the basis of their involvement in the Learning Organisation.

Course process

In his description of the Learning Community, Boydell (1976) referred to five phases of its development: establishing the appropriate climate; identifying needs; identifying resources; meeting needs and evaluation. The phases provide a useful framework with which to describe the mechanics of our approach.

Establishing the appropriate climate

The right climate is both an essential prerequisite for success and yet is difficult to achieve. Burgoyne et al. (1978) noted that ' . . . teacher/ trainer control is deeply rooted in both attitudes and institutional structures'. The architecture and furniture of most educational institutions further reinforce the idea of students' dependence on tutors. A lot of unlearning has to occur on the student side. For example, they have to accept that learning is not about passing exams but about being a better manager; that learning takes place both inside and outside of the classroom; and that the tutor is not the only learning resource available to students. In developing this approach, we found that as tutors we had also to make changes in our attitudes and methods. Perhaps the most significant change was in the way we perceived our roles. We no longer purported to be 'experts' telling students how they ought to solve their managerial problems. We have tried to move away from the 'teacher' position so as to encourage group members to be more independent and confident in thinking and self-expression. The idea that students and tutors are jointly responsible for learning outcomes is frequently greeted with a mixture of incomprehension and disbelief by students. Hence the need for the teacher to demonstrate this philosophy. During one of the first seminar sessions the group failed to prepare adequately for the session and, following a shallow discussion, looked to me as the tutor to salvage the situation, which I declined to do. At the debriefing session, participants agreed that they had wasted their own and each other's time. They accepted the responsibility for making these seminar sessions useful and there was no repetition of inadequate preclass preparation during the rest of the course. A second important aspect of climate is the development of trust, mutual support and acceptance of the individual. It is a climate in which the learner can take risks (in the sense of trying out new behaviours), admit to difficulties and problems, give and receive feedback, and cope with allied stresses. Our evaluation suggests that such a climate was partly achieved, but mainly amongst the students themselves rather than between students and tutors. This may be a function of the part time nature of the course.

There is no formula for achieving desired learning climate. Boydell has suggested the use of warming-up sessions, getting to know people, and trust building activities. While these may sound somewhat contrived, we were surprised how little students knew each other despite being in their second year — a point with which they themselves concurred. In the absence of any special 'tips' I have tried to be honest and open to the class members about the approach, especially when I thought it was going wrong. Romey (1972) wrote that for students the learning environment can be fearful, filled with doubt and uncertainty. If the tutor shares his own feelings of uncertainty, then this can establish the basis of a strong working relationship. I certainly find it difficult to deal with anybody who feels he knows all the answers.

Identify needs

The idea of students identifying their own learning goals in a course can constitute a threat to those teachers who are used to a predefined syllabus. However, since needs identification is the first stage in any self-development process, it should not be avoided even in graduating programmes. Can student free choice and the university requirement for some published syllabuses be reconciled? In practice we have found this problem less intractable than in theory. Asking students to select learning goals within a specified subject field (e.g. human behaviour in organisations) has led to the design of a 'class group syllabus' which often resembles a tutor-designed one. Tl.e important difference is that this agenda has been student generated and not tutor imposed. We found that it was more useful if members framed their goals in terms of questions rather than subject fields. Thus, 'how do I motivate a person with a boring job?' was preferred to an aim of 'knowing about current theories of motivation'. By experience we found that the same aims came up annually, and that it was possible for university regulation and planning and purposes, to outline subject fields, e.g. individual influences on organisational behaviour. So in practice, students are able to specify and update their learning needs within an accepted broad framework of topics.

Working in groups, members then sought to design a class syllabus. Individual contributions were selected on the basis of prior reading, work problem analysis and role-set analysis. We encouraged members to retain their own question list since items which were unique to the students and not shared by others, could be considered either during the work-related session, or in the block assignment.

Groups have generally been able to develop a syllabus in the cognitive content area with little difficulty. We have encountered greater problems in trying to help students set learning objectives in the affective and process spheres. Before one can realistically ask members to make decisions and identify priorities on aspects of learning they are less familiar with it is necessary to educate them in the options available so that they can make a sensible choice. Towards this end we have circulated a pre-course paper to students. This lists process objectives and asks the students to select those which they consider most currently relevant to them. This checklist approach is not ideal but, since these process goals constitute the criteria on which learning resources and methods are selected, they are an essential element in the operation of the Learning Organisation. As with all goals, these can be redefined during the course. We are, however, currently exploring more satisfactory ways of introducing them into the course.

Identifying resources

With traditional teaching approaches students are not required to identify any learning resources but are presented with them by the teacher. Amongst the resources available to students are themselves, their class colleagues, their organisations, the university library, the tutors, and the departmental teaching equipment (video, films, handouts). What expertise has the student to decide which resource to use and should he be asked to do so? We believe that the identification of resources to help achieve objectives is an important part of any manager's job. After a year's study, most students know enough about the potential of a learning resource to be able to make a choice. The subject of management union conflict, for example, can be explored through the use of a case study, a role-play, or by inviting a guest speaker. If the process goal is to help students develop self-confidence then the role-play would be the most appropriate. If the aim is to develop analytical skills, then a case study might be more suitable. Thus, learning resources are identified and used with reference to process goals and, as Figure 10.2 suggests, any single content objective can be achieved through the use of different learning methods depending on which process goals the group wishes to concentrate on at that time.

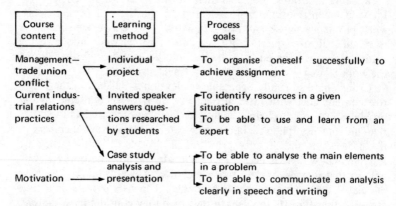

Figure 10.2

We have found in the past that members of the learning organisation tend to overvalue staff and what they can provide, and undervalue both themselves and other students.

Meeting needs

The fact that the course has predefined timetable slots and exists alongside other more traditional courses does not mean that the students need all go through the same learning experiences. During the early phases of our experiments there was less heterogeneity of activities than there is at present. Logically, identification of different learning objectives by members should mean students working on differing tasks. On a recent course the 'organisation' of twenty students decided to break into three 'departments' who worked independently of one another to achieve their group goals. Because of this parallel working, report-back sessions were instituted to keep everybody in touch, and the organisation as a whole met to take part in sessions which the tutors had been asked to provide and which had a relevance to all three groups. Paralleling a real organisation, the attempt was to mediate between and seek to meet needs at the individual group, inter-group and organisational level.

Evaluation

We have built in evaluation as an ongoing process and each class meeting concludes with a debriefing — planning session. Good and bad points of the organisation's performance are identified and plans and changes for the future are suggested. Such evaluations allow modifications to be introduced in an ongoing way. Moreover, they reinforce the view that staff and students are jointly in control of the Learning Organisation, and are thus jointly responsible for its achievements and its failures. Tutor comments on written work constitute only one form of feedback. During these debriefing sessions, members try to comment non-judgementally on the effect that other individuals' behaviour is having on them. Students see that they can take in such comments and survive. The information helps them to obtain a realistic self-assessment of themselves, contributes to an increase in their self-awareness and encourages them to become self-directing in their learning.

Assessment

Have we as tutors met the objectives we set ourselves? What have the students' reactions been to this approach? We have tried to measure the learner-centredness of the course using Boydell's (1975) scale which has the following dimensions:

1   Goals: whether goals were set by the tutor alone or with learners.
2   Homogeneity: whether all learners went through the same learning experiences or not.
3   Sequencing: whether the order in which things were taught was flexible or fixed.
4   Control: whether decisions were made by the tutors or with learners.
5   Evaluation: whether evaluation by the tutor was based on his or the learner's goals.

6   Methods: whether a few or a wide variety of teaching methods were used.

7   Tutor-learning relationships: whether the relationships between tutors and students were distant and formal or close and personal.

8   Group: whether or not people trusted and supported each other.

9   Tutor: whether the tutor was seen as a role or a person.

10   Feelings: whether the expression of feelings was thought legitimate and encouraged.

11   Expository discovery approach: whether a discovery or an expository approach was used.

12   Certainty: whether ideas were presented in a positivistic or a relativistic manner.

Figure 10.3 shows the profiles of three successive courses run using this method. The rightwards shift of the profiles reflects the learning we have acquired as tutors as well as the confidence we have gained. It also serves to emphasise the point that the approach has evolved progressively over a number of years. The changes that we have made over time have included an increased attention to individual goal setting, regular debriefing/planning meetings and the conscious emphasis on the expression and discussion of individuals' feelings within the group. A learner-centred course in our view demonstrates to participants the potential each member has to carry on learning beyond both the course and the Master's programme. It also prepares him to take the responsibility for that life-long learning. Other evaluation comments were obtained from members and these are reported in the context of what we see as some of the main issues to be resolved by the tutor applying this approach.

Role of the tutor as member

The role of the tutor as a facilitating member is a difficult one to establish and sustain. There is an element of ambiguity in the role of the 'member with the power of assessment'. Such ambiguity can inhibit the development of the leadership roles in the group.

> The leadership function of the group was the next stage of development and in this the group failed. No competition for leadership emerged and the group performed in a very united and democratic style of action. This was a disadvantage at times when decisions had to be made, but was an advantage in that a team spirit existed.

The way in which the staff member manages his role within the Learning Organisation will depend on a number of factors, amongst the most

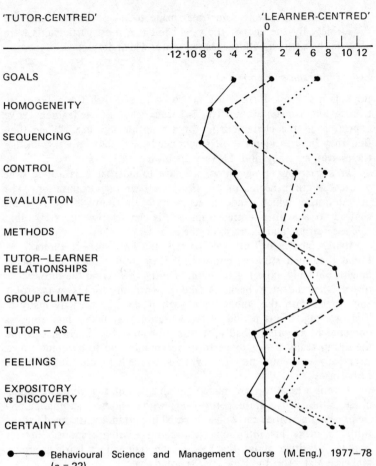

Figure 10.3   Scale for measuring and learner-centredness of a course

important of which is his own personality. This change of role also produces difficulties for students who also have to adapt.

At this stage the group had still not really resolved the power vacuum which had been left by the lecturer participating rather than leading and indeed this was a conflict never fully resolved and attempts were sometimes made to take over the leadership role. By the end of the year I felt that most participants were fairly satisfied with the shared power which developed.

Establishing shared responsibility

Boydell has stressed the need not only to establish the appropriate climate but to maintain it. This is because: ' . . . most learners arrive expecting all the characteristics of a traditional course. When they find they have to identify their own needs, help each other, think for themselves, etc. they find this very disturbing'.

On a part-time programme, we have found that it is a long time before the group begins to function as a Learning Organisation. The period during which students reorientate themselves from a tutor-centred to a learner-centred approach is characterised by confusion, role redefinition and a certain degree of anger.

Abercrombie and Terry (1978) reported how some lecturers ' . . . found that their students complain if they are not subjected to being taught, but only expected to learn.' During this period the tutor needs to help the student to begin to take responsibility for his own learning and persist with this aim even though it may be seen by many as 'time-wasting'. This period of reorientation may take a long time, as one student reported: 'Sadly, it was probably after Christmas before the group really began to perform acceptably and to be used as constructively as it could be. This was due to the high role-conflict in the early stages'.

There is a limit to how much one can speed up the 'group storming' phase, although we are experimenting with various trust-building and ice-breaking activities early on. Of equal importance is the need for the tutor to make his intention clear about sharing responsibility for learners. Writing about the role of the trainer in a learning group, McLeish, Matheson and Park (1973) noted that:

> The process of devolving responsibility to the individual group members seems to be the most difficult task facing the trainer. Not all trainers are prepared to yield their responsibility. It is part of the trainer role to abdicate authority, and become more and more a member. This means that he must train the group to accept responsibility for their own learning. If he does not incorporate this as an objective, he does the members a disservice; their learning process will be handicapped because of their continued dependence on him.

To achieve this, we are prepared to be relatively directive during the early stages of the course by, for example, suggesting different work structures, provided that we feel we are helping the individuals move towards a position of independence. This does not mean throwing students in at the deep end without preparation. Douglas (1978) stated that:

> It is not a good thing to think that people can be self-directing without some help in first recognising what such a way of existing actually entails . . . the development (in self-sufficiency) should be allowed to conform to the needs of those involved and not be imposed as part of some philosophy which sees self-direction as a desirable end in itself without reference to the needs and abilities of group members.

It is inevitable that students will initially experience difficulty and will seek to push tutors back into the stereotype roles they are familiar with. These were amongst the most difficult pressures we had to deal with. One student summarised his own experience:

> It took several weeks for this difference in perception and its implication to strike the group and it floundered badly – not only was the method of learning new to our experience but also many of our (original) goals had changed in priority.

Discussions of learner-controlled learning rarely refer to the process by which control is given up by the tutor and taken up by the students. Douglas referred to the need for the tutor to show that this possibility existed, while Koberg and Bagnall (1978) commented on the need for tutors to give students the 'authority' to act in a self-directing manner which they would not otherwise do. A learner-centred approach involves the gradual withdrawal of tutor direction which matches the students' growing confidence and ability to take it up. Our aim is to provide the initial structure to allow them freedom and progressively withdraw our own frameworks as we see them making their own. This sharing by students in the teacher's authority role helps them to end the idea that authority is absolute and they begin to accept it in a relative sense. In our view this prepares them to take on responsibility for their own self-development.

Conclusion

The period since the end of the Second World War has been one of continuing and accelerating technological, social and economic change. How has the educational system responded to this challenge? In essence it has provided more of the same. While student numbers in post-compulsory education have risen and some new technology has been introduced into the classroom, there has been little fundamental change. If colleges and universities are seriously to prepare students to meet the as yet unknown challenges of the future then some fundamental changes are necessary. In our view what is called for is an altering of the tutor–learner relationship so as to provide a learner-centred educational approach which encourages the independence of the learner in the classroom and engenders in him a commitment to self-development in the future. Regrettably, our qualification programmes, geared as many of them are to outdated examination systems, produce institution-centred learning which produces learner-dependence.

References and notes

The writer gratefully acknowledges the help and support of his colleague David Boddy who has been jointly involved in the development and implementation of the approach described in this chapter.

Abercrombie, M. L. J. and Terry, P. M. (1978), 'Talking to Learn: Improving Teaching and Learning in Small Groups', Society for Research into Higher Education.

Boddy, D. (1979), 'Human Behaviour in Organizations – Objectives', Working Paper, Department of Management Studies, University of Glasgow, mimeo.

Boydell, T. (1975), 'Questionnaire for Measuring the Learner-Centredness of a Course', *Management Education and Development*, vol. 6, no. 3.

Boydell, T. (1976), 'Experiential Learning', Manchester Monographs No. 5, Department of Adult Education, University of Manchester.

Burgoyne, J., Boydell, T. and Pedler, M. (1978), 'Self-Development: theory and applications for practitioners', Association of Teachers of Management, Polytechnic of Central London.

Douglas, T. (1978), *Basic Groupwork*, Tavistock Publications.

Dunbar, R. L. M., 'A Proposal to the AACSB Western Electric Fund Award Program for Educational Innovation in Higher Education for Business Administration', Southern Methodist University, USA mimeo (no date).

Handy, C. B. (1973), 'Reflections on the Way to a Philosophy of Education', London Business School, mimeo.

Harrison, R. and Hopkins, R. (1967), 'The Design of Cross-Cultural Training: An Alternative to the University Model', *Journal of Applied Behavioral Sciences*, vol. 3, no. 4.

Heron, J. (1974), 'The Concept of the Peer Learning Community', Department of Adult Education, University of Surrey.

Hill, Fawcett, W. (1977), 'Learning Thru Discussion: Guide for Leaders and Members of Discussion Groups', Sage Publications.

Huczynski, A. A. (1979), 'Utilising the Work Experiences of Adults in the Learning Process', *Adult Education*, vol. 51, no. 6.

Juch, A. H. (1979), 'Self Development within the Organization', *Management Education and Development*, vol. 10, no. 1.

Koberg, D. and Bagnall, J. (1976), 'Values Tech.: a portable school for discovering and developing decision-making skills and self-enhancing potential', William Kaufmann Inc., Los Altos, California.

Kolb, D. A., Rubin, I. M. and McIntyre, J. N. (1971), *Organizational Psychology: An Experiential Approach*, Prentice-Hall, London.

McDonald, R. and Knights, S. (1979), 'Learning from Tapes: The Experience of Home-Based Students', *Programmed Learning and Educational Technology*, vol. 16, no. 1.

McLeish, J., Matheson, W. and Park, J. (1973), *The Psychology of the Learning Group*, Hutchinson.

Megginson, D. and Pedler, M. (1976), 'Developing structures and technology for the learning community', *Journal of European Training*, vol. 5, no. 5.

Pedler, M. (1974), 'Learning in Management Education', *Journal of European Training*, vol. 3, no. 3.

Romey, W. D. (1972), *Risk—Trust—Love: Learning in a Humane Environment*, Charles E. Merrill, Columbus, Ohio, USA.

Suessmuth, P. (1978), 'Ideas for Training Managers and Supervisors', University Associates of Europe.

11   Learning as a subversive activity

Philip Boxer

What is meant by 'subversive'?   Is it the challenging of established forms of knowledge, or does it imply the undermining of the establishment values around the authority-figure teacher/learner relationship?   In either case it can clearly be seen as a movement towards the integration of knower and known, of learner and learned.   This chapter describes one approach to this movement, which is also a very clear example of the use of social processes to aid individual development, through co-counselling.   It is all the more intriguing in that these personal and social processes are assisted by modern technology, by computer-assisted reflective learning.   It can thus be seen to be related to the learning community (Chapter 5) and to certain aspects of learning conversation (Chapter 15).

Introduction

At the beginning of the 1979/80 academic year, a new programme director took over the Master's degree programme at the London Business School.   One of the initiatives introduced to the programme was a series of Creativity and Learning Workshops in the first term (McQuillan, 1979).   These workshops had four objectives: first to make it easier for students to manage a highly structured and impersonal first term by providing them with private space and some help in using this for reflection; secondly to provide alternative forms of experiential and student-centred learning; thirdly to use facilitators who had a direct relationship with the School as a whole; and fourthly to contribute to the climate of the programme by providing opportunities which surfaced and explored issues in an arena which was essentially integrative rather than win–lose.   The end result of this initiative was that three alternative forms of workshop were offered: using and writing poetry as a way of exploring ideas and experiences; exploring feelings, attitudes and forms of action through drama; and exploring different learning needs and styles in relation to the School as an environment. The aim of this chapter is to describe this last workshop, which I ran under the title: 'Learning as a Subversive Activity'.

Aims and objectives

The title of the workshop was derived from Postman and Weingartner's book (1971): *Teaching as a Subversive Activity*. Weingartner's point was that for teachers to be effective, they had to challenge and question established forms of knowledge, and thus imbue their pupils with the same attitude of mind. My aim was to enable the workshop participants to challenge and question established teachers in relation to a conscious awareness of their own learning needs, so that they were better able to digest the forms of knowledge being offered to them within the two year MSc. experience.

The workshop therefore was designed to develop an active approach to learning. It was intended to be of use to those 'who were feeling flatulent or who were suffering from indigestion as a result of consuming too much pre-packaged knowledge'. Its design was based on the assumption that different people had different learning needs originating in the particular forms of experience they had acquired and the intentions they had for their own future. The implication of this assumption was that unless people could become conscious of the ways in which their intentions and experience influenced their learning needs, they would be unable to subvert to their own ends what was undoubtedly a very rich learning environment.

The workshop was intended for a maximum of ten people, and the specific objectives were:

(a) to find ways of describing the School as a learning environment both in terms of the activities available and also in terms of their relevance to personal goals;

(b) to discover what learning needs existed, and how different people went about meeting them differently;

(c) to explore how different people had learnt differently from their past experience;

(d) to use the insights gained in the workshop to create new ways of relating learning activities to personal goals.

What follows describes the workshop from, as far as possible, the participants' point of view. To do this I have used participants' own comments, and a particular example of one participant's reflections. Writing about this kind of process is very difficult however, not only because the written medium is wholly inadequate for representing the quality of different individuals' experience, but also because what I write can only be my view among many other equally legitimate views. Keeping this in mind therefore, I hope to leave you, the reader, with my impression of the value of the workshop experience.

The context to the workshop

All three of the alternative forms of workshop offered were seen as having a marginal contribution by the School. This was reflected in the location for the workshop: a basement room with a window looking up at a noisy main road within 20 feet; and their timing — seven sessions last thing on Friday afternoons. The MSc.'s term was ten weeks of formal teaching occupying about 30 hours per week. Their second week was set aside exclusively to Accounting, culminating in an exam. After that, Data Analysis, Macro-Economics and Organisational Behaviour occupied about 75 per cent of their time; and Working with Computers and Business Environment occupied a further 20 per cent. The 5 per cent of formal time allocated to the workshops was intended as 'private' space, and therefore it was competing with all the other demands placed on the MSc.'s for reading, case studies, and the various other forms of assignment generated by the formal teaching.

There were about 80 of the 100 MSc. students in the lecture theatre where we three teachers presented the alternative workshops. I enlarged on the aims and emphasised the contract: we would work together on the basis that participants would do what they chose, express themselves in their own way, and be responsible for their own learning. At the end, 19 students signed up, and when we met two weeks later, 10 actually turned up, and 6 worked through all the sessions. This depletion in numbers was both an expression of the kind of pressure MSc.'s were already under in the School and also a necessary consequence of the contracting process — those who remained had chosen to stay. Some indication of the reasons for the MSc.'s initial choice can be seen in the following:

> I had no idea what I was going to get out of it, but I wanted to get to know people better and to be known better.

> Boxer seemed cynical, quite amusing and reasonably bright. I tried his workshop because the best fun people were joining up, and because it seemed the best.

A clue to the importance the group had to the contracting in of participants was that four out of the eventual six came from the same first term study group. My main concern in designing the workshop was that the group's cohesiveness and intensity built up during sessions would be destroyed by the pressure placed on individuals through assessment and the fragmented and low energy timing of the sessions: there were no interdependencies created by the institution which supported or legitimised the group's existence. I planned to counter this influence by developing their awareness of their interdependency in terms of the two-year experience as a whole, and enabling them to see the extent to which their individual differences were a valuable learning resource to each other. Beyond that I felt I had to accept that there would be a considerable overhead of time that would have to be spent re-establishing the group's 'here-and-now' presence each time we started a session. After the first two sessions however, the process would depend on individuals opting into a focal role in order to work with their own experience. The quality of learning which they would then derive would depend on their commitment to learning and the extent to which the other participants could contribute their insights to that learning.

The workshop

The workshop started with us seated around a large magnetic white-board which was on the floor. Around it were piles of magnetic tiles and pens. The object of the session was to identify as many different learning activities — things which students could be observed doing — as possible. These activities had to be written on the tiles, and then arranged on the board so that their positioning on the board reflected their relationship to each other. The board therefore was a kind of map of the LBS terrain over which the various activities would be experienced. The process thus disabled forms of thought which sought to categorise and classify because the board only allowed the expression of boundaries and relationships. It also helped the participants to distinguish between on the one hand the activities and on the other hand how they experienced the activities.

> I felt frustrated having to consider others' ideas. I had a prevailingly anxious feeling because we concentrated on school.

> The group seemed very interesting, and I began to realise that I learnt more from extra-curricular activities than programmed learning.

> Reticent, strained atmosphere which asked 'who is this guy?' (i.e. Philip). I played fool to relax. Very unclear on what it was all aiming at eventually. I was relieved those I didn't get on with did not turn up.

> I was pretty sceptical about this board game thing; persevered as it might lead somewhere.

There were eight participants at the first session. Of these two did not come again, leaving the six participants who stayed with the workshop throughout. Two further participants came along to the second session who had not been able to attend the first one. Neither of these continued with the workshop. The new arrivals meant that the terrain mapping process had to continue into the second session. The fact that they both left was of course part of the contracting in process, but it was also due to their experiencing themselves as slight outsiders in relation to the others, and the fact (I felt subsequently) that I had allowed the process to deepen too quickly.

Table 11.1
A sample of the 137 activities and their groupings

A	Making dinner Injections	K	Peer discussion Coffee breaks
B	Going to bank Loan getting	L	Theatre Restaurant
C	Tennis Gliding	M	Walk in park Getting away
D	TV Reading letters	N	Socialising with corporate people LBS discussion with expert
E	Assess my performance Having an identity crisis	O	Selling yourself Being polite
F	Visiting family Special occasion – a wedding	P	Committing crimes Stopping stealing
G	Co-operative projects Listening to lectures	Q	Projects overseas Domestic travel
H	Explain late work Library	R	Socialising with lecturers Organising revue
I	Earning money Paying for course	S	Communicating Hustling
J	Formal group discussions Making presentations	T	Being mentally and physically ill

Getting bearings on each other

By half way through the second session, the activities had been formed into twenty groups. Each group expressed some underlying theme, a feel for which can be gained from Table 11.1, which shows a sample from each group. Participants were then asked to express some of their learning goals – ways in which they would evaluate their learning looking back over the two-year experience as a whole – and to discuss what these goals meant for each other. They were asked to select one goal which was particularly important to them as an individual, and to rate the degree to which each group of activities contributed to attaining that goal. The rating took the form of a pattern of letters along a continuum. Figure 11.1 is one example. The others were then asked to create patterns expressing how they felt the activities contributed to that participant's goal, and the different patterns were then compared. The participant ended up with different feedback on how the others' views of the activities differed in relation to his own goal. The marked differences were discussed, and then the process was repeated for another participant.

LOW   HIGH

< Getting | ...L....DM....K...T...S.E.R.FG......A.C...J.HNQBP.I.O. |
tough | |

Figure 11.1   An example of the degree to which one participant experienced the learning activities as contributing to his learning goal

> I have found that exercise revealing for myself, in trying to quantify how much 'jogging in the park' helped me to 'examine my intelligence'. It made me aware of the many different ways I do learn, and where I didn't feel I was learning. The other side was discovering in a fairly specific way how my attitudes differed from others. It's a great process for getting to know others in a group. I'm sorry we didn't do more at the time.
>
> I had no idea that anyone 'like me' would be so different . . . he had totally different ideas on things I thought were conventional wisdom. I must not assume so much.
>
> At last I began to see where the workshop was going — even though I only approximated all my classifications, when I compared them with other people I found some very great differences. I can see bits of myself in other people, though I don't understand why they think so differently from me.
>
> I'm realising something. Can't put my finger on it but it's good.
>
> If this whole thing means opening up, I think I can handle that.

At the end of the second session, one of the participants agreed to take on the focal role in the next session. The preparation for taking on this role had to be done outside the sessions. Part of this preparation involved two participants getting together to discuss each other's learning goals and to help the other to identify the particular past learning experiences which he or she felt were significant in influencing his or her approach to those learning goals. The process involved distinguishing a set of relevant experiences and then through active listening, enabling the other to condense into conceptual form particular ways in which he or she had experienced those experiences. Figure 11.2

EVALUATIONS OF PAST EXPERIENCES:

a - A-LEVELS   b - OUTSIDE SCHOOL
c - 1ST YEAR UNIVERSITY   d - E.I.U. HOME PROJECTS
e - E.I.U. OVERSEAS PROJECTS   f - LISBON
g - MONASTERY   h - L.C.
i - FACTORY   j - L.B.S.
k - STUDY GROUP   l - FAMILY VISITS
m - SCHOOL DAYS   n - FAMILY ABROAD
o - MID-UNIVERSITY   p - SEVILLE
q - BED-SITTER   r - DOLE
s - MULE   t - 4TH YEAR UNIVERSITY

```
                   LOW                                                    HIGH

SAFE               :-cm-------d--ijpr-----ek--qs----gobfhlnt---a------:

OUT OF SYSTEM      :-am----qj-h1rngoi--kt---d-e---c--f--p-s---------b-:

CONFUSING          :-----bsao--f-nkriht-l-e-jqd-gp---m---------c------:

STEADY             :-------cedj-lop--i-knm--fqtbrsh------g--a--------:

PRACTICAL          :-------n--m--oq-pc--al--tbr-g-jfsk--hi----e--d----:

EXCITING           :q---m--l------o-n--jakrgc-ib-fh-dtp-se-----------:

MINDLESS           :-ghisetfbmdkpocn-j--a-l-------r----------------q-:

STERILE            :--s-gh-kbedptil-fjrc---a-om--qn------------------:

OUT OF THIS WORLD  :--a--q-r-m---jo--cli-b---kn--dt-h-pef-g------s----:

REPLETE            :---m-q--o---l--nr--j---k-a--icp-tbfs-d-he-g------:

CAREFUL            :----m-nq-c--bo-s--pa-fr--te-d-jh--g----li------k--:

QUIET PAIN         :----------fspb--nec-kd-air-t-h--jg-qol--m--------:

JOLLY              :------ma--q-o--ct-rs1k--b-djn-pi-------e-g--f-h---:

LOVED              :-----------ma-qk---jlrbin-ceopd-sf-t---h-g--------:

ORIENTING          :-------c--q-n-m-a--obr-l-sfd--ketgp-----ijh-------:

PLUSH              :--------s-rmc--tq--a--o-i-b-kp---d-j-fhen1g-------:

LAZY RUSH          :--------s--qr-a-m-j--oi-b-k1t-d-p-e-ch-g--f-n-----:

LIBERATING         :----ma-q---l-nr-k-cjb-o--tdig-e-h-f----p-s--------:

BASIC              :------n-a-m-c-ol--q--btpe-fdk-gjs-h-----r-i-------:

QUIET              :-------c-mn-a--l-d-o-k-bj-pie---hq--frt--s--g-----:
```

Figure 11.2   The concepts produced by one participant reflecting on past experience relevant to his particular learning goals

shows the outcome of this process for one participant. Each continuum expressed the degree to which each experience was experienced in terms of that concept. The preparation involved inputting these patterns into a computer in order to use it to discover the patterns implicit in how the participant had patterned his experiences – a computer assisted reflective learning technique (CARL for short) was used which supported the reflective process (Boxer 1979).

Enter CARL

Each session lasted about 1½ to 2 hours. During sessions 3, 4, 5 and 6 we worked with three participants in the focal role. It was decided to move the final scheduled session to a Saturday – which came immediately after the MSc.'s end of term 'binge' – and it went on for about 8 hours. About 2 hours were spent by each participant in the focal role, although much more time than this was spent with the earlier ones. The average was slightly more than my previous experience had suggested, which fitted with my feeling that the group was never really able to settle down. The essence of the reflective learning process was in developing the participant's consciousness – the size of whole he or she could think in terms of, whether in relation to self or others (Boxer, 1980). Although the process was focused on one participant's views, the process of empathising with and enabling the thinking of that participant was equally as important a part of the learning process. My role was therefore to model the process of empathising myself and through this to influence the forms of communication through which the others sought to enable the thinking of the focal participant. Before discussing this process further, however, it will help to consider what the focal participant was focusing on.

The co-counselling process which produced the patterns shown in Figure 11.2 developed a mutual understanding and awareness between the two participants involved. In order to achieve the aim of using the group to help the focal participant to develop his own understanding and awareness, the group had first to share the context defined by the set of past experiences. The computer was used to provide a focus for this process by generating a printout shown in Figure 11.3 based on the patterns in Figure 11.2. This printout showed the ways in which the focal participant had experienced the experiences as similar in terms of his own concepts. The focal participant was asked to explain the significance to himself of each experience and then to try and rationalise the groupings. The notes generated by this process for this particular focal participant are shown alongside the computer printout. This rationalising was felt at times to be very irrational since there was no obvious connection between the experiences grouped together. It was only after the group had understood *how* the focal participant had

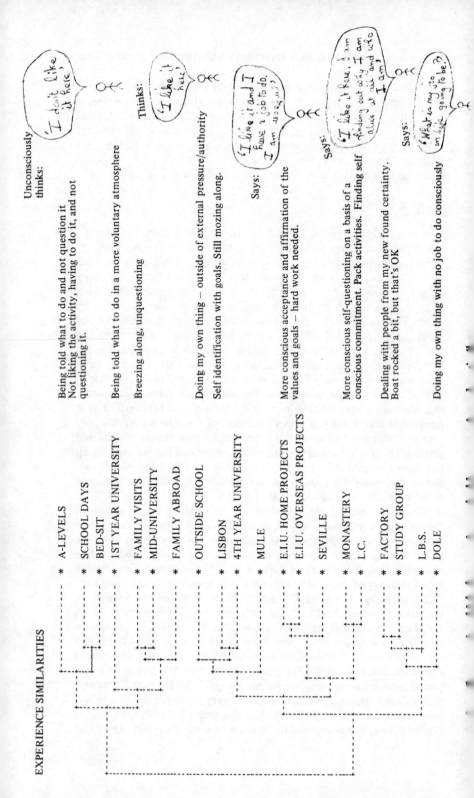

experienced the experience that the connections became apparent.

> Tenderised somewhat. Immediately afterwards I didn't feel helped or hindered for that matter. Just a bit exposed. I had great difficulty finding words to express areas of experience. Those used were all others' suggestions, not mine. No absolutely new discoveries, but made certain things more conscious and thus easier to deal with.

> I was very surprised to find so little in common — deep down — though at the time I couldn't see what was important to me.

> Getting to know him through his important events and activities was fascinating. Self-analysis by computer? The idea is ridiculous, the concept intriguing, the practice quite practical. The objective viewpoint given him by the computer printout distanced him enough to allow him to see his activities in a new light. The juxtaposition of perhaps less likely events forced him to really analyse what happened in those events, and how he learned from them . . . I learned from helping him to learn. Trying to open new approaches to his experiences with him was a stimulating experience for me.

The effect of working through the focal participant's experiences in this way was to generate the feeling of a shared consciousness: it felt as if we were all on the 'inside'. This provided the foundation on which the group could develop a way of describing the gestalt in how the focal participant patterned his experience. This 'way' took the form of language which the group negotiated with the focal participant so that it had appropriate connotations with how he experienced. The computer printout which supports this process is shown in Figure 11.4. Based on the patterns in Figure 11.2, it showed both the gestalt in pictorial form, and also as a list, so that the patterning concepts could be related in terms of larger patterning concepts. The significant thing for the focal participant was not the accuracy or 'truth' of the groupings but rather the extent to which he could develop forms of meaning which could embrace the concepts — the reflective learning process.

At some point the focal participant felt unable to identify any larger patterns which felt solid. The writing in Figure 11.4 indicates the point at which he stopped. What was left then was a number of large patterns describing different ways in which he patterned his experience — different modalities. Some of these modalities supported each other, and some conflicted and created tensions between them. The reflective learning process for the focal role ended when the ways in which the modalities supported and conflicted with each other had been recognised and owned. Figure 11.5 shows the result of this process on paper for the focal participant.

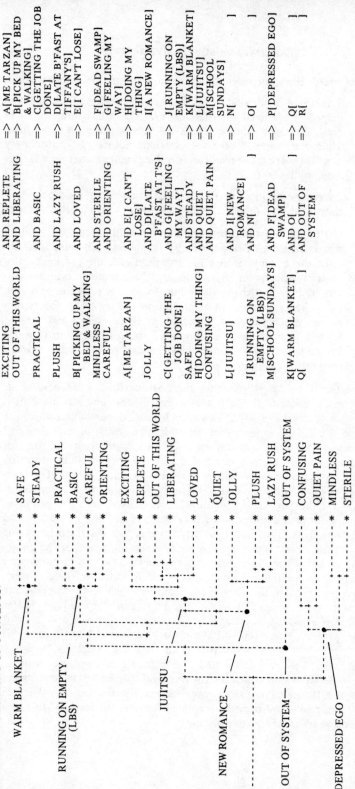

SIMILARITY GROUPING OF CONCEPTS:

Figure 11.4   The gestalt in how the focal participant patterned his experience

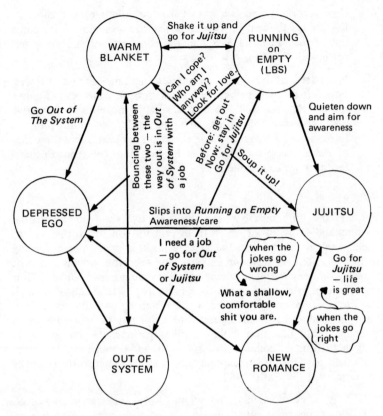

Figure 11.5   **The forms of support and conflict between the different modalities identified in Figure 11.4**

Absorbing work getting out modality relationships. That need for love was OK, but the extent to which it occurred with me betrayed an excessive lack of self-confidence. I stop seeking strokes the whole time now from all and sundry. Others can take me or leave me. I am me — not who others want me to be.

Useful? I don't know. The experience got me thinking about myself in new ways — a 'good' thing. No decisions were made. Again, the major result was a deeper knowledge and appreciation of him. Very worthwhile.

His feel for introspection was tremendous. Far greater than mine. I've always thought introspection I've had was mine, as it's come out of me. In fact I have much in common with him only he's better at it than me.

Fascinated at how valid computer's linking of concepts was. Found it difficult to help him work through concepts as I didn't know him too well. Was struck with the potential negative implications of this in a hostile 'real world'. From his printout I could see he was more able to act on his own internal feelings of right/wrong, good/bad than I. I'm more tuned into others' feedback which sets me up.

Being a catalyst

For me, the difference between this reflective form of experiential learning and those forms which focus primarily on structuring experiencing itself is that whereas the latter feels like a focus on *being* leading to new possibilities for *consciousness*, the reflective process is one of focusing on *consciousness* leading to re-interpretations of *being*. Thus my intention in relation to the focal participant was to empathise with the forms of meaning which he was transferring onto the representations he had created, and thereby to help him to articulate those meanings. My intention with the other participants was to model congruent forms of communication myself, and through that to enable the other participants to express their insights congruently (Bandler and Grinder, 1975; Satir, 1967).

Why is everyone laughing at me? My values seem so logical. Don't people want to be loved and in control of their own destinies? I feel much younger than them. Now I know why she left.

He is irritating. He asserts himself *and* looks for approval at the same time – one or the other, OK; but both together is irritating.

He was absolutely shocking. His egocentricity and lack of self-esteem seemed to be major contradictions. He was revolving around a void or insignificant centre. Found some inadequacies very funny as they were so classically textbook. I didn't think people would be able to function half way as effectively as he does with all these problems.

A very different process. Where working with the one before was interesting, analytical and slightly detached, the process with him was, for me, involving, emotional, and more demanding. He needed our help more . . . demands were made on us as a group. It was more like work. A little frightening – I wasn't sure enough of Philip to be confident that he (the focal participant) wouldn't start something *we* couldn't handle. We were responsible. But he had enough trouble relaxing that it seemed likely he wasn't going to push himself too far. There were times when I heartily disliked him, but by the end I felt closer to him, warts and all. I think he needed some fairly strong persuading; the computer output was too easy to ignore. It only suggested, it did not demand anything of him. If he was to get anything from the experience, he was going to have to *experience* it himself.

The original contract was essential to the legitimacy of my actions: you do what you choose, you express yourself your way, and you are responsible for your actions. It also meant that I did not intervene directly on the structure of their actions itself. There were times however when I felt that the focal participant was experiencing confusion between different forms of consciousness — consciousness of reality as he experienced it, consciousness of symbolic forms of thought, and consciousness of his own desires. Two of the participants chose to use a gestalt 'empty chair' technique in order to distinguish between these forms of consciousness in order that they could make better use of their insights.

> In the hot seats. I can identify two characters in me. One I call 'the Fish' and he's a thoughtful intelligent chap with a keen eye for change. 'The Lad' is a popular external chap who generally operates pretty well with 'the Fish'. I only know the outlier I'm aware of as occasional intrusions of hate. 'The Lad' has to try to deal with him on his own. I *think* this picture is me. What does it all mean?

> He is thoroughly into this, acting as 'Fish', 'the Lad' and 'God'. Trying to show the bad characters the inconsistency of their positions through questions. Socratic method.

Concluding

The last day together had both the warm feeling of a reunion and a sense of truncation. The last two focal participants had stayed on the margins of the group and never really took much time in the focal role — both their choice and a constraint placed on them by the workshop. They were left with varying degrees of unfinished business, and my concern was that the School should provide other spaces and other ways of enabling them to work that through.

We did not spend time re-examining their relationship with the School. There was therefore no closure placed on the process of the group — neither did the participants choose to create any. I did feel however (following the metaphor in the title) that they had in a sense been liberated from a dependent relationship with the institution. A learning cell had formed.

The open-endedness of the workshop as a whole was intentional. It was an active way of enabling a reflective process which would be part of their learning style throughout the two-year experience, and hopefully beyond. As a particular application of computer assisted reflective learning it was however a first time in the MSc. context. It left me with concerns over the extent to which we had been able to move from a macro to a micro learning focus, but otherwise the workshop was a successful transfer of the application of this approach from an organisational context to an institutional one (Boot and Boxer, 1980). There were however, definite problems in how the participants were able to see my role as legitimate in the context of the first term; and the cultural pressures of the School combined with forms of learning media which do not have an explicit place for reflective learning will inevitably dissipate some of the benefits which could be gained. My aim now is to build on the outcomes of the workshop by enabling the workshop's participants to work with other students in their year, using myself and the technology as a way of supporting this process. To end the chapter however it seems appropriate to add a postscript written by the participants about a month after it ended.

Postscript

I am now able to analyse why I make a decision in ways I could not before. When faced with a task I now have the ability to look at the problem in context, while at the same time being able to get on and accomplish it. In relation to the course, I feel able to see interrelationships between subjects much more strongly, and why we are taught in different ways. I also more fully realise that I am going to learn more from other students than from the course itself. The group is a very strong base of support for the next two years, offering physical and moral support in a 'sea of troubles'.

I feel more self-confident in that I have a clearer perspective of myself. I have more understanding of my behaviour and feelings. I was never able to pinpoint my motivations and energy sources as clearly as I am now. I feel I will be successful in changing old coping behaviour that I no longer need and is at times very negative. I feel that being myself is OK and even great at times. I feel entitled to feel uncomfortable and anxious without thinking I'm going into a major depression.

I have discovered that I am not here to be subverted to the School and its system, but to subvert the School to my uses. I feel the group has been an oasis of learning in a sea of knowledge. It has been productive to have a place to meet a small group of confrères and to attack our problems. Its comforting to discover there actually are others who have the same problems. We are not alone!

All in all I have no plans to change myself but I'm stronger through awareness. These sessions have really been a source of power through self knowledge and not, as they might be envisaged by outsiders, a weekly couch session with the local head shrinker.

I really don't feel I was able to contribute much due to my own introverted state but that the experience of the Saturday was so disturbing to me in what the others said and did that it forced me to go and seek help and to realise that I'm not an island and other people can help me. I can't think my way out of everything! I only hope I can accept this idea and put it into practice. It's so easy to fall back into the ways of twenty-five years of experience.

Acknowledgement

I could not have written this chapter without the support and invaluable feedback of those involved in the workshop.

References

Bandler, R. and Grinder, J., *The Structure of Magic, I and II*. Science and Behaviour Books, California, 1975.

Boot, R. L. and Boxer, P. J., 'Reflective Learning' in Beck, J. and Cox, C. (eds), *Advances in Management Development*, Wiley & Sons, 1980.

Boxer, P. J., 'Reflective Analysis', *International Journal of Man-Machine Studies*, 1979, 11, pp. 547–84.

Boxer, P. J., 'Supporting Reflective Learning: Towards a Reflexive Theory of Form', *Human Relations*, 1980.

McQuillan, W. F., *Creativity and Learning Workshops*, London Business School Working Paper, July 1979.

Postman, N. and Weingartner, C., *Teaching as a Subversive Activity*, Penguin, 1971.

Satir, V., *Conjoint Family Therapy*, Science and Behaviour Books, California, 1967.

12 Self-managed learning in independent study

Ian Cunningham

In contrast to the two previous chapters, this is an account of one attempt to build a complete programme – and, indeed, a whole division of an institution – on the concept of self-development. Such a system of independent study is, however, much more than is normally indicated by the term, such as the ubiquitous correspondence course. The latter may well lead to self-development in the sense used in this book, but this will be in spite of the system, rather than as a direct, planned outcome. Cunningham's approach is therefore much broader than mere distance learning, and it will be seen to incorporate elements that are similar to those described in other chapters, e.g. biography work (cf Chapter 7), action projects (cf Chapter 13), and, once again, the social processes of a peer learning community. In this context, Cunningham's reluctance to involve himself in one-to-one counselling is of interest. He also raises pertinent questions about the middle-classes – their domination of management and their monopoly of educational opportunity.

In this chapter I discuss an approach to self-development that has emerged in a college setting. I am not going to argue in detail here the case for the approach we have used: the theoretical and philosophical basis of our work is written up elsewhere (see Foy, 1978; Cunningham, 1978). I want to explore strategies I believe provide a more useful and satisfying experience for potential and practising managers than the traditional prestructured course. Particularly my interest is in pro-grammes which provide (a) an opportunity for learners to develop clear ideas about their needs and (b) assistance in meeting those needs. One implication of this is my mistrust of 'hit and run' short course provision. Finding out what people really need to learn takes time, and I am mostly interested in programmes of at least two or three months duration (part time or full time). Berger (1977) has shown that clarity about learning needs is a crucial factor in making certain that management development programmes are effective, so I want to emphasise particularly the importance of diagnostic procedures.

The chapter is centred on my experience of developing 'independent study' at North East London Polytechnic and on how that experience has influenced our current 'Self-Managed Learning' programmes for managers. I have written elsewhere about the full time and part time programmes of independent study (Cunningham, 1975; Cunningham, 1976). Also I have analysed the processes whereby these innovations came into being (Cunningham, 1979). Here I attempt to interpret the specific use of independent study and Self Managed Learning as it might affect the field of management education. It is my perspective and does not necessarily match those of my ex-colleagues in the School for Independent Study at North East London Polytechnic (for an alternative view see Burgess, 1977).

I want to say something about the development of the School and of its independent study programmes, quoting some examples of students doing work in the field of management. In the concluding parts of the chapter I try to indicate how we are attempting to apply the lessons learned in the School for Independent Study (SIS) to the work of the newly formed Personal Development Division of the Anglian Regional Management Centre. (The Centre operates as the management faculty of North East London Polytechnic.)

The School for Independent Study

The School provides three undergraduate courses: a two-year full time Diploma of Higher Education (Dip.HE) which started in 1974; a BA by Independent Study which is a one-year honours degree (with the entry requirement of a Dip.HE from North East London Polytechnic); and a part time Dip.HE which started in 1977. These two later programmes have some particular features which are improvements on the earlier (full time Dip.HE) design. However, the overall approach has not been changed. The characteristics of the School's programmes can be distinguished from traditional courses as shown in Table 12.1.

SIS in operation – diagnosis and planning

The diagnosis of learning needs and the planning to meet these occupies a considerable part of each student's time in the early stages of the programme. Initially we allowed six weeks on the full time Dip.HE for this, but this time has now been extended because it does seem to take many people nearly a term to do this work effectively.

Table 12.1

	Traditional course	SIS
Curriculum	Staff determined Mainly cognitive Knowledge based	Student determined Cognitive and affective Skills based
Staff roles	Teach subjects plus possibly provide personal tutoring	Two roles: 1) Help students develop and carry out own programmes 2) Provide specialist help as needed
Teaching	Prescribed – lectures, seminars, practicals, case studies, tutorials	Students choose what is appropriate except that tutorial contact is required
Location of learning	Lecture theatre, labora- tory, seminar room, controlled field trips, library	Anywhere – instruction in the lecture theatre is the exception rather than the rule
Timing of learning	Prescribed timetable Learning in blocks/ periods through the day/week	By negotiation – loose timetable, e.g. meet tutors or other students for collaborative activity – otherwise students choose
Assessment	Examinations plus possibly dissertation/ thesis or course work	Student negotiates with staff. Recommended that students undertake a project as part of final assessment

We asked students to answer five questions about themselves:

1   Where have I been? i.e. what past experiences have I had that make me as I am?
2   Where am I now? i.e. what are my current strengths and weaknesses?
3   Where do I want to get to? i.e. what goals do I have in life (short or long term)? What do I want to do in the future?
4   How do I get there? i.e. what do I need to learn to achieve my goals? What abilities do I need to gain and how am I going to do this?
5   How will I know if I have arrived? i.e. what criteria do I have to evaluate my progress? How can I assess my performance?

In answering these five questions the student has to write an extensive document called a 'statement': the process of doing this is for most people quite arduous. However, our experience is that if this early analysis is skimped, then the student may end up pursuing an inappropriate course of study. This point relates to my opening remarks about the need for thorough diagnostic activity prior to embarking on a programme of learning.

We have found that many students revise these initial statements at a later date. It is indeed desirable that students continually review their programmes of activity in order to make changes that result from their development on the course. This does not invalidate the effort put in on the initial statement, because the crucial aspect of the first term is that students learn to plan for themselves. Thus the process of diagnosis and planning is more important than the product of that process (the written statement).

Two case studies

Students on the full time Dip.HE are expected to divide their programme into two approximately equal portions. One half is for 'group work' where students undertake projects in small groups (typically about five in a group). The other half is 'individual work' where the student negotiates a programme of activity with a tutor (who could be anyone in the Polytechnic).

To give something of the flavour of individual work programmes I will refer to two specific students. Joyce started on the part time Dip.HE and switched to the full time course after one year. She had, until then, spent most of her adult life bringing up a family though she had had a part time job as a school secretary for a short while. She had felt bored at home and had considered evening classes as an escape.

However, she learned about the Dip.HE and having surprised herself by getting accepted, she joined the first intake of the part time Dip.HE in April 1976.

She found the writing of a statement quite an effort, and had a great deal of trouble in working out what she wanted to do. She felt that 'something with numbers' might suit her and after a while she linked up with an accountancy tutor in the Management Centre. She attended sessions he ran on the Diploma in Management Studies and found that she could keep up with the other students on the course. Then she started to evolve the idea of running her own catering or hotel business after she had finished the Dip.HE. She negotiated a placement in the Polytechnic refectory and worked alongside the manageress in the refectory learning from her about managing such an operation.

The next step in her development was to change tutor (having learned enough accountancy). She linked up with another member of staff of the Management Centre who has experience of small business management, in order to broaden her learning activities to include the problems of setting up a business (e.g. marketing, legal aspects, etc.).

She is near the end of her Diploma now, and is making serious plans to start a catering business as soon as she has finished.

In making this brief sketch of Joyce's development on the Dip.HE I have left out a great deal about how she has changed. The important aspect is not just that she has evolved her ideas from an unambitious goal of keeping herself from getting bored to a much more challenging one of running her own business. Rather it is the marked personal change that has occurred in her. She was always lively and pleasant but now she is more self-confident, more assured and much more in touch with herself and her abilities. She had to work through a great deal to achieve this: initially she was confronted with weaknesses she had glossed over and she found that very uncomfortable. However, she did work at it and later I want to mention a crucial factor in how she was assisted in her learning.

Before I do, I want to take another case, that of Diane. She joined the part time Dip.HE at the same time as Joyce, but she was in a full time job (as a cashier) so she stayed on the part time programme throughout. She chose initially to make a broad study of personnel management and the behavioural sciences.

She linked up with a tutor in the Management Centre and attended his lectures on the Diploma in Management Studies. She also had tutorials, undertook reading and essay writing and attended a weekend residential course on interpersonal skills. She took the examination at the end of the course with the other students (in order to test her learning) and passed fairly easily.

Gradually she started to narrow down her individual work to take an interest in organisation development (OD), group processes, etc. She met some OD people from a large British company (at a conference) and visited them to find out about their work. This confirmed her decision to move away from the orthodox personnel management area.

By now she was coming up to her final assessment, and had to pick on a piece of work to present at the end of her course. She decided that something on life planning/career development would be appropriate. At this time Capital Radio (a London commercial radio station) started to do work with young unemployed. She contacted Capital Radio and discussed the way in which the Dip.HE tried to provide help for people to make informed choices about their future. She then joined a scheme that the radio station was running to provide guidance for young unemployed. At the time of writing she is working with a number of young people in the East End of London (where she lives). She is writing up her experience of helping people get jobs and relating this to the theory, so that her piece of work for assessment will be an extensive dissertation based on her 'action research'.

The reason I picked these two cases out of the many that I could have chosen is that:

(a)   they are both women and I would like to see more women getting the opportunity to become managers;

(b)   they both have no educational qualifications (each having left school at 15);

(c)   they have both been undertaking 'pre-entry development' rather than 'post experience training', i.e. they are learning to be managers but neither has experience of managing in an organisation.

There is a danger that self-development approaches might come to be seen as appropriate only for those who have had some initial higher educational experience (degree or professional training) and/or some experience of managing. The classic action learning model implies this: one has to have some managerial experience in order to share problems with others.

I am not criticising other self-development activities here, rather I want to argue that the whole self-development philosophy can be applied in a wider context than some people have imagined. I could have chosen to refer to some of the practising managers who have used the part time Dip.HE, but I felt that it was more interesting to draw attention to the fact that colleges and universities offering MBAs, undergraduate business studies degrees, etc., could all operate a self-development approach along the lines of independent study, if they so wanted;

(d)   they are both from working class backgrounds in the East End of London. Managerial positions in this country are dominated by the middle class, and I believe that management teachers and trainers too easily confirm and enhance the élitism of management by not assisting working class people to gain entry into management. One way they do this is to require entry qualifications like degrees which are beyond the reach of most working class people. (The Open University is no answer as it provides inadequate support mechanisms to assist people who are unused to academic education.)

Last year I worked as a tutor with three students on the BA (by independent study) and although they did not have an 'O'-level between them their final results were two upper twos and one lower two.

It is quite clear that the entry requirements of most educational institutions exclude people who deserve the chance to be there.

Group work in SIS

The idea of students doing projects in groups had a noble aim. We were convinced that the traditional individualistic, competitive mode of education was wrong, and we wanted to provide an opportunity for people not only to undertake a piece of work on their own but also to balance this with collaborative activity. The investment by organisations in OD, T-groups, interpersonal skills training, transactional analysis, etc. is all evidence of the distorting effect that educational (and other) experiences have on people such that they are unable to work effectively with others.

We wanted to tackle this issue, and group projects seemed the ideal answer. In the event this side of SIS's work has been less successful than the individual work. There are a number of reasons for this: I will refer to one of the main ones.

The wrong kind of project work

Two kinds of project work emerged in the School. I have called these 'Investigative Projects' and 'Action Projects' respectively. The former seem to provide very little opportunity for learning but have been the kinds most favoured by students.

Investigative projects are those where a group investigates a situation and usually writes a report on it. There is no attempt to change the situation; to take action. At their worst they mirror third rate sociological research studies. At best groups write interesting impressionistic reports on 'social issues' like pollution or homelessness. Such reports may result from library based 'research' or questionnaire/interview research in the field. Hence students can learn to do literature searches, to conduct surveys and to write reports. However such projects are 'low risk' — students, by not taking action and testing ideas can play safe and merely make recommendations (which as a rule are not acted upon by anyone).

Also the groups often do not have to tackle issues of working together; each person can go off and do his bit for the project and then it can all be thrown together for a final report. Hence genuine collaborative working is never faced — people do not have to take action together to try to get something done.

Action projects are closer to the best of the action learning kind of project, i.e. there is an expectation that there will be an attempt to do something about a problem. Such projects are small scale, and concerned with issues which can feasibly be solved in the time available (usually at most one term).

Groups doing such projects may not produce a report at all (or if there is one, it is a minor feature of the activity). By having to work together to get something done, the group is forced to face issues of personal relationships (and these have to be solved in order for the group to be effective). Also the group may have to tackle a wide range of learning problems, some of which will be unpredictable before the project starts.

One project of this nature that I was involved in was a group of three students who decided to study problems of survival. They researched the subject thoroughly (including visiting RAF survival training specialists). They then tested out their ideas in two contexts. First they attempted to survive in urban structured environments by seeing how far they could get from central London with no money. In the event they reached Belgium and returned safely, without a penny between them the whole time. Next they tested their ideas in a hostile, non-urban environment by seeing if they could survive for two weeks on a Scottish island (in the middle of a loch) without taking any food with them. In the event they encountered some of the worst weather ever for that time of year (blizzards, etc.) but managed to last out for most of their planned time (they did return to the mainland a bit short of their target). (The project was written up by Charlotte Gray in *Psychology Today* and anyone interested in reading more about it can get information from that article.)

The students concerned gained a great deal from their experience. Hence it was more rigorous and demanding although the absence of superficially 'scientific' data such as produced in investigative projects made it less apparently so. This, indeed, has been one problem. When students have attempted to do more interesting and useful action projects, the more traditionalist staff have found it unacceptable because there is not an emphasis on library use or traditional sociological research based analysis.

Another factor is that most students' previous experience of learning has been in the false situations used in investigative projects. Nearly all the fashionable 'discovery learning' is nothing of the kind. It is safely controlled by teachers who have predefined objectives of their own which students are expected to meet. Hence it is not surprising that students entering the School for Independent Study should find the combined pressure of their earlier educational experiences and conservative tutors pushing them into investigative projects.

Table 12.2 summarises the key distinctions between the two types of project.

Table 12.2
Two kinds of project

Characteristics	Investigative	Action
1 Orientation	Liberal arts, sociological or journalistic	Learning by doing, scientific and problem solving
2 Product	A report	Anything
3 Type of problem	Global	Discrete, specific
4 Risk to learner, i.e. potential for failure	Low	High
5 Group working	'Co-acting' – low level of interaction	'Cohesive' – high level level of interaction
6 Possible learning	Literature searching, sociological survey methods, report writing	Wide range of competencies, but especially the ability to take action

Changes in SIS programmes

The part time Dip.HE started in April 1977 and as the first head of that programme I was determined to avoid some of the problems of the full time Dip.HE. I want to indicate, in outline, some of these problems and a few of the solutions that we attempted on the part time programme.

1   Problem: diagnosis and planning is difficult for students

Writing a 'statement' is not easy, and two aspects that I felt were lacking in the full time Dip.HE were (a) adequate peer group support and (b) effective induction into the programme.

One solution: We initiated a weekend induction residential for new students in order to develop a supportive community within which there was a high level of peer group support. This by and large worked, the evidence for this being that part time students were able to complete statements in the same time as full time students (even though most had full time jobs and could only give a few hours each week to studying).

2   Problem: tutorial support was ineffective

The arrangements on the full time Dip.HE for tutorial support within SIS were a weekly half-day 'tutor group' meeting (tutor plus about 12 to 15 students) and one-to-one tutorials. (*N.B.* I am excluding from consideration here the specialist academic tutoring that students receive from their 'individual work' tutors.) Tutor groups have proved too large to give real support and assistance to students and attendance at these meetings has often been poor.

The one-to-one tutorial arrangements maintain a dependence on the tutor, and hence are inimical to genuine self-development activity. Also one-to-one tutorials undermine mutual peer group support and enhance differences between tutors and learners. I became convinced that we had to move away from this mode of operating.

One solution: Prior to taking on the task of starting up the part time Dip.HE I have acted as a set adviser on the GEC action learning programme (see Casey and Pearce, 1977). I decided to transplant the 'set' concept from the action learning world into the part time Dip.HE. This decision was probably the most important one in terms of raising the quality of the programme (see Cunningham, 1977).

At the residential weekend students negotiated a place in a set with a set tutor. The set then replaced *both* the tutor group and the one-to-one tutorial. Unless a student is in need of urgent help (a very rare occurrence) I refuse to conduct one-to-one sessions: all problems are raised in the set meetings.

One student I worked with (Maureen) who transferred from the part time Dip.HE to the full time programme commented:

> The biggest plus on the part time course, which sadly does not seem to have been incorporated in the full time course, is the formation of sets — approximately 6 students and 1 tutor. I found my set was most important, particularly at the start when everyone was floundering trying to make sense of the course and battling with their statement. Our part time set was a group where we could discuss problems which might be affecting our work, air our views on any matter, and generally turn to the other members for support. I know that I would have left the part time course quite early on without the support of my set. The tutor group which I have been involved with on the full time course (14 students and 1 tutor) does not fulfil the same function, mainly I think because the group is too large. . . . This makes it difficult for a sense of closeness and trust to be built up.   (FitzHenry, 1979, p. 150)

I mentioned earlier that Joyce's struggles to cope with the programme were assisted by another 'factor'. Joyce commented to me about her experience as follows:

> Although I knew it was a course designed for independent study and that to do my own thing was what appealed to me, it was literally easier said than done. To make up one's own course instead of being heaven as I first thought, was turning into, not quite hell, but a bad dream or nightmare. At times I wished I'd never started and was all ready to give up when I would give myself a target, say if nothing happened by next term then I would make a decision whether to give up or stay. The other factor that helped me finally to stay the course and gave me so much support were the others in my set. Knowing that they were all willing to help, however big or small my problem was, and that I could call on them and be sure that they would be there when I needed them. Without their help I wouldn't have got where I am, I'm sure.

3   Problem: tutors retained too much power over the programme

Although SIS students have more power than most over their own personal activities, the tutors retained control of the overall structure and policies of the full time Dip.HE. Any changes in course procedures were decided by staff and then imposed on students in the same way as most other courses. The students became very frustrated with this but because of the way in which educational institutions operate (e.g. jargon ridden meetings, behind the scenes politics, complex multi-stage decision-making processes) students have found it difficult to have any influence on decisions affecting the whole School.

One solution: The course committee (established to oversee the course) consisted of three staff and three students. I arranged with the students that they would agree a nominee for chairperson amongst themselves, and I would then second that person. My idea was that as staff tend to have more power just by virtue of their greater knowledge of the system, we would not redress this merely by establishing equal numbers of staff and students on the course committee. There had to be a positive move to give students more power.

In the event, the decision worked out fairly well, but it was often more symbolic than anything. As the course evolved we tended to use the course committee mainly as the formal 'rubber stamp' to decisions that evolved through sets or through meetings of all students.

These meetings were held on what we called a 'core evening' when all students were asked to attend so that we could deal with general problems affecting everyone, e.g. giving information about learning resources in the Polytechnic. These meetings evolved as a forum to work out policy matters and by and large were more effective than the 'representative' system (i.e. staff and students elected to 'represent' their colleagues on a course committee).

It seems to me that issues of power and control are often ignored in considering self-development programmes. There is usually the assumption that by giving individuals more control over their own learning, this is all that is needed. However if learners have no influence on the overall structures and methods of management developing being used, then this can dilute and undermine the whole approach. One can identify four basic positions:

1   *The traditional course.*   The learner has little or no control over personal learning methods and over the content of learning. Also the learner has no say in course design, structure and policies.

2   *SIS full time Dip.HE, many self-development programmes etc.* The learner has a high level of control over his own personal learning, but it is within a structure imposed on him (over which he has little or no influence).

3   *Summerhill-style schools.*   Students at A. S. Neill's school (Summerhill) have a high level of involvement in general policy and structural decisions. The meetings, which all students can attend, genuinely do give a great deal of power to the learners. However, this is all done within the context of fairly traditional approaches to teaching.

4   *SIS part time Dip.HE, Carl Rogers' person centred workshops (Rogers, 1977), some learning community events.*   Here learners have a high level of involvement in decisions affecting their own personal learning and affecting the overall structure of the event. Clearly it is not possible to separate control of one's own learning from the level of one's influence on structures and policies. To that extent the other three situations must provide less opportunity for genuine self-development than this one.

Table 12.3 summarises the issue.

Self-managed learning

Outstanding problems in SIS

Although the part time Dip.HE marked a step forward it did not go far enough. Constraints within SIS meant that some outstanding problems could not be tackled. These included:

1   *Group projects.*   The School was committed to them, and it was impossible to engineer any appropriate changes in the way group projects were organised (or alternatively to get them scrapped).

Table 12.3

	Learner influence over learning methods and course content	Learner influence over course structure, policies and procedures
Traditional course	Low	Low
SIS full time Dip.HE, many self-development programmes	High	Low
Summerhill-style schools	Low	High
SIS part time Dip.HE, Rogers' person centred workshops (Rogers, 1977)	High	High

2   *Qualifications.* The whole of SIS's effort was geared to assisting people who wanted to do qualification courses. It seemed to me that many people would like the opportunity to design their own learning programmes, but not have to register for a qualification in order to do it. (This was indeed true for a number of people who joined the part time Dip.HE: they really wanted a method of continuing their learning in their own way without doing a diploma. Mostly such students dropped out early on as they found the whole process geared too much to final assessment.)

3   *Assessment.* Students were not sufficiently involved in their own assessment for my liking. The whole procedure tended to push the process back into the traditional mode, i.e. staff and external examiners imposing their personal judgements on students under a cloak of secrecy and a facade of objectivity.

4   *Making choices.* Students on the Dip.HE can choose to study anything, provided their final assessment material is up to the level of the second year of an honours degree. However the way people make choices can be quite haphazard. An interest might be sparked off by seeing a television programme, or parental influence might be a strong factor, or the advice of a friend might persuade someone to undertake a particular course of action. If staff take a very non-directive stance it can mean that students are influenced by often ill-informed sources. However the alternative is not to be highly directive (a trap that many staff fall into). I will refer later to what I regard as the best way of solving this problem.

The very openness of the opportunities available in SIS is both a strength and a weakness. The strength is that there are no artificial boundaries imposed on what can be learned: this is especially valuable in a practical area like management. Managerial problems do not respect the subject boundaries that academics have artificially established. Problems in organisations are rarely (if ever) wholly economic or wholly behavioural: rather the solutions to problems need to be drawn from a range of subject areas.

The weakness of this openness is that it is difficult to provide information to learners on what is available for them to study. The logistic problems of introducing people to the whole range of human knowledge are enormous. Hence in practice the choice of learning activity can become quite random and chaotic (even after intensive diagnosis and planning).

The establishment of the Personal Development Division

When the Anglian Regional Management Centre (ARMC) decided to commit itself to provide independent study programmes at the post experience level, I took the opportunity to return to the Management Centre (I had originally joined the Polytechnic as a member of the Management Centre in 1972 before transferring to SIS). One immediate advantage of operating only in the management field (as opposed to covering everything, as in SIS) was to provide a much easier context in which to run programmes (see point 4 above). The Personal Development Division was established in January 1979 to provide a focus for independent study programmes, and it soon became apparent that we would be diverging quite a bit from the SIS view of independent study. Hence we coined the term 'Self-Managed Learning' to describe the kinds of activity we would be promoting.

I will describe here some features of our 'general management' programmes and leave aside reference to our specialist and in-company work. I want to draw attention particularly to how we have tried to solve the problems that arose in SIS.

1   *Group Projects.* We have dropped the idea of encouraging group projects. Our experience of using 'sets' is that they provide much the best way to facilitate collaborative activity. Hence we see the use of sets as an important corner-stone of most of our programmes.

2   *Qualifications.* We have decided to offer a range of part time programmes of increasing intensity and, initially at least, to place a low emphasis on qualification courses. We described these programmes in terms of 'levels'.

Level A programmes provide managers with access to learning resources in the Centre plus a minimal (usually twice termly) tutorial contact. Thus for £5 a term a manager can use the facilities of the Management Centre, attend events and get some assistance from staff of the Division. This level of involvement has proved particularly appropriate for ex-students of the Centre, e.g. those who have gained a diploma in Management Studies and who want to continue their learning at their own pace and in their own way.

Level B programmes provide managers with all of Level A plus the use of a weekly set meeting. This type of programme has proved valuable for those who want to undertake some diagnostic and planning work as well as use the learning resources of the Centre.

Level C programmes provide all of Levels A and B plus the opportunity to have specialist tutorial assistance along the lines of the 'individual work' component of the Dip.HE. Our experience so far is that people usually need to operate on Level B for one term before they can switch to Level C. This is in keeping with the SIS experience and confirms that 'practising managers' are no different from 'potential managers' in their need for extended diagnostic and planning activity prior to launching on a particular learning programme.

Our next step will be to start a Level D programme which will cover all of Levels A, B and C plus provide the opportunity for the learner to present work for assessment in order to gain a postgraduate diploma (after 2 years' part time study). In design it will have some features in common with the part time Dip.HE (e.g. sets, induction residential, individual work) but there are some important differences, two of which I will mention below.

3   *Assessment.* We believe that final assessment to award a diploma or not should be made on the basis of a consensual agreement between the learner, his peers, his tutors and his external assessor. The person's self assessment should be the starting point and external judgements are best used to help the learner reach his own conclusions about his competence.

We already use a similar process in dealing with the assessment of individual work on SIS programmes, where students are located in the Management Centre with us as tutors. Basically the procedure is to copy all the students' work and distribute it to his set colleagues and to his tutors. Then we have a set meeting and the student first announces his own judgement on his work.

Then we go round the set, each person (tutor or student) in turn commenting on the work, and summing up by announcing their judgement of it. At the end of this process we discuss any differences until we have reached a consensus.

The students have commented that, for them, this has been one of the high spots of the course. Rather than submitting work and then anxiously waiting for results (with no useful feedback on the work) they have had a chance to discuss their performance and know that a fair, honest decision has been reached to which they are committed.

4   *Making choices.* As I mentioned earlier, there is a real problem about how a learner chooses what he is going to learn. He may make a thorough analysis of his problems through the process of diagnosis and

planning, but he may not be aware of what solutions are available. There is a genuine danger that in some self-development programmes managers can engage in 'rediscovering the wheel'.

Clearly there can be much learning in rediscovering knowledge that already exists (unbeknown to the learner). However our life-time is limited and it may be more fruitful if people can use existing know-ledge, where appropriate, in order to save themselves time. My experience is that most managers expect management trainers and teachers to help them make short-cuts to optimal solutions to their problems.

Burgoyne (1977) has studied the problem of managers making choices of learning goals. He suggests:

> The idea of a person setting learning goals implies that the person in some way 'knows what he does not know'. This is not a paradox since it is possible to know of an area of knowledge or expertise without having that knowledge or expertise. It is however equally possible for a person not to know what he does not know, in which case it seems likely that this would consti-tute a block to self development. It follows from this that one possible characteristic of the self-development manager is a *rich cognitive map of the possible skills, qualities and competences which could be useful to him in performing a managerial function.*   (p. 18)

Burgoyne's research confirms this view.

In keeping with this finding, our plan is to use part of the first term of the diploma to assist managers to develop richer cognitive maps. We intend to use a variety of methods though we favour the idea of sets (a) interviewing practising senior managers (e.g. personnel managers, financial managers, production managers) to find out about the abilities needed to do their jobs and (b) interviewing expert manage-ment teachers (in economics, production management quantitative methods, behavioural sciences etc.) to find out what these bodies of knowledge can contribute to managerial effectiveness.

If this process continues throughout the first term along with the diagnostic and planning activity, we believe this will provide a better basis for managers to develop appropriate learning goals. I should stress that there will be no attempt to *teach* anything to the learners: rather the emphasis is on letting people know what is available so that their planning can be more realistic and fruitful.

Conclusion

In some 'self-development' approaches there is a danger of throwing the baby out with the bath water. Structured educational courses in institutions are the wrong way to go about developing managers, but educational institutions do have resources (e.g. libraries, staff, computers) that can be of use to managers for their own learning. Therefore I am not sympathetic to overly anti-academic 'self-developers'. College and university resources can be used, but it needs a wholly different relationship between the institution and the manager than has hitherto been the case. I believe that the Self Managed Learning mode offers the basis for just such a relationship.

References

Berger, M. (1977), 'Training and the Organisational Context', *Journal of European Industrial Training*, 1, 2, pp. 7–12.

Burgess, T. (1977), *Education After School*, Penguin, London.

Burgoyne, J. G. (1977), 'Self Development, Managerial Success and Effectiveness: Some Empirical Evidence', *Management Education and Development*, 8, 1, (April 1977), pp. 16–20.

Casey, D. and Pearce, D. (eds), (1977), *More than Management Development: Action Learning at GEC*, Gower, Farnborough.

Cunningham, I. (1975), 'The NELP Experiment with Dip.H.E.', *Education and Training*, 17, 5 (May 1975), pp. 114–117.

Cunningham, I. (1976), 'College/Employer Relations – A New Approach', *The Training Officer*, 12, 9, (September/October 1976), pp. 226–228.

Cunningham, I. (1977), 'The Use of Action Learning Principles in Undergraduate Education', *Action Learning Newsletter*, 2, p. 1.

Cunningham, I. (1978), *Self Managed Learning*, Anglian Regional Management Centre, Working Paper (June 1978).

Cunningham, I. (1979), 'Educational Change and the NELP Dip.H.E.', *Educational Change and Development*, 1, 3 (Spring 1979), pp. 26–36.

FitzHenry, M. (1979), 'My Experience of Dip.H.E.', *The NELP Experience of Independent Study*, North East London Polytechnic: School for Independent Study.

Foy, N. (1978), *The Missing Links. British Management Education in the Eighties*, Centre for Management Studies, Oxford.

Gray, C. (1975), 'The Psychology of Survival', *Psychology Today*, 5, (August 1978), p. 61.

Rogers, C. (1977), *On Personal Power*, Dell, New York.

PART IV

SELF-DEVELOPMENT AND EVERYDAY EXPERIENCE

Overview

Each of us is faced, every day, with opportunities for development — far more such opportunities than we are ever going to have on formal courses. What, then, can be done to help people make the most of these?

Paul Temporal (Chapter 3) has shown some of the barriers that hinder such development. In this part of the book we present three chapters on what might perhaps be called the interface between formal, planned activities and Temporal's non-contrived learning events. Each of the three approaches — action learning, counselling and learning conversations — may be seen as ways of helping the individual to learn from his normal work tasks and experiences.

13 Action learning and the development of the self

Reg Revans

Revans, in his inimitable style, shows how action learning integrates knowing and doing. He is critical of our educational system, which emphasises knowing about things, rather than mastery over them. Once again I find that I need to engage with others if I, as an individual, am to develop – these others, comrades in adversity, bringing their own unique selves into relationship with mine. In so doing they help me to shock myself, to question myself and my goals, forcing me to 'move between familiar detail and the uncharted labyrinths' of my total lived experience. For without such shocks, I might preserve 'my dependence on the dead and on the past', but I will not develop.

Here lies another feature of action learning – the participant's task really matters to him. Because it is a real task, it is by definition messy – there is no neat programmable solution. Rather, the individual has to 'get away from the detailed security of the programme . . . into the open wilderness of the totality of mastery over, . . . of creativity for the future'. Such is self-development.

Reference to and mastery over

There is a distinction between verbal acquaintance with something (such as correctly stating the height of the world pole vault record) and realising something, in whole or in part, at some specific here-and-now (such as getting within ten centimetres of that record while a brass band is playing on August Bank Holiday, 1980, at Wath-on-Dearne). If the distinction is overlooked or ignored – as it often is in a culture such as ours, whose literate bureaucracy is paid more for writing letters about jet engines than are its engineers for making them – we may fall into serious error. Many teachers, for example, continue, with unclouded consciences, to draw higher pay than the local managers who come to listen to them because those teachers believe themselves to be equipping those managers to solve, say, the costing problems of their factories. All, in fact, they do is air ideas in elementary arithmetic, disguised in familiar terms to hold the attention of their audience. Because it is no longer a class of fidgety children that sits in front of them, the talk is no longer of bowls of apples or baskets of oranges, but of work volumes and budgets and variances. While these, like the statement about the pole vault record, are related (in some particulars) to what goes on in the factory across the street, there is no evidence that any time devoted to them in the classroom will be more than offset by improved performance at the workplace . . . unless a vast array of other things are also taken into account. What contribution, one might ask, to the future success of the aspiring pole vaulter is made by his knowledge of the present record? Some, no doubt, but how much in terms of the time available to him? He may need to know that it is over 18 feet, but this is also known to thousands of others who will never pick up a pole; whether he will be the first over 19 feet depends almost exclusively upon things that have nothing to do with arithmetical awareness. *Reference to* and *mastery over* are very different, as are conditions *necessary* and conditions *sufficient*; to conquer their differences is the mission of *action learning*.

Some formidable barriers

Between, on the one hand, the words of the teacher and, on the other, the actions the boss has to take in the factory to pay *real* money to *real* people for providing him with *real* services are interposed some vast and largely unexplored divides: every manager setting out on a new task stands before his own uncharted Himalayas. On closer study these turn out to include:

(a)   the unique self of the manager;
(b)   the unique selves of his collaborators, such as his teacher and his supervisors;
(c)   whatever is unknown about his working conditions, both present and future.

Each of these is in turn a vast catalogue of doubt and ambiguity, and what carries the stamp of truth may, in itself, be the most doubtful and ambiguous of all. For example, although its logic may appear impeccable the teacher may show by his behaviour that he does not practise his own lesson; many are the professors of managerial psychology who lose their tempers when faced with alternative explanations of the data. Indeed, the emerging gap between reference to and mastery over has brought a new word to our language: 'iatrogenesis', or the aggravation of the malady by the healer called to cure it.   The physician may exacerbate the disease, although it is over a century since Florence Nightingale first warned her nurses not to do the patient further harm; the jailer, so far from reforming the criminal, still further degrades him; the minister of religion, surrounded by political strife, calls his flock not to humility and repentance, but to arrogance and revenge; the psychiatrist laboriously trains his client to deviations anew; and the business expert, consulted about some minor fault, vamps up trouble enough throughout the firm to fill a ten-year contract.

Kennenship and könnenship

Before exploring the barriers of the previous paragraph, we note a troublesome semantic equivocation. Modern English seems to make a clear distinction between the verb 'to do' and the verb 'to know'; since action learning insists that to know anything in the operational world of mastering one's surroundings implies the ability to do it — so making action indispensable to learning — we must examine the breach that seems to have opened up between the flimsy web of *reference to* and the iron battlefield of *mastery over*.   All Germanic languages trace the two words to the same source; in German itself the relationship is at once apparent: *kennen* is to know or recognise, *können* is to be able. In English *know* and *can* are both cognate with the Latin *gnosco*, although the connection is not immediately obvious; it has been further obscured by an educational system which depends upon exploiting the distinctions between *reference to* and *mastery over*.   The Scot, of course, still uses *ken* in the sense of recognition, and this word also retains its archaistic and elegant overtones in English usage, as in 'beyond my ken' or 'when a new planet swims into his ken'. There is, however, one robust survival: the Authorised Version tells of the patriarchs who *knew* their women, while we hear today in the discothèque 'She come in while the fourth number was on and I done her by the sixth'. These reminders serve still to associate a knowledge of things with some power to command them; knowing and doing may still occasionally be seen as different aspects of the same total activity.

But with the growth of compulsory schooling the link between knowing and doing has become greatly attenuated, expressed as slabs of print recited from memory, inexorably creeping away from mastery over towards reference to. The very multiplication and durability of these slabs slowly force more widely open the semantic breach, for when the processes of technology and arts of commerce spread a million copies of the same text across the world, those who refer to it must get the same lesson wherever it is read. This gives an uncritical impression of innate truth, since, according to John Locke, truth is that on which all men agree. Nor is this all: the impression upon the page today will be the same impression tomorrow. Thus the message is not only veneered with truth by constant repetition; it is also bolstered by the permanence of the page on which it stands, so that what is agreed as true today must also be agreed as true tomorrow. *Reference to*, by the very nature of the books that make it possible, is not only constantly accepted as immemorial reality, but, among the risks of management education, preferred as something easier. Thus it is that the value of ideas promising to promote *mastery over* our surroundings, like action learning, can be measured by the animosity with which they are saluted by management teachers; and thus it is that those who produce such ideas are confirmed in their worthwhileness by the opposition of their colleagues at home and by the ridicule of their enemies elsewhere. When such detraction has for long enough matured, those skilled in manipulating the *reference to* acquire leisure enough and authority enough to out-manoeuvre those preoccupied with and responsible for *mastery over*. But the hour eventually must come (as it has come in Britain) when society as a whole loses command of its environment as a whole; there is a surfeit of civil servants and a dearth of colliery managers; left purely to market forces in a culture of *reference to*, the education industry moves sharply from *könnenship* into *kennenship*; action learning seeks to reverse this trend, preparing its apprentices for könnenship, while traditional schooling is an endless treadmill of kennenship. No sooner has its young teacher copied out the canonical slabs than he takes his children around the same scriptorium in the same unchanging cycle.

The self as referent and as master

It was written in the Temple at Delphi: 'Know thyself', but it is not clear whether the knowledge that the gods advised their pilgrims to acquire was kennenship or könnenship. Those who, over two thousand years later, may relish writing themselves up for the first time in *Who's Who*, have probably thought little upon the distinction. Most of those whom I know can (even when the subject of themselves has not been raised for discussion) recite a catalogue of personal *reference to* from which any item, to be omitted, must be of monumental triviality. It might not, however, occur to them that what they know about themselves could be of little use were they unexpectedly forced to act in the face of some dire and unfamiliar peril. Indeed, those who insist that they *do* know how they would so respond are not only ill-acquainted with themselves but can have had little experience of what it means to be in a tight corner. Those who pass through life without needing to ask themselves who they think they are, or why they say the things they say or do the things they do, must merely drift along the backwaters of inconsequence, like the case-jockeys of fashionable business schools. Just as only in real adversity can one discover what one really values because only then may it be really threatened, so does real adversity alone force one to read between those same lines in *Who's Who*. It may equally illuminate the integrity of others, enabling us to discriminate between kennenship, as their lofty advice, and könnenship, as their active help; as it is put by the intelligence of France: 'Only because we misunderstand others so much do we hate them so little'.

Our distinction between reference and mastery was emphasised by Samuel Johnson on hearing that a celebrated preacher, William Dodd, had been sentenced to death for forgery: 'Depend upon it, Sir, when a man knows he is to be hanged in a fortnight, it concentrates his mind wonderfully'; action learning tries to induce a little of the same application by methods which encourage its survival. For those personal memorials advertised as public knowledge, called image-building, merely repeat one's known achievements, called bio-data, and may suffice for pursuing one's lawful occasions. But there is no guarantee that, faced with sudden calamity, they will be found either adequate or true. Since most managers in Britain now walk in the shadow of calamity, it would be helpful if more of them could say who they are and in what, if anything, they believe. Their education, if it is to be seriously attempted, should thus engender in them some curiosity over these affairs, and this it is the mission of action learning to attempt. Nowhere is the distinction between kennenship and könnenship more critical than in this particular field, but nowhere is the quest for kennenship more singleminded. Yet it is no excuse to insist that könnenship must be postponed until some arbitrary syllabus of kennenship has been completed; it is agreed that no architect is likely to design a cathedral before he has been shown how to sharpen a pencil, nor can the composer start on his symphonies without first being told where to find the manuscript paper. But these are lessons for the immature, and I, for one, do not believe that the managers of Britain are as immature as our present educational policies suggest. Indeed, the immaturity lies elsewhere, among those who run the system; they have no wish to shock their clients, so safeguarding their own acceptability, and less wish to shock themselves, so preserving their dependence on the dead and on the past.

Self-acquaintance a social process

I cannot learn much about myself — apart from what I draft for *Who's Who* — without help from others, nor can they learn who they may be without what I have to give them. The news that I am to be hanged within the fortnight might well concentrate my mind without help from others. But upon what? If my imagination is charged with little but self-deceit behind the file of *references to* myself, perhaps the concentration will but enrich the self-deception. Unless my thoughts are strictly and continuously monitored for me by some independent judge free of my illusions, although no doubt well equipped with his own, and unless, additionally, those partly dis-hallucinated thoughts are then reflected in my observable strivings towards some external goal, I cannot assess their practical worth. To make my point I compose a parable:

> About a year ago I was put in charge of a factory making toys for children and assembly games for psychology courses in business schools. Since taking over I have brought in a few new designs and sales have steadily risen. But, despite this success, some of the staff I found there have left, and others are following them. At first I am not concerned, but then I hear that a few have set up on their own to exploit my new designs. I must do something to strengthen my relations with the remaining staff and the expanding business. But what? If I begin by asking those still with me why the others have gone, however objectively I put my questions and however attentively I listen to the replies, ought I not to have a third party to monitor the conversations? What about another manager also anxious to understand some trouble closing in upon himself? Might he not be able, were he to attend, to say afterwards 'By coming here to see how you and your staff interpret what seems to be going on, I hoped to pick up something to help sort out my own mess. But to tell the truth, I cannot understand the questions you seem to be putting to the foremen. Perhaps it's because I'm not in the musical giraffe trade; perhaps it's because I've never made psychology machines. But the foremen were also confused; they couldn't get what you were driving at half the time. All that about the men who left being jealous of your new ideas . . . ' My interruption to deny that I was imputing jealousy to anybody might well be silenced with 'Well, I'm glad to hear I misunderstood you. But if that was my impression; what did the others feel? . . . '

It is unnecessary to prolong the narrative. An independent critic, disinterested in the proper sense of that misused word, giving me his time because he, too, wants to understand the behaviour of *real* people facing *real* problems to be treated in *real* time, can monitor for me the messages I transmit to and receive from others, so that I may read them afresh against the objective problems around me and my emotional traits from within. But how to be sure that his views are any more reliable than my own? Is he, too, not a fabric of self-deception and misjudged values that explain his own predicament?

I cannot, of course, ever be sure. But I can reduce the risk of being gravely wrong. I can visit him at his place of work to discover how clear he seems to me about his goals, his problems, and his resources. Perhaps if I try to tell him how I see his condition, I bring up weaknesses not only in him, but also in myself; a series of exchanges is launched in which each helps the other towards a more accurate self-evaluation, tempted by the rewards of an interested self-disclosure. I do not pay him to tell me what I should like to hear; he is frank with me exactly because I am frank with him. We have stripped ourselves of the degradation of dependence and the imposture of acceptability, those besetting sins of the academy. But may not this exchange become merely the swapping of one set of illusions for another, like the celebrated case study? For unless what the pair of us arrive at can be checked against some outside reality that regards our opinions with contemptuous indifference, none can judge any point of view more useful than any other in *mastering reality* . . . I return to the musical giraffes:

My talks with the staff, given new meaning by my fellow manager have changed my possible fears that the old hands were jealous of my new ideas. Perhaps our new products were not due to me at all, but were evolved by the old hands who have now left, after years of fruitlessly trying to persuade the previous boss to try them out. What ought I to do, faced with this new view of my predicament, this fresh detraction from my power? . . . Whatever my intention, it seems imperative to me now that I sense its impact on the remaining staff, so that I must find some way of discussing it with them. Perhaps a chat would not only forestall misunderstanding, but also improve my plans? . . . But I do not seem a very good judge of my effect upon other people in the factory. Ought I not, then, to talk about my intentions first with my outside manager, the colleague with his own troubles? As a practical man who has to make things work, he will have ideas — or at least questions — about how my plan (reference to) is likely to operate (mastery over). He will criticise and amend and, perhaps, suggest new points altogether, but, when all has been argued out, he will say of my final proposal, 'Try it! I think there's some hope, but not as much as you do. I think you're still too sensitive about where the idea of the psychology machinery came from; you still feel it was yours — even though you also admit reading about it years ago in some management magazine — while the foreman sticks to his point that he and a couple who've now left had been pushing it for years at the old boss. Didn't one of them say they'd made a pilot model of it and tried it out at night, in the Stamford Arms, until the landlord said it brought all those long-haired undesirables up from the teachers' training college? So, if you are thinking of a chat with some of the men who left, I feel it may get you somewhere . . . and so on . . . and so forth'.

Although I may still flounder in the greyness of the zone between *reference to* and *mastery over*, I have now at least made some effort to rid my plans of those fantasies most likely to be apparent to an outside observer himself much concerned to guard against his own fantasisings; in the action learning programmes that I have developed over the past twenty years, this mutual insurance against self-deception has been fortified within the set of four or five comrades in adversity, rather than between the pair imagined in the parable of musical giraffes. The multiplying effect of the set is prodigious; each participant has four counsellors, each of whom is counselled by three others as well as by the given participant; each becomes as interested in the progress of his colleagues as in his own. But not until some plan of action, purged by my colleagues of my grosser illusions and enriched beyond my wit by their suggestions, is tried out in the *real here-and-now* of my factory can it be known whether that plan is of any use.

If we are to rise above the sophistries of mere speculation, or the even more dangerous assertions of speciously similar past experience, it is imperative to test our conclusions in some reality of which we ourselves are part. Otherwise we may as well return to the case study and save ourselves the trouble of trying to improve the world beyond it. And, as soon as possible after having tried the new line of action, the outcome of it must be reviewed by those whose arguments helped in its design, because we need not only to know how far it worked, but how far the experiences of others in the set are confirmed or denied by the observable outcome. It is not only that we are all interested in improving conditions in my factory; we are also interested in the processes by which we contribute to the improvement, and the review will soon touch upon our capacities to learn as much as upon the prospects of rescuing my factory. Thus a recursive cycle will be started, and will continue, not only until the real-time outcomes of the trial decisions hammered out in the conclave match our expectations, but also until the participating managers begin to disclose freely to each other the changes they feel within themselves. (It may be noted that mutual learning of this kind, between equals, is recorded by Solomon in

Proverbs, ch. 27, v. 17: 'Iron sharpeneth iron; so a man sharpeneth the countenance of his friend'.)

Action learning and self-development

Action learning is a means of extending *reference to* into *mastery over* and thus inexplicable in a chapter like this which cannot be more than *reference to* — even if reference to how to go beyond reference to. In practice, the extension is achieved by helping others master themselves in the hope of mastering their world, and being reciprocally helped in the same way. All are involved in their own separate tasks, to do something worthwhile about a serious threat or a tempting opportunity, but all become involved in the parallel progress of the others. Each informs himself about the problems and opportunities of his colleagues, and concentrates on the reports given by their owners about their progress; they try to attribute any differences arising between themselves to such influences as imperfect information from the owner, lack of attentiveness in a colleague, lack of realism in another, and so forth. Slowly it will emerge that some differences between members of the 'set' are more profound than can be explained by communication variables alone, such as readiness to listen, to question and to offer help; differing mental schemata begin to emerge, so that five different persons, all sober, honest and intelligent, begin to draw quite different conclusions from what is agreed to be the same data, and to advocate divergent lines of action as a result. While small divergences can contribute to variety of approach and to richness of outcome, beyond a certain tolerance they may need to be classed as fantasy; it then is up to other members of the set to help in correcting them and so to learn a little about themselves as well. We see that there are three distinct steps in these processes of mutual aid and self-development:

(a)   to help each manager observe more keenly his present condition, by obliging him to explain it to his colleagues, and to evaluate his proposed course of action more realistically, by obliging him to list for them his goals, the obstructions that bar those goals and the means by which he intends to remove those obstructions. In the real worlds in which these exchanges occur, there will be seen among these goals, these obstructions and these means, like the jokers in a pack of cards, much contaminating fantasy which all will conspire to dispel;

(b)   to help each manager employ the more realistic view of his present condition gained from his keener and more realistic observation, by an improved assessment of the uncertainties of the condition he is trying to change in his own favour; the objects of attention throughout the set are no longer mainly the individual self-deceptions of predisposing mental schemata, but the confusions entangled with them by the inscrutability of the real world around. Faced with conditions that none has faced before, how does any manager make an intelligent guess as to his next move, or choose the most useful question to alleviate his ignorance? If, in stage (a) above, several courses of action were suggested (not all by the manager who would have to settle which) how are their relative utilities to be estimated? As these are evaluated in turn, the discussion will constantly bring home to him the methods and standards he uses to make up his mind, and in a way that brings order where all before was intuitive; above everything, he will be obliged to estimate the risks he is ready to accept, and so disclose his sense of values.   To have his mental apparatus dismantled, cleaned and restored in this way by sympathetic colleagues, who then proceed to offer a more reliable list of instructions as to its use, is a second reward of action learning in a small set;

(c)   to help each manager review the outcome of the action taken after stage (b) above. In the first two stages, of de-fantasising the manager's perception and of sharpening his guesswork, the dialogue has largely been with other managers, with his comrades in adversity, even if each was but an hour before in contest with a hard and unyielding world to which he will shortly return. But, after the second stage, the manager must bring his clearer vision and his stricter logic to bear upon reality, which will soon make known how far he is yet at variance with it. The level of surprise with which the response of reality is greeted measures the shortcomings of all, the other managers no less than he who took the action. For reality cannot be condemned for having unrealistic perceptions of itself, as can other managers, howsoever successful their past record. Thus, the post-mortems on the operations successively carried out by each manager after the first two stages above provide, with rigorous austerity, the further spring-cleaning of the imaginations. Action learning alone can offer this; the case study, for example, allows of no post operational review, since there is no operation, and the outcome of the computer game is determined, not by some indifferent reality, but by a programme fabricated by some interested expert aiming to please those with seminars to sell.

Programmed and unprogrammed; answers and questions

By now it should be clear that action learning is what is needed to extend *reference to* into *mastery over*, at least in terms of purely managerial resources, since real achievement will also call for real resources such as manpower and machinery. Since it is the pathway out of kennenship into könnenship that I see as the range of action learning, it is often said that kennenship is unnecessary within its programmes. Insofar as this implies that no time is set aside in advance to 'teach' any predetermined syllabus of *reference to*, this may be true. But, as soon as the problems of any particular manager are taken up by his set, he will be asked all kinds of questions that had never occurred to him, some of which will be in fields that are not familiar. He is therefore bound to need a richer kennenship to explore the field he is already in. But — and it is the heart of the argument — he knows in what quarters to look for it, and he will soon know whether he is getting what he needs. This is a very different entry to the slabs of print from being crushed under an avalanche of lectures. The difference is cardinal to action learning which is concerned to help managers pose the proper questions; it is then for the answers to be traced in the records. Whereas kennenship will provide the answers to the questions that have been specifically put, it is the quest for könnenship, or action learning, that will help to identify what are the most discriminating questions to be raised. Activities found to obey the laws of orderly search may be called 'programmed' and lead to the answering of known questions; activities that are still largely the exploration of ignorance, risk and confusion, out of which known questions will emerge, may be called 'unprogrammed'. They are essentially the probings towards discovery.

This distinction, between search and instruction, question and answer, reference to and mastery over, kennenship and könnenship, suggests the essence of creativity. It should help to exorcise the false dichotomy between art and science, and the solecism encouraged thereby: that scientists are logical, working only in accordance with rules available to all (if too difficult to be grasped by all), that they depend entirely upon observation and measurement, and so forth; that they are slaves to self-imposed disciplines, rigid, formal and dispassionate in their work never displaying their feelings in their cult of themselves as calculating machines programmed for years in advance . . . and that artists, on the contrary, are extravagantly undisciplined, constantly demented by the inspiration of wayward muses with questionable moral standards, liable on the instant to be carried away by the most irrelevant remark, but able, from time to time and as the agent of some celestial power, to produce great works of art as timeless memorials to their short stay among the rest of us. This is hardly the place to go into the popular misconception of art *v* science, whether as subjectivity *v* objectivity, passion *v* austerity, imagination *v* logic, romance *v* research, poetry *v* calculation, and a score of other contrasts. What is intended by them all is the dichotomy between behaviour that is programmed and that which is not. Programmed knowledge, for example, must already be classified and on the record, brought down from the past — even if as late as yesterday evening. It is just as much to be found in the history of music or painting or drama as in that of chemistry, physics or philosophy, and has led no less firmly to the consolidation of practice in the arts than in the sciences. Indeed, tradition in the arts, following in father's footsteps, has been immeasurably more powerful than it has in science; so much is this the case that, when some painter today is as ingenious as he is hard up, the quickest way for him to come into some money is to copy some master of the past (follow precisely the canonical programme) and release upon the world what is called by the Director of Public Prosecutions a cunning forgery. Until about the time of Galileo the same could be inferred in science, for all questions were then settled by reference to the writings of Aristotle; if his programme did not contain, for example, a reference to sunspots then there could be no spots upon the sun.

But when, under the influence of forces both historically and culturally determined, the consolidated practices, whether in art or in science, are no longer equal to the calls of the day, the existing stocks of programmed knowledge are insufficient. Those who, in a changing world, continue to live as if they were (as has Britain for half a century) soon find themselves in trouble; new values, new problems, new opportunities, new alliances, new discoveries reinforce the failure of programmed knowledge and the insufficiency of behaviour based on it. But the results of following different codes lie in the future and cannot be foreseen; yet we must decide now, in our ignorance and confusion, about what will still be uncertain tomorrow. It is our only alternative to idolising the past by adhering to yesterday's programmes; we must discover new responses to change, so that we do not remain expert in yesterday's business. In a rapidly changing world, when the rate of new discovery must also be rapid, we are obliged to enquire into the nature of creativity, or the fruitful departure from the programmes of the past that may help us adapt to the demands of the future. What, in simpler terms, are the questions most likely to lead to those fruitful departures and how are they most readily stimulated? To explore this is to enter into the very secrets of Nature.

We may examine the conditions of creativity by asking, for example, how Isaac Newton discovered the law of gravitation. Before his time many people must have noticed that the moon stays with the earth, even if it seems to wander most erratically about the sky; those who lived in temperate climates must also have observed that apples fall to the ground. What Newton suggested was that the force pulling the apple downwards was essentially the same as that which obliged the moon to hug the earth in its monthly cycle. He posed a question where no question had been posed before, and he posed it of existing pro-grammed knowledge. (It is incidental that some of that programmed knowledge was inaccurate, so that it returned to him a disappointingly inappropriate reply.) It is this willingness, surging up in a bout of curiosity — or even fear — to address new questions to the familiar patterns, or to read the existing slabs under a new light, that is the core of creative behaviour. The loathing of unconvention, the deriding of the *enfant terrible*, the adulation of the conformist and the schooling for acceptability that mark each ageing culture are but its insistence upon the canonical programmes, which it has lost the ability to question for new arrangements within themselves. The dichotomy is not between art and science (were they not, only yesterday, spoken of as 'The Two Vultures'?), but between programme-worship and programme-interrogation. An ancient illustration is to be found, long before Newton, in the story of David and Goliath; the Israelite soldiers, idolising their past glories, could see no way of dealing with the giant except by finding a bigger man to fight in heavier armour. When David, the boy, offered to take him on, they still insisted that he be dressed in the smallest suit of it to be found in their camp, since they had grown unable to ask the fresh question: 'How do we dispose of Goliath, not necessarily by insisting upon the rules and programmes of the past?' It was David, untrammelled by any worship of tradition, who was able to answer this — but only because he was first free to pose it. His mind, in other words, was *free* to search his own experience; it was not constrained by programme-worship useless-ly to run to and fro in useless channels. He shows us today the keys of creativity.

The difference, which I personally have observed among the artists, engineers, politicians and scientists of twenty different nations, between those who worship the programmes handed down to them and those disposed, from time to time, to challenge and extend those programmes, is so clear and so sharp that its origins must be traceable in some physical characteristic of the human frame. I cannot believe that the animosity and detraction that has saluted my efforts to get British professors of management studies to ask themselves what they imagine they are trying to do can spring from any shallow or temporary source. I was therefore encouraged when, some years ago, I read of the suggestion that the cerebral hemispheres have quite different functions; the left is concerned with detail, with logic, with sequence, or, in the terminology I have been using, with programmed knowledge and its manipulation, while the right makes intelligible the significance of the whole, of the pattern and of the gestalt; it is concerned with judgement, with taking in the tune as well as the sound of the individu-al note, and with seeing relationships between what may at first sight not be related — like the apple and the moon before Newton. The communications between hemispheres may apparently be severed and the subject still survive, a being with two complete half-brains. If this is so, may it not be that others who survive without having undergone such surgery are, nevertheless, grossly underusing the nerve fibres of the *corpus callosum* that link the hemispheres together? If so, we have a physical explanation of programme-worship and at the same time an explanation for the success of action learning.

For action learning is an effort to get away from the detailed security of the programme, of reference to, of kennenship and of inherited modes of thinking, into the open wilderness of the totality, of mastery over, of könnenship and of creativity for the future. It rejects the narrow sterility of local exactitude and seeks the exciting risk of foreign exploration, and, although its conjectures are often wrong, they are never barren. By going for the whole rather than for the part, by questioning the self as well as the goal, and by engaging others as well as the self, the subject is constantly obliged to move between familiar detail and the uncharted labyrinths of his total lived experience. He seems to make this trip, both ways, across the fibres of the *corpus callosum*, of which there are, in each of us, a number about the same as the population of the United States of America. It is to free this multitude of channels, by forcing upon the manager the need to explain what he thinks he is trying to do in the face of what conditions he imagines surround him, and then obliging him to review what happened when he did it, that is (at least in terms of cerebrology) the first objective of action learning. The explanation by invoking the cerebral hemispheres may be entirely modern, but action learning, if illustrated over two thousand years ago by the boy David, would also have met with approval over two thousand years ago from Aristotle himself. In his *Ethics* he expounded a form of eudemonism that held the supreme virtue to be a blend of contemplation and activity, an idea that the modern Chinese force upon their professors by having them work on the land and in the factories. While I cannot believe that the British establishment will ever permit so robust a solution to arrest the galloping decay of our economy, there is also a little evidence that our national thinking may be towards the right in more senses than one.

14 Counselling senior managers' development

Alan Mumford

Coaching and counselling provide, normally in a one-to-one setting, excellent opportunities for learning from everyday experiences. Mumford describes how he has spent time with senior managers acting as a catalyst to enable them to reflect on their experiences and hence identify their own development needs. He then acts as a neutral third party when the manager discusses these needs with his immediate boss.

Clearly Mumford sees the main purpose of such counselling as an aid to self-diagnosis. No doubt it can also help by becoming part of the development process itself.

The chapter discusses a number of issues related to the role of the self-development counsellor, confidentiality, and problems of appraisal.

In this chapter I shall be looking at a particular process for identifying the development needs of senior managers, which occurred in a particular organisation for particular reasons. In order to give readers the best opportunity to assess the validity of the process for the circumstances which might apply in their own organisation, I shall first give some reasons why the process of identifying development needs for senior managers is in general terms difficult. I shall then look at the reasons why this particular process was chosen in this case, before going on to describe the details of the process.

The problem of identifying needs

There are three main methods of identifying manager development needs:

A general analysis, usually through some form of questionnaire, conducted across a group of managers. The questionnaire may often be based on a list of required skills.

Individual discussion of needs between boss and subordinate often conducted as part of an appraisal session.

Self-analysis by a manager, sometimes as part of the appraisal process, sometimes as a self-initiated process perhaps based on questions derived from a book or course.

In many large organisations these methods of assessing needs are, in practice, subordinate to what have become 'norms' for manager development. It may have become standard practice for a manager to attend an internal course on interviewing skills or, at a more senior level, to attend a course at the London Business School or Harvard.

The problems involved tend to be similar whatever level of manager is being considered. The general analysis of needs is by definition good at finding those needs which are common to large groups of managers; it is however relatively prescriptive and less good at helping individual managers in unique situations. Discussions between a boss and his subordinate manager which ought, in principle, to provide exactly the detailed discussion of particular circumstances not offered by the first method, in practice are often not very effective. Neither party may be committed to either the time or the depth of discussion; this approach seems often to produce an unacknowledged conspiracy to avoid discussing the real issues. Self-analysis of needs is still a relatively rare phenomenon and produces problems of knowing how to start and with whom to share the information.

The contribution made by general analyses of training needs inevitably becomes less as the needs of more senior managers are considered; the number of jobs which have essentially similar accountabilities and job content becomes very small. Equally, boss/subordinate discussions become more inhibited. In many organisations there is a degree of reluctance to accept that managers in the two or three top levels actually have development needs. These are the levels of management occupied by people who see themselves, and are seen by others, as 'having arrived'. It is therefore, I believe, quite normal for managers at this level to have no real commitment to any process for identifying possible development needs. Appraisal quite often is not carried out in these most senior levels, and therefore does not provide even in principle a route to the successful identification of development needs through perceived shortfalls in performance. (Appraisal is not, in practice, a very good route for this purpose anyway, but it is often the only one available.)

If it was true that senior managers did not in fact have significant development needs, either for their current jobs or for future promotion, the absence of any process to identify needs would clearly not be a cause for concern. Of course in fact senior managers are at least as subject as other managers to problems of changing job content, of new demands for different or improved managerial skills, of meeting situations which require an enhancement of those skills which secured them promotion. All these factors suggest that it cannot be accepted that people in the most senior positions in an organisation have in fact been developed to the limit of their capacity to act effectively as managers.

It might seem therefore in many organisations that an impasse has been reached; a man from Mars might recognise that senior managers have development needs while tradition, status and general organisational culture inhibit the identification of such needs. There are a number of different ways in which this impasse might in principle be overcome in many organisations. In the particular case I am describing, I believe the main factor to have been the degree of 'felt hurt' at the top of the organisation. The number of feasible candidates for the most senior jobs in the business seemed to be diminishing at a time when the number of jobs which needed to be filled showed no signs of diminishing and indeed the longer term business plans identified growth and therefore the need for more top level managers. The organisation had put a great deal of effort into securing effective placement decisions, but now found itself with fewer choices about placement. It also recognised that the development of the most senior managers had occurred largely as a result of movement and exposure to new experiences; there had been, at senior level, very few formal inputs in the sense of internal management training or external management education, and there was little planned use of major formative experience on committees, working parties or similar events. The organisation therefore reached a stage at which it questioned whether more could and should be done to ensure that top levels of management were equipped both to meet the existing needs of their jobs and were also in appropriate cases developed for the possibility of more senior roles.

Choosing a process for identifying needs

When I reviewed the situation on joining the organisation, it seemed to me that no general analysis of development needs would be relevant for the group of forty or so senior executives with whom I was concerned. Nor did it seem to me that an approach through appraisal would be likely to be successful; although unusually for many organisations appraisal was in fact carried out from the chief executive downwards, identification of, and action on development needs was not one of the results of the existing appraisal scheme. An attempt to improve the quality of the development need section of appraisal would, it seemed to me, inevitably raise major questions about the appraisal process itself, questions which I felt would get in the way of the need to improve manager development. The problems of the multi-purpose nature of appraisal are well known and do not need to be repeated here, so although I would not necessarily write off appraisal as a suitable route in all organisations, I felt it inappropriate in the particular circumstances. An alternative route which has been used in other organisations is to take development as a separate issue from appraisal, and design forms and processes which require managers to discuss strengths, weaknesses and development needs with their subordinates. I rejected this option because it seemed to me that asking managers who had no substantial experience of management development to take the subject more seriously, for example by requiring them to have a discussion with their subordinates, was unlikely to be productive. Their lack of experience in the intimacy of that kind of discussion, and lack of knowledge of the kind of development needs which might arise or the kind of solutions which could be identified, would not give an effective base for the discussion.

Another possibility was to undertake a kind of individual training need analysis in which, as adviser and expert, I would go round and interview a number of managers in order to identify what their needs were, against a check list of required management skills.

Experience with this kind of approach however suggested to me that the list of skills tends to inhibit thought about individual situations and needs; it helps with generalisations, but is less appropriate where generalisation is not an objective.

I finally decided to design a process in which I took a much stronger role as catalyst helping individual managers to identify their own needs, but a process which pushed the responsibility back towards the manager and his boss after the initial catalytic action in helping the manager to look at his own development needs.

The process in question was used for a small group of very senior people. If the chief executive is described as level one and his subordinates as level two, then the client group was largely executives at levels three and four. The group for whom the process was potentially appropriate was around thirty. One of the issues involved in this kind of intervention is obviously that it is time consuming for all the parties. The case for accepting the relative luxury involved in the use of the adviser's time now was simply that the seniority of those involved made the question of cost acceptable.

Selection of participants

One of the first issues, once the process had been described and accepted by top management, was deciding which managers should be given the opportunity of taking part first. The potential group could have been chosen from the most senior or the slightly less senior, from those thought most suitable for future promotion or those most recently appointed to their current job, or from those most at risk because of existing questions about their managerial effectiveness. The question of selection was, of course, particularly important since the early participants would, in effect, determine both the future of the particular process as a means of identifying manager development and also conceivably the future of the relatively new adviser in the business. The first dozen or so participants were in the end chosen on a broad mix of status, of perceived promotion possibility and of managers about whom there were some questions in terms of performance.

Characteristics of the process

The two essential characteristics of the process are that a manager is asked to identify his own development needs and that he is taken through that process of self-identification by an adviser in a private discussion. Self-identification of needs is an absolute prerequisite for any form of self-development. Too often, even if managers are asked to look at their own strengths and weaknesses and therefore to identify their development needs, the subsequent discussion between themselves and their boss is made ineffective by defensiveness on the part of the manager and superficiality on the part of both manager and boss. The process in which a manager is asked to look more seriously and more deeply at himself, his own performance and his own needs should be more productive but of course it can be risky.

Instead of leaving the manager on his own to think about his needs, or alternatively giving him some kind of questionnaire on which he could mark his perceptions of his skills and requirements for his job, the adviser chose a process which combined a degree of informality with a basic form of structure. Instead of imposing on the manager a set questionnaire which would in effect determine the kind of answers he could give, the basis for the discussion was to provide the manager in advance with a series of headings (given later in this chapter) which would be discussed but then take him over the ground with only a light guiding hand so that the manager could talk about those things which were important to him and look at those aspects of his current and future needs which were significant to him.

The role of the adviser in this situation, once having proposed and secured agreement for the whole process, was to provide an effective stimulus in discussion with each individual manager so that the manager could look at himself, his environment and his needs. The adviser chose to act as stimulus and listener, to play down any appearance of being highly analytical and to avoid any temptation to judge the manager. The adviser can ask searching questions, but can do so without the appearance of storing information for judgements on effectiveness, promotion or salary – those aspects which tend to be perceived as the major concern of the boss. As will be seen when I describe the later stages of the process, his role changed in the later stages of discussion towards that of interpreter and identifier of solutions.

Stages in the process

The policy for choosing individual participants has been mentioned above. One of the practical problems which arose was inevitable in a managerial hierarchy. Grandfather A could wish that grandson C should participate in the process, but father B, while not necessarily disagreeing with the choice, might feel put out that the decision had been made by grandfather A. Nor does selection by even the most important executive in an organisation mean that the manager selected will necessarily want to participate. Given the nature of the process involved, it is important that potential participants are given the right to say whether they want to take part or not. In practice so far only two potential participants have declined the opportunity to take part out of a total group now of about twenty-five.

Acceptance of the invitation of course depends in part on the way in which the invitation has been tendered, which means the kind of briefing given to the individual on what the purpose of the exercise is, what he can expect from it, and what safeguards will operate. In an attempt to emphasise the relatively informal and unthreatening nature of the discussion, early briefing was done by the manager's direct boss, usually orally. Experience showed that this was not done very well, so on later occasions a written note was sent by the adviser to the manager after the initial approach made by the manager's boss. The note explained why the process had been set up and gave some illustrations of the kind of things which had been identified through such discussions. The note also gave assurances on the nature of the confidentiality involved in the first discussion, a point outlined in more detail below.

Discussions between the manager and the adviser took place in nearly all cases in the manager's office, partly because of the extra psychological comfort involved for the manager and partly because the manager in his own office seems to talk more fluently about concrete current experiences; he is also able to refer to documents. The discussion was based on general headings rather than on a long list of specific questions as follows:

> past experience
> content of current job
> skills and knowledge required for current job
> own perception of strengths and areas for improvement
> current development needs
> career interests
> future development needs
> possible solutions to the needs

Managers were advised through the written note that these were the headings that would be used and in some cases, but not in many, they prepared themselves with their own notes for the discussion. Discussions varied in length but averaged around 2 hours. The shortest was 1¼ hours and the longest 4 hours.

Confidentiality was perhaps one of the most crucial issues, both in originally agreeing the purpose of the process and in carrying it out with individuals. Managers may have perceptions about themselves, about their colleagues, about their boss, which could be significant in identifying and determining their development needs, but which they would not necessarily wish to discuss with their boss or wish to be passed on to a wider circle within the organisation. In order to give the manager full opportunity to discuss these intimate and dangerous topics, it was agreed as part of the process that what he said to the adviser would be treated as confidential. The specific assurance was that nothing would be passed on to anyone else either in written or in oral form which had not been agreed by the manager. The main reassurance on confidentiality was represented by the fact that notes on the discussion written by the adviser were cleared by the manager and were appropriately amended by him before they went to his boss. The adviser also said, and hoped to be believed, that he gave no oral comments which might be harmful to the individual. In nearly every case, something has been said by the manager which he does not want passed on.

The report on the discussion used the headings given above. The adviser could make his own judgements on which parts of the discussion to expurgate on the grounds of either confidentiality or usefulness. The only additional comments made in the notes which would not necessarily have arisen directly in the discussion would normally be under the heading of 'Possible Solutions'. Some of these might have been discussed between the adviser and the manager but often the adviser would have developed potential solutions as a result of further reflection and review after the discussion.

Full notes were sent to the manager for his comment and if necessary, amendment. He was not asked to commit himself at this stage to the solutions but merely to accept that these would be relevant for discussion with his boss presuming agreement was reached on the earlier points in the report.

Discussion between the manager and his boss

The report was then sent, after the manager's approval, to his boss with the suggestion that he would meet his subordinate to discuss it. At this stage the adviser would emphasise that his own presence at the discussion was optional. In practice in all cases except some overseas based managers, the adviser has been present. The overt reasons for this are that often the manager and his boss want to discuss the meaning of some aspect of the note, and particularly that they want to discuss some of the solutions with the man they often regard as 'expert' in the nature and content of solutions suggested. In addition there is often a recognition of the fact that presence of a third party believed to be potentially helpful by both boss and manager, can be useful in tackling some of the difficult issues which can arise during a discussion. The boss is of course committed to the discussion and not to acceptance of the notes as they stand; he may feel that his subordinate has additional strength or additional requirements for improvement, or may feel a career ambition is entirely misplaced. Sometimes the notes bring out issues of relationships between subordinate and boss where the presence of an interpreter can help them understand each other better. The presence of the adviser, while justified by these kind of considerations, is of course an intervention in the normal relationship between the boss and his subordinate. On the most basic level it was often necessary at least on the first occasion of a boss meeting one of his subordinates, to make sure that it was understood that this was a meeting between the boss and his subordinate and a meeting run by the boss and not a meeting called by and run by the adviser.

At the end of the meeting the adviser would offer to record any actions which have been agreed, some of which might well lie with the boss, some with the manager, and some with the adviser himself. Strictly speaking of course, either boss or manager ought to accept the commitment involved in recording actions, but in practice it is probably more helpful for the adviser to take the responsibility of recording, so long as he emphasises the responsibility for action rests with the boss and the manager rather than with himself.

The adviser might be involved further in informal discussions with either boss or manager about the nature of the discussion that has occurred. Rather more frequently he would be involved in developing solutions and in undertaking an informal monitoring of progress on the actual plans agreed.

Examples of development plans

The kind of development plans which can be drawn up are of course highly specific to the needs of the individual and to practicalities within the organisation. In this organisation solutions have ranged from setting up special projects for individuals, involving a real piece of work with associated learning objectives, to selection for an important committee or working party which would enhance their knowledge of some aspect of the business, to nomination for a management training or educational course. In some cases it involved more individual work on issues such as analysing use of time, analysing managerial behaviour at meetings, setting targets for improved relationship between boss and subordinate. The kind of individual development activities which can be undertaken are now very well known from the literature. The particular feature of the process described here is its concentration on identifying specific activities which will help specific individuals rather than trying to push everybody through the same kind of experience.

Some issues arising from the process

The third man

Some of the reasons for the involvement of the third man, the adviser, have been identified earlier. In addition to those reasons it seems to me that the role of the third party is particularly significant in helping a manager to identify his own needs at a more than superficial level. Few managers have really been asked to assess themselves seriously, and to be asked to do so by their direct line boss can cause anxiety and defensiveness. To undertake self-analysis with a disinterested adviser, seen really as an outsider in many respects, is a much less risky way of starting the self-analysis. A manager can experiment with the degree of frankness he is prepared to use in describing himself, and almost certainly is able to be more adventurous in talking to a third party when he knows that if he goes too far, he can in practice, effectively recall the words which he subsequently wishes he had not said.

The third man can also be used as a sympathetic listener, something which many managers feel the need of. He can be used for those who wish to do so, as a sort of personal consultant on issues which the manager does not feel able to discuss with his boss or with his colleagues. He can also be used as a way of testing out possibilities for the future. Finally he can be given messages in confidence which the manager hopes will be used to affect the environment in which he lives. The manager, for example, may not wish to tell his boss directly that he has been working for him long enough, but may feel able to indicate to a third man both the fact and the reasons for it and expect the third man to make appropriate use of the information given in confidence.

Can a manager identify his own needs?

The risk of the broad headings which were used in these discussions is that managers who are after all not very used to analysing themselves in detail, will remain at a level of relative superficiality in assessing themselves and their own needs. The case for the involvement of a third party is of course precisely that the manager might otherwise be superficial. Even with the presence of a third man however, it could be argued that these broad headings give insufficient opportunity to assess in depth what the manager really needs. In practice this depends on the kind of subsidiary questions which the adviser asks in the course of discussion and particularly his ability to identify things the manager has not said about his past experiences or about the current issues arising in his job which might indicate gaps in either experience or skill. In principle I would go so far as to say that only those needs which a manager can identify himself are really likely to be acted on by him. Only those needs will lead to commitment by him to undertake appropriate action to meet the needs. A more sophisticated analysis, however carefully contrived, which was in effect pushed on the manager, would not cause him to have commitment and would therefore not lead to useful actions.

Adviser credibility

Clearly one of the major issues is the credibility of the adviser seen both in prospect before these kinds of discussions occur and after they have occurred. This is of course particularly important given the level of seniority of the managers involved in the particular exercise described here; age, past experience, status and the culture of the organisation all contribute to credibility. In the end credibility is achieved and sustained through the quality of the discussion which the adviser has with managers and with the contribution he makes to the subsequent discussion between manager and boss.

A relationship to appraisal

An attempt to build development needs and solutions on current and future performance requirements inevitably brings out issues of what the current level of performance is. It is necessary to distinguish this process from that of appraisal if appraisal is a current activity between the boss and subordinate. The most desirable situation is for the development discussion to occur after the appraisal discussion, since then there need be no clash of information arising from the two discussions and no confusion about what the adviser is really about. However, in practice it is not always feasible to postpone the development discussion until after appraisal since this might mean waiting too long. In that case it is extremely important to establish with the manager's boss at least whether there are any major reservations about the manager's performance which could lead to difficulties if raised through the development discussion. For example, the sections on strengths and areas for improvement have a considerable resemblance to the kind of issues which would normally be raised in appraisal. The boss must be helped to see that such issues can and ought to come through the development discussion and be prepared to accept that he will undertake some discussion of them rather than being surprised that they should come up and being made uncomfortable that they should have done so through this particular route. In my experience the relationship between this process and appraisal or other methods of assessing performance has been the least tidy and on one or two occasions the most explosive feature of the whole process.

Uncomfortable issues

In addition to the problems of the assessing of performance I just mentioned, other uncomfortable issues may arise when, for example, a manager says that he is not getting sufficient development experience from his current job or identifies a career path for himself which is not felt to be feasible or appropriate, or indicates that he is not interested in a potential promotion.

These can be uncomfortable areas for those bosses who would prefer to ignore such issues. One or two senior executives have, in my experience, become disturbed at the prospects of, as they put it, one of their people being stirred up as a result of this discussion. It is best for the adviser to face and to articulate the fact that some uncomfortable issues will arise and either secure acceptance that a boss is prepared to face such uncomfortable issues or, alternatively, that he would prefer that the discussion should not go ahead. Many bosses presume that if no discussion takes place with a manager whose career ambitions exceed the organisation's view of his potential, somehow the manager will remain undisturbed and relatively happy. While an adviser may feel that such a view is unrealistic and unhelpful, he should not in fact undertake this kind of process without the agreement of the line boss that he is prepared to face this kind of issue. It is not in my view right for the adviser to impose his own values of what the organisation should be saying to the individual and the individual to the organisation.

Who is offering – who is risking?

It is important to notice that a number of people are making a different kind of offer in relation to manager development through this process. The difference in the role offer made by the adviser in this process compared with that offered by many management development advisers is no doubt clear. It should also be clear that both boss and manager are offering more of themselves to each other in terms of revealing their real thoughts. More is being offered to the manager in terms of the possibility of further development and he is offering more of himself to the possibilities of development. Equally, however, each of these offers contains risks for those making the offer. Risks to the adviser include rejection, or being actually unable to be helpful, or the possibility that greater visibility will lead to a decision not to allow him to undertake such sensitive work. The risks to the manager himself are also fairly clear; in revealing more of himself he is likely to be saying that he is not the perfectly equipped fully rounded well-balanced manager which organisational mythology may feel he ought to claim to be. In recognising his own needs he may be causing the organisation to recognise that he is not effective enough for his current job or for some future promotion that he might otherwise have secured in greater ignorance. The risk for the boss is that he is faced with the need to have a more thorough going discussion with his subordinate on sensitive issues which may reveal the lack of confidence on his own part in handling such a discussion. In addition he faces the risk of meeting requests for help or guarantees of future career growth which he is unwilling to make but which he cannot now avoid committing himself on.

A contingency or situational approach

I hope that both my early description of the factors which led to the choice of this particular approach, and my later description of some of the problems which have to be faced, together show the circumstances in which this relatively high risk approach to self-development may be appropriate. It is relatively unusual because of the seniority of those involved, and because of the approach to self-identification of needs through a dialogue with a catalyst. The situation largely determined the method; I did not have a predetermined method I wanted to apply to the situation.

15 Learning conversations

Sheila Harri-Augstein and Laurie F. Thomas

Self-development involves the construction of personally relevant and viable meaning – the integration of the knower and the known. To do this I need to become a self-organised learner – one who 'expects to go on learning, to make independent judgements and to question'. I can be helped to become a self-organised learner through a number of techniques which enable me to develop the ability to converse with myself about the processes of learning. Learning to learn can be facilitated by such learning conversations.

The chapter describes a number of learning conversation techniques, and then looks at a number of implications for trainers. In particular, the trainer must first learn to view and experience himself or herself as a self-organised learner.

The authors also suggest that self-development is not just a 'flavour of the month', but that in 'the crisis-ridden conditions which prevail in contemporary industry', learning to learn becomes an 'important selective factor in the struggle for personal and industrial survival' – a point also made by Reg Revans in Chapter 13.

Self-development and self-organisation

The capacity to learn from experience and to take control of the direction, quality and content of one's learning is central to making the best of management opportunities. The skilled manager learns to construe a wide variety of events, people and technical systems in ways that enable the participating individuals to achieve their organisationally defined purposes more economically and effectively. In our view this is best achieved by encouraging and enabling managers to become more aware of themselves as learners. Insight into personal learning processes experienced at work is a prerequisite not only for self-development but also for enabling others to develop their competence. The concern then becomes that of developing means for becoming more aware of personal learning processes within the context of the socio-technical environment of management. Self-development in management implies learning with others and this depends on the practice of techniques which not only facilitate self-awareness but also enable the exchange and effective negotiation of personal meaning systems amongst groups, which work more or less permanently together within a given set of purposes, determined by the institution's shorter and longer term goals.

This chapter introduces a number of awareness-raising techniques and content-free conversational heuristics which have been developed at the Centre for the Study of Human Learning in the last ten years. In a number of action-based projects, managers in a wide variety of institutional settings and pursuing diverse purposes, have applied these conversational techniques to explore, review and develop their competence. Case studies illustrate how individual managers, a management team, and a company as a whole can learn to change in directions which may be mutually advantageous.

In educational and industrial settings, self-organisation is with us. Let us accept and use it. Institutions have to adapt to self-organised learners and towards the end of this chapter the implications of this challenge for the dynamic and creative growth of an organisation will be discussed. The examples also serve to illustrate the theoretical and practical implications of the dynamics of 'Learning Conversations'.

The final part of the chapter outlines a conversational theory and associated heuristics which we have developed for enabling personal growth in men and women at work. The implications of this approach for trainers is discussed within this context.

Self-organisation and the learning conversation

If we are to encourage people to learn from experience, to think about their needs and purposes, to plan their strategies, to evaluate their success, and to review, revise and improve their methods of learning, then inevitably we are emphasising self-organisation. Self-organised learners expect to go on learning, to make independent judgements and to question. This makes them potentially more useful. The company or institution can effectively harness the rich variety of available experience so that it itself becomes enriched and capable of dynamic change. Everyone has to learn to adapt and develop. This depends on the recruitment of procedures which facilitate personal growth.

In our view an emphasis on 'process' rather than 'product' enables the development of a 'metalanguage' which is itself content-free and which once acquired enables individuals, often for the first time, to take control of the ways they learn from experience. In the crisis-ridden conditions which prevail in contemporary industry, where 'the products' of today can easily become the chains restricting tomorrow's growth, the development of a language which enables a way of thinking about personal learning processes becomes an important selective factor in the struggle for personal and industrial survival.

How can this be achieved?

First, let us examine briefly what learning is, and what we mean by the process of becoming self-organised.

Learning is not a fact that can be directly observed. It must be inferred, either from behaviour or experience: preferably it is inferred participatively from both. The observer of behaviour sees things which the learner often cannot, but only the learner has access to his or her own experience. In the 1960s the psychology of learning became obsessed with measurement in terms of *behavioural objectives*. Learning in this sense is measured in terms of how well the *trainer* achieves *his* objectives. 'Training' is really what is measured by the trainer when he reviews the learner's behaviour in terms of how well it demonstrates changes which 'the trainer' was trying to achieve. Let us call this learning *Type T*. Now, if we consult self-organised learners, our effective managers, they would argue that learning was something only they, as learners, could assess. Expressed in terms of experience or behaviour they would believe themselves to be successful learners if they had learned something which they themselves valued. This might be very different from what the expert or their boss intended! Let us call this learning *Type L*. Self-organised learners, who have learnt how to develop in their own terms (Type L) may or may not do well in their jobs. It depends on the extent to which their purposes and strategies include or overlap with those of others with whom they work. What the self-organised learner can do is learn from his or her experience, and use these methods to facilitate others to learn. It is this view of learning which led the authors to define it as 'the construction and exchange of personally relevant and viable meanings'. This gives emphasis to both behaviour (viability) and experience (personally significant meanings) in the person's own terms (Type L).

Now we approach the core issue. How can people be enabled to think, feel and act more effectively, and thus live more fully? How can people learn-to-learn?

Listening, discussion, consultation, problem-solving, decision-making, reading and writing reports, are some managerial skills that can be recruited for the development of greater self-organisation in learning. *Learning-to-learn consists in an ability to converse with oneself about the processes of learning*; to observe, search, analyse, formulate, review, judge, decide and act on the basis of personal encounters. This involves

as much feeling as thought. Unaided, most of us are not able to generate effective learning conversations with ourselves. Many develop an
'unwillingness to learn' that owes little to their potential capacity. It
may be withdrawal from an intolerable situation or even boredom at
having done the same job for a long time.

Our studies show that people of all ages can be encouraged to break
existing habits which have become self-validating and inhibiting to
personal growth. A variety of awareness-raising techniques have been
developed to negotiate this process of learning-to-learn in each area of
learning skill. This chapter focuses on *conversational* 'repertory grid'
and 'structure of meaning' procedures which are specifically designed
to elicit, display and reflect upon personal systems of meaning. These
have been used to extend a person's range of meaning and to exchange
more effectively their meanings with others.

The learning conversation is designed to assist in the acquisition of
new skills as well as in achieving effective review and development of
deeply-embedded habitual skills. It is conducted as a *meta-commentary*
around a learning event. This term is used to indicate the nature of the
conversation. This is concerned primarily with the processes of learning
so that the learner can be more aware of these processes. The learning
conversation is only concerned with the content of the learning event
(e.g. decision-making, problem-solving, chairing a meeting, writing a
report) in as much as this can be used to illustrate, emphasise and
concretise the processes by which the participant learner(s) construct
their meanings. The creation of a language in which to converse about
learning processes requires much more than a dictionary of terms and
a syntax in which to string terms together into conversationally agreed
phrases. The language must arise out of the sharing of personally
meaningful experience. The focus of the learning conversation is the
reflection on process, and the repertory grid techniques and structures
of meaning procedures are used as mirrors of process, heightened
awareness enables the learner to explore skills and attitudes in a
particular area of central importance, thus achieving greater compet-
ency. The conversation is based on a systematic control, guidance and
exchange of experiences within a learning event.

It is useful to describe the learning event in terms of phrases such as:

1   Negotiating personal needs into articulated learning purposes.
2   Developing and reviewing the processes of learning in terms of
    skills, strategies and tactics.
3   Recognising, revising and improving the outcomes of the learn-
    ing processes and the criteria by which they may be evaluated.

It is important to recognise that such a 'phrases description' is concerned only with one cycle of the process at one level of event. Effective
learning almost always consists of a series of such cycles in which the

purposes become progressively more clearly articulated and the outcomes become more precise and determined and well mapped onto the purposes. Thus a meta-language dealing with learning requires a structure that acknowledges phases, cycles and the levels of a learning event.

As a learner becomes more self-organised, the learning conversation is internalised. He or she becomes his or her own mentor and tutor. Self-organised learners use a model of the process of learning to review and improve performance. They can identify needs and translate these into realistic learning purposes. They are able to plan how to go about the learning task, recognise personal limitations of skill, develop effective strategies which overcome these. They must be able to generate criteria of success which match purposes and which can be applied to the outcomes of the learning efforts. Self-organisation depends on evaluating one's own performance. Periodically, learning processes in given areas must be reviewed, to prevent a take-over of habitual mechanisms which stabilise and inhibit further development. This is difficult. External conversations can re-establish contact and this may best be aided by a trainer. The trainer can help the learner to draw a 'learning contract' and then by acting as tutor or coach, he can aid the periodic reviews of progress. This organising role of the trainer as an aid to maintaining and developing greater self-organisation in learning has enormous repercussions for the structure and organisation of industrial training departments. It is beyond the scope of this chapter to discuss these in detail, but various papers by the authors (Thomas and Harri-Augstein, 1976, 1978, 1979a) refer to the theory of 'Learning Conversations' and the impact of this on training and tutoring.

In this chapter some examples of the conversational use of awareness-raising techniques serve to illustrate that the heuristics of learning conversations can be applied to any area. It is a matter of selecting the appropriate procedures for raising awareness and review of learning processes. The conversation takes on different forms depending on the requirements of the lecturers and the content of the learning event. Within this paradigm we have explored job appraisal, selection interviews, problem-solving discussions, quality control, and a wide range of other management events as learning experiences for individuals and groups.

A   Techniques which allow self-organised learning

People operate through a system of personal meaning. The more self-organised one is, the more one acts as a personal scientist (Kelly, 1955) differentiating, categorising and theorising about the world and people in it. Personal theories (meanings) are constructed and form the basis of anticipation and action. During learning these are tested and revised in the context of ongoing experiences. Only when the same situation has the same meaning for two people will they react similarly to it. Five members of a management team working on a practical problem such as job appraisal, selection, forward planning, quality control or marketing will in all probability perceive the situation differently and draw different inferences from it. One may see it as a chance to demonstrate his competence to his superiors, one as an opportunity to explore a part of the organisation to which he normally does not have access, another may see it as a learning event, while another may well see it as a chore to be endured. The fifth may see it as part of a larger and more intractable problem.

The position, responsibilities, and past experience of each manager have led to a development of different meaning systems. Each system influences the way in which a situation is perceived, to select certain aspects and ignore others, to give more emphasis to some characteristics than others, and it determines the way in which the perceived dimensions combine into an overall meaning. The five managers not only perceive the situation differently, but also tackle the problem from five different points of view.

Using the Repertory Grid to explore changing views of management

The Repertory Grid procedures provide a basis for identifying the dimensions in a person's meaning system. They can also be used for comparison of two or more individual systems of meaning, so that groups can explore areas of agreement and disagreement. Rarely is an individual fully aware of these dimensions and they are usually inaccessible. Questionnaire and interview techniques force the respondent's answers into the inquirer's meaning system. Normal discussion often results in one or more participants taking over the structure or content with the result that most participants' views remain hidden.

The repertory grid is a two-dimensional matrix in which events (elements) representing a given (chosen) universe are interlaced with abstractions (constructs). These constructs are bipolar dimensions along which events can be placed according to the similarities and differences in a person's frame of reference. An individual's repertoire of constructs cluster into patterns which underlie his or her meaning system (Thomas and Harri-Augstein, 1977).

The content of the grid is determined during the elicitation conversation. It will be as significant or as trivial as the quality of the interaction between elicitor and subject. Both must fully participate in the conversational process (Thomas, 1978). This aspect is often under-emphasised. Before any content is entered into the grid, the purpose of the exercise must be negotiated. In this context the grid should be seen as contributing to the solution of a learning problem experienced by the subject. The nature of the problem is explored and an understanding of it shared. This understanding forms the basis of guiding, controlling and selecting the 'elements' and 'constructs' in a grid conversation.

Studies carried out at the Centre illustrate the range of management topics that can be explored.

1   Industrial inspectors used windscreen wiper blades as elements to explore the meanings which each assigned to the acceptable/defective criteria of subjective quality assessment.

2   Wine and tea tasters and whisky blenders used their 'products' as elements to explore the meanings (verbal and non-verbal) they assigned to the qualities of each product.

3   A quality assurance manager, market researcher, production manager, research and development manager, factory manager, sales manager and training manager explored their view of quality (faults) of a well known food product.

4   Industrial trainers used 'training situations' such as 'on the job', 'lecture', 'project', 'film', 'discussion', 'demonstrations', 'case studies' as the elements in a grid to explore the assumptions they brought to the designing of a course.

5   A group of managers in the paints division of a major company used as elements 'people to be appraised' in order to explore the range of their construings and to relate these to the standard appraisal form which each was compelled to use.

6   Shop managers in a shoe company used the repertory grid to explore their views on managing a retail business.

7   The constructs obtained in example 6 were used as a starting point for further grid conversations to identify criteria for effective recruitment.

8   A wide ranging group of middle managers in an international company used 'management events' as elements for identifying their ideas of effective management.

9   Managers in a research and development pharmaceutical company used learning events to explore ways of identifying criteria for setting up a 'high creativity' environment for their research teams.

The 'appraisal grid' will be used to illustrate how the awareness-raising grid conversation is carried through. The main phases of the conversation are:

(a)   negotiating the purpose,
(b)   eliciting and agreeing the elements,
(c)   eliciting the bipolar constructs,
(d)   assigning elements to positions on the constructs.

The appraisal grid

In this study the elements are the people to be appraised.

In the following example Mr Donaldson and his subordinates are invented; but his constructs are a small sample of those most widely shared by the managers who took part in this study. Mr Donaldson has subordinates Mr Smith, Miss Jones, Mr Brown, Mrs Green, Dr Black and Ms White. To begin to elicit a repertory grid from Mr Donaldson three elements are selected (say Mr Smith, Miss Jones and Mr Brown). He is asked to consider them as people working for him. 'Now if you consider each of them as people that you know well and who work for you, which two seem most alike and which one seems most different from the other two?' Mr Donaldson thinks about this for some time and then he replies, 'Mr Smith and Miss Jones are similar and Mr Brown is different'. He is then asked what it is about these two which make them similar and he replies, 'They are poor at planning and analysing problems'.

Mr Donaldson is then asked what it is about Mr Brown that makes him different. He says, 'Oh, Brown has good planning and creative ability'. Mr Donaldson has now revealed his first bipolar construct:

Poor at planning and v Good planning and
analysing problems   creative ability

Mr Donaldson's own terminology is faithfully recorded. The repertory grid and each construct in it are taken to be samples of how Mr Donaldson thinks and feels about his subordinates *in his own terms*. He is now asked to assign the three remaining elements, Mrs Green, Dr Black and Ms White to one or other pole of the construct.

The second construct is elicited in the same way. Mrs Green, Dr Black and Ms White are used as the second triad. Mr Donaldson puts Ms White and Mrs Green together as 'followers' and calls Dr Black a 'leader'. Four more constructs are elicited and each time all the elements were assigned to one or other pole.

In its raw form (not shown) the repertory grid presents the elements in the order in which they were originally named and the constructs in the order in which they were elicted. But this is not the best form of presentation from which to abstract the full meaning of the responses. Visual comparison of the element columns in the raw grid reveals that Mr Smith and Ms White have been similarly assigned to all the constructs. Dr Black and Mr Brown have also been assigned similarly. The meaning of the grid is partly clarified by re-ordering the elements. Now visual inspection reveals that Constructs C2 and C5 contain a similar pattern of responses.

FOCUSing is a two-way sorting procedure developed at the Centre. One paper and pencil form of this method of analysis has been introduced by Margaret Neal and Peter Honey in earlier articles. The procedure is described in detail in a Centre Working Paper. A Manual Grid Sorter or a 'FOCUS' computer program are available to facilitate this analysis. The fully FOCUSED grid is presented so that the meaning contained in the responses recorded in the raw grid is made explicit.

FOCUSED							REPERTORY GRID	
STAFF APPRAISAL PROJECT								
o .... Pole 1 .... o	E6	E1	E4	E2	E3	E5	x .... Pole 2 x	
C2 Follower	o	o	o	o	x	x	Leader	C2
C5 Poor communicator	o	o	o	o	x	x	Good communicator	C5
C4 Lacks determination	o	o	o	x	x	x	Persistent	C4
C1 Poor at planning and analysing problems	o	o	x	o	x	x	Good planning and creative ability	C1
R C3 Unintelligent R	o	o	x	x	x	x	Intelligent	R C3 R
R C6 Dislikes pressure R	o	o	x	x	x	x	Accepts pressure	R C6 R
					Dr Black			
				Mr Brown				
			Miss Jones					
		Mrs Green						
	Mr Smith							
Ms White								

Figure 15.1 Mr Donaldson's FOCUSED grid

The FOCUSed grid shows that Mr Donaldson sees Dr Black and Mr Brown as intelligent creative persistent leaders, good at planning and communicating and who are well able to accept pressure. On the other hand, he sees Ms White and Mr Smith as unintelligent followers, lacking in determination, who dislike pressure, are poor at planning, analysing problems and communicating. He sees Mrs Green and Miss Jones as having some good and some bad characteristics. But the grid reveals as much about Mr Donaldson as it does about his subordinates. It shows the terms in which he thinks and feels about subordinates. (In practice a grid usually contains more than six elements and six constructs.) It shows how his different thoughts and feelings relate to each other. On the evidence of these six elements, Mr Donaldson feels that:

(a)   followers are poor communicators and leaders are good communicators;

(b)   intelligent people can accept pressure and unintelligent ones dislike it.

A series of learning conversations was conducted with Mr Donaldson and his colleagues. Each conversation started from the individual's FOCUSed grid and raised his awareness of his own construing. Figure 15.2 illustrates a talk-back heuristic for a focused grid.

The managers then went on to pool their experience by comparing and contrasting systems of constructs. Various additional 'grid procedures' were used to enable this group of managers to develop a psychologically, as well as procedurally, shared system of appraisal.

Learning conversations with the FOCUSed grid

Eliciting and focusing the grid offers unique opportunities for learning-to-learn. Used to create conversations with oneself it is both a method for achieving personally relevant changes and a paradigm of how this can be done more informally.

Seven 'grid games' are outlined as examples of extensions of this self-conversational technique.

1   *Elaboration*
     When a grid is focused clusters of elements and constructs emerge. If each cluster is split by introducing new constructs to differentiate between similar elements and new elements to split constructs the meaning represented is elaborated.

2   *Brainstorming with the grid*
     An exercise in divergent thinking is to look for elements and constructs which would form into additional clusters to those already in the grid.

3   *Superordination*
     Another approach to the focused grid is to look for unifying concepts, which adequately subsume a whole cluster of elements or constructs.

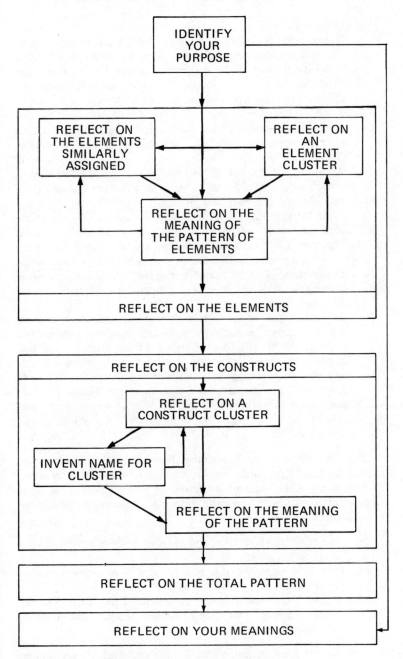

Figure 15.2   Talk-back heuristic for a FOCUSED grid

4   *Cross-grids*
If two grids A and B containing different but related sets of elements are combined, all the A elements can be placed on the B constructs and all the B elements on the A constructs. The combined grid can be focused to reveal how the 'different' elements and constructs cluster with each other.

5   *Types of construct*
A procedure similar to that in 4 can be used to explore how different *types* or *levels* of construing relate one to another.

6   *Non-verbal construing*
An interesting perceptual exercise is to collect together a set of objects that are important to one. Now one can take any three and identify the two that are most alike; but one must not name the similarity, even silently in one's head. Next, one can sort the rest of the objects on to operationally defined poles. The exercise can be continued with new triads. The usual result is a greatly heightened awareness of visual and/or tactile phenomena. This technique has proved particularly useful in training for subjective aspects of industrial inspection.

7   *The change grid*
The change grid serves to raise awareness of change in construing over time. Specifically, it is a comparison between two grids displayed on a focused version of the later one. In addition to the direct comparison of ratings on the initial elements and constructs (change in rating is shown by circling ○ changed responses), new elements and constructs are displayed. These are shown in their relationship to original elements and constructs. The change grid shows how a person's view of a topic varies over time.

This example of *Type L* learning illustrates how individuals can explore an area of personally important understandings without initially having committed himself or herself to any clear-cut ideas about what would constitute a successful outcome. This process of exploration has three aspects:

(1)   the revision, elaboration and extension of one's own personal construct system;

(2)   the close regarding of others' systems of construings to compare and contrast with one's own;

(3)   1 and 2 eventually stabilise to produce a new pattern of personal meanings. Out of this emerges a retrospective definition of needs and purposes.

Later in the chapter, procedures for the exchange of meanings are briefly outlined. The examples so far have concentrated on procedures which facilitate the process of becoming aware of one's own system of meaning, exploring it and differentiating it. This enables one to become more flexible and amenable to growth.

Details of conversational talk-back heuristics are published elsewhere (Thomas and Harri-Augstein, 1976b). Conversational heuristics have been embodied in content-free computer programs which have the capacity to encourage and control conversation as vigorously and systematically as behavioural modification techniques and other instruction-based procedures control behaviour. The FOCUS program re-orders a completed grid for feed-back purposes. The pattern of responses is highlighted. PEGASUS is an interactive program which elicits a grid and gives a feedback commentary immediately the responses are entered. ARGUS elicits several grids simultaneously from one person from different points of view. Other BASIC 'grid games' are built into programs and paper and pencil techniques.

B   Techniques for enabling groups to exchange and share meaning

Effective processes of learning Type L consist of the creative search for personally viable meanings within an informed context of established knowledge (in management appraisal forms, selection criteria, behavioural modification techniques, problem solving heuristics) and the reported experiences of others. But one has to learn that to understand a position does not necessitate finally agreeing with it and that initial disagreement need not be a barrier to understanding. The exchange of meanings can take many forms.

Learning to learn from the experience of others requires that we learn how to enter into another's reality.

Exchange grids

The 'exchange grid' procedures are methods for generating a variety of systematically controlled conversations about a mutually agreed topic, for example with ICI managers about 'appraisal' or with the people working for M & S suppliers about 'quality of underwear'.

For simplicity of explanation a two person exchange is described.

> Sid and Arthur have each separately completed grids on the topic of 'problem solving', have reflected upon their FOCUSed grids and played some grid games to make themselves more aware of and creative about the implications of their own 'problem handling' experience. They now get together. Sid describes his elements (items from his own experience) to Arthur and Arthur explains his to Sid. Each now fills in a new grid form with his own element names and construct pole descriptions. They do not

fill in the cells (the 'o's and 'x's) of the grid. They then swap grid forms and each completes the other's grid. Comparison of Sid's own grid with Arthur's attempt to enter into Sid's pattern of meaning is revealing. The PAIRS DIFFERENCE and CORE procedures can be used to facilitate the comparison (Analysis Programs).

Three forms of exchange grid are:

Understanding – misunderstanding where Sid attempts to complete Arthur's grid as he believes Arthur would have originally completed it.

Agreement – disagreement where Sid fills in Arthur's grid as he believes it should be completed.

True exchange where Sid and Arthur pool their resources to produce a new shared understanding.

These controlled encounter techniques may produce:

(a) takeover: 'I understand what you mean. I had it wrong (or at least I cannot see how what you are saying is wrong and I do not believe in myself sufficiently to work it through). Let's agree to see it your way.'

(b) giveover: 'I understand what you are saying but you cannot really mean it'; or

(c) compromise: 'I understand you and you seem to understand me, we differ, now what shall we do about it?'.

But such conversations increase the possibility of:

(d) a creative encounter: 'I understand you, you understand me, and we differ. Let us see if we can throw our meanings into the melting pot and create something new that transcends our separate positions and achieves it all'.

These techniques, particularly when they achieve a creative encounter, enable us truly to learn from another's experience. The other may even be 'the expert' or an acknowledged source of publicly recognised know-how, knowledge or expertise. The real lesson is to learn not to be (passively) instructed but to enter fully into their world, explore it, and then create a new system of personally relevant and viable meanings of one's own. If the expert source is acknowledged, and included in subsequent developments, the isolated encounters can gel into a coherent enterprise. If creative encounter is in reality a 'pirate raid', communication closes down and the rat race is perpetuated.

Implications: the achievement of self-organised change

This chapter has sketched out a paradigm for self-organised change. Examples illustrate how this can be carried out in practice. Specific conversational techniques are recruited to heighten awareness and to develop a meta-language to converse about learning processes.

We are unskilled as change agents and we are unskilled in collaborating to initiate and sustain processes of change. Preplanned instructional paradigms tend to produce efficient robots. A conversational paradigm acknowledges each participant as a semi-independent mode of control and influence. Only by fully embracing this approach can we hope to sustain a process of creative change.

Some view of the self-organised learning system is essential as a model on which conversational encounters can be based. One aspect of this relates to the change process itself. The personal system of meaning which is creating a certain level of competence is ultra-stable. Figure 15.3 shows how, when an attempt to change is made, the whole system compensates, creating strong pressures to return to a stable condition.

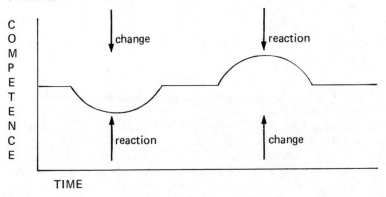

Figure 15.3

The established methods of work, and the existing systems of relationship, are familiar, and provide a cosy escape hole from the winds of change. Any sustained attempt to change is bound to go through periods of relative discouragement when lack of skill compounds with inevitable difficulties to produce almost unresistable pressures for a return to the *status quo*. Indeed, in the most insidious forms of failure, it is the apparent successful completion of the 'planned change' which enables everybody to absorb it comfortably without allowing it to disturb the fundamental habits of thoughts and work.

When a habitual skill is disrupted, performance drops and the learner becomes emotionally vulnerable. He or she requires support and discipline from inside and outside to continue down into the trough of the process of change and to enter into the positive reconstructive phase of growth. Figure 15.4 illustrates this.

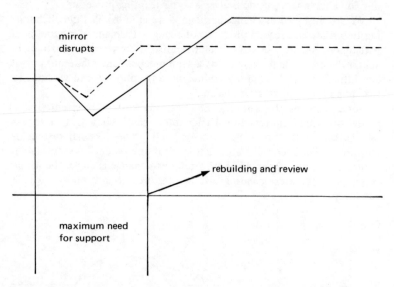

Figure 15.4   The disintegration of performance before improvement

Any system of thought, feeling and action can usefully be classified as either habitual or flexible. Change depends upon flexibility but this can be very time-consuming if it is too tentative and exploratory. Habits occupy no attention but people can easily become imprisoned by them.   A characteristic of self-organised learners and fully-functioning people is their resolution of this dilemma. It is conveniently designated the 'hour glass phenomenon'. Provisionality during the exploratory period is followed by decisiveness (Figure 15.5). This establishes new habits which cope with the new situation until a need for further review and growth is recognised.

The trainer who is interested in effective change, both in individuals and in the performance of a group working together, must, in our opinion, treat people singly or together, as self-organised learning systems. The conversational paradigm would further require that to achieve this, the trainer must first learn to view and experience himself or herself in the same way.

It is the purpose of this chapter to indicate that the effective agent of change is a self-organised learner. This capacity enables him or her to identify personally valued learning processes in others. Effective change is the product of personally valued learning.

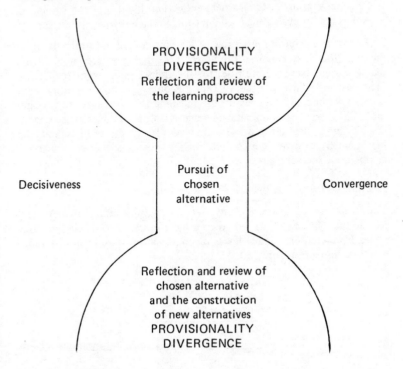

Figure 15.5   The 'hour-glass' phenomenon of 'process'

The skills by which learning is achieved must themselves be learnt, but they are seldom encouraged in training departments or educational institutions. A 'scientific' understanding of the self-organised learning system and of the conversational process is essential. The Centre has developed a theory and awareness-raising tools for enabling people to learn-to-learn. The conversational repertory grid and structure of meaning procedures are two such tools. A 'learning conversation' is designed to achieve effective review of deeply embedded and partially developed skills. This requires three parallel dialogues. Together these reflect the learning processes to the learner, support him or her through painful periods of change, and encourage the development of appropriate referents which anchor judgement about the quality of the experience (Harri-Augstein, 1976). The three dialogues can be described as:

Commentaries on the learning process (Purpose (P); Strategy (S); Outcome (O); Review (R)
Personal support of the learner's reflection
Referents for evaluating learning competence.

Tools for exhibiting processes of learning contribute to the development of the meta-language on which these dialogues are based. Each dialogue signposts separate roles for the trainer as an agent for change (Thomas and Harri-Augstein, 1977). People do not necessarily learn from experience, it depends on the meaning they attribute to this and on their capacity to reflect and review. Most organisations tend to disable us as learners and the onus is clearly on trainers and top management to provide a context within which learning conversations can be nourished and sustained.

Learning-to-learn, tutorial and life conversations

The structure of 'learning conversations' within short, medium and longer time intervals has led us to a hierarchical view of the learning-to-learn encounter. Three levels of conversation have been differentiated, as shown in Figure 15.6.

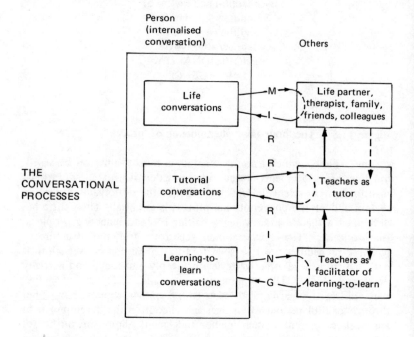

Figure 15.6   Levels of conversation

The 'learning-to-learn conversation' is primarily concerned with skills by which personal understanding is achieved. The detailed interaction by which habits can be broken, reviewed and rebuilt, becomes the focus of attention. The 'tutorial conversation' on the other hand is more concerned with the long term strategic aspects of learning; the planning of goals and the execution of purposes over a period of weeks, months or years. It depends on the establishment of explicit learning contracts where the content of the learning is negotiated, the needs articulated into specific purposes, the resources identified and the strategies put into action. The deployment of basic learning skills forms part of the conversation. It can also raise the issue of when a learner should spend time in raising his level of competence in any one skill. It is when such decisions are made that the 'tutorial conversation' refers back to the 'learning-to-learn conversation'.

Questions about the relevance of what is being learnt are raised in the 'life conversation'. In training this deals with issues of self-development and with the learner's perception of his role, job and tasks.

The emphasis on self-development and the practice of learning conversations has enormous implications for trainers. This section highlights some of the issues involved. As managers of self-development they must play a key role in any organisation. They become the catalysts for change at all levels including top management. Such people will need guidance for their own development and will also need encouragement and assistance in providing an organisational context for all participants to grow and change. To act as 'managers of learning', trainers will require new skills, sensitivity, a wide knowledge of learning methods and considerable resources, and above all, they will need to be self-organised learners themselves. One major responsibility of industrial organisations is to meet the challenge involved in enabling training staff to adapt themselves to the changing scene. For an organisation to achieve creative growth and change it must work as a system of corporate, self-organised learners. It is not too far-fetched to envisage 'conversational networks' made up of semi-autonomous modes at all levels in an organisation. Each mode defines its own responsibilities within the context of the total network and achieves this by conversational interactions between modes. Some of the techniques and philosophy described in this chapter could be recruited to achieve this. A fully participative corpus, made up of supporting self-organised groups is feasible. To meet the demands of today's society and the challenges of the micro-processer revolution which is almost on us, the trajectory to growth must involve the management of people as self-organised learners and fully-functioning beings. Only by moving into this unexplored terrain can industrial society survive and grow.

References and notes

Details of computer programs mentioned in the text and a list of Technical Papers (1–100) are available from The Centre for the Study of Human Learning, Brunel University, Uxbridge, Middlesex.

Augstein, E. S. Harri- and Thomas, L. F. (July 1978), 'Learning conversations: a person centred approach to self-organsed learning', *British Journal of Guidance and Counselling.*

Augstein, E. S. Harri- and Thomas, L. F. in conjunction with Chell, N. (1978), *Learning-to-learn: the Conversational Use of the Repertory Grid and Structures of Meaning in Developing Man-Management Skills.*

Augstein, E. S. Harri- and Thomas, L. F. (1979a), *Self-organised Learning and the Relativity of Knowing: Towards a Conversational Methodology*, eds D. Bannister and P. Stringer, Academic Press.

Kelly, G. A. (1955), *The Psychology of Personal Constructs*, vols. I and II, Norton, New York.

Thomas, L. F. and Augstein, E. S. Harri- (June 1976), 'The self organised learner at work', *Personnel Management*, vol. 8, no. 6.

Thomas, L. F. and Augstein, E. S. Harri- (1977), 'Learning to learn: the personal constructs and exchange of meaning', *Adult Learning*, ed. M. Howe, Wiley.

Thomas, L. F. (May 1978), 'A personal construct approach to learning in education, therapy and training', *Proceedings of the Second International Congress on Personal Construct Theory*, ed. Fay Fransella, Academic Press.

Thomas, L. F. and Augstein, E. S. Harri- (1979b), 'Notes on the use of the repertory grid for self-development and evaluation of courses', *Report to SSRC.*

Thomas, L. F. and Chell, N. (1979), 'Exploring the meaning of a job', *CSHL Research Report.*